I0866660

PENGUIN BOOKS

DIVINING DUTERTE

Edilberto C. de Jesus served as president of: Far Eastern University (1995-2002); the University of the Cordilleras (2008-2009); and the Asian Institute of Management (2009-2012), where he now holds a Professor Emeritus appointment.

In 1987, President Corazon Aquino appointed him Deputy Peace Commissioner, on secondment from AIM, where he was Chair of the Rural Development Management Program. In 1988, he received a concurrent appointment in the Cabinet as Presidential Adviser on Rural Development (1988-1992). Returning to AIM, he served as Associate Dean for Research and established its Policy Center.

He was president of the Philippine Association of Colleges and Universities and a board member of the Coordinating Council of Private Educational Associations when he was appointed Secretary of Education (2002-2004). He was President of the Council of Southeast Asia Ministers of Education Organization (SEAMEO) in 2003, later serving as its Secretariat Director in Bangkok (2005-2007). He served in the Asia-Europe Education Hub established by the Asia Europe Foundation for the ASEM (Asia Europe Ministerial Meetings) and has been on the Advisory Committee of the Philippine Business for Education since its inception in 2006.

He obtained a B.A., Honors Course in the Humanities, cum laude, from the Ateneo de Manila University and the M. Phil. and Ph.D. degrees in History from Yale University. He is the author of *The Tobacco Monopoly in the Philippines: Bureaucratic Enterprise and Social Changes, 1766-1880.* (Ateneo de Manila University Press, 1980) and co-edited, with Alfred McCoy, *Philippine Social History: Global Trade and Local Transformations* (Ateneo de Manila University, 1982).

ADVANCE PRAISE FOR THE BOOK

University Professor at Claremont Graduate University. Formerly Dean of the Pardee RAND Graduate School and a professor at Harvard and Yale, he consults around the world on government reform and economic strategy. His eleven books include *The Culture and Development Manifesto* (Oxford University Press, 2021) and *Tropical Gangsters*, which was named one of the *New York Times*' Books of the Century.

A master class in contemporaneous history from one of the Philippines' most distinguished voices. With the panache of a mystery writer, de Jesus takes you inside the dramas of the Duterte years—the corruption and extrajudicial killings, the insurrections and international upheavals, and the tragedies of Covid-19. There are big doses of Duterte himself, who "tends to speak in tongues, blending Tagalog, Cebuano and English in one verbal flow, with digressions and parenthetical phrases, often of a profane or scurrilous nature." *Divining Duterte* provides both unique insights into the Philippines and a vivid appreciation of the challenges ahead.

—Robert Klitgaard, Ph.D.

Prof. de Jesus masterfully combines a contemporary insider's insights with a scholar's deliberative analysis and a historian's reflective perspective, to highlight not just the disappointing policy outcomes of the mercurial Duterte administration, but also their causes, deeply embedded in longstanding power structures, governance systems and personality politics in the Philippines. He is well-placed to comment on the implications of the regional and international context and constraints for Duterte's policies, and his deep understanding, lively prose and unflinching cut-and-thrust style help sort through the opacity which so often confounds outside observers while stimulating Filipinos to reconsider their own experience and interpretation of these tumultuous years.

—Linda Lim, Ph.D. Professor Emerita of Corporate Strategy
and International Business, Stephen M. Ross School of Business,
University of Michigan

Every other enigmatic personality attracts both followers and detractors, but the narrative that has created the sui generis persona of the Mayor from Davao may be an unfathomable tale. Thus, *Divining Duterte* may be a futile venture and a most frustrating goal. But whether you consider yourself a DDS or Dilawan, a political animal, social scientist, or concerned citizen, D.J. de Jesus's insights into Dutertismo—much like the Delphic oracle—should bring the reader closer to the holy grail of understanding the Filipino psyche. For, in the end, a people's choice of its leader reveals the profile of its electorate and unravels the heart and soul of the nation.

—Br Armin A. Luistro, FSC, Ph.D.
Former Secretary, Department of Education, Philippines

Historian, university president, cabinet minister under two Philippine presidents, and columnist, Edilberto C. de Jesus combines an exceptional set of virtues, a scholar's depth of perspective, an inside view of how political and governmental power works, and a passion for staying in the moment in the twists and turns of a nation's life.

In a time (and not just in the Philippines) when politics seems to be taking the strangest turns and the quality of public discourse is at a historic low, we sorely need a voice such as that of de Jesus, intellectually honest, sane, modulated yet deeply felt and thought.

—Resil Mojares, Ph.D.
Philippine National Artist for Literature (2018)

De Jesus draws upon years in government service and his doctorate in history for penetrating insights into a tempestuous time that has plunged the Philippines from exceptional growth to extraordinary violence. Each well-crafted essay balances the details of successive scandals with insight into the art of governance, the profession of politics, or the imperative of an educated electorate. Probing the many excesses of Duterte's precedent-shattering presidency, de Jesus reminds us that democracy has the resilience to overcome even the most egregious of derelictions.

—Alfred W. McCoy
Fred Harvey Harrington Professor of History
University of WIsconsin-Madison
Author, *The Politics of Heroin in Southeast Asia*

The appearance of *Divining Duterte* could not be timelier. Filipino voters—both those living in the country and those working overseas—will go to the polls in 2022 to replace the most puzzling head of state in their country's history. As Filipinos prepare to cast their ballots, Edilberto de Jesus's book will offer them a calm and carefully reasoned review of the Rodrigo Duterte years—of the president's murderous war on low-level drug users, his fruitless courtship of the People's Republic of China, his still-born promise to work toward federalism, and his dependence on military men to meet the demands of civilian governance.

The story that de Jesus tells is, ultimately, one of failure. While diligently manipulated social media depicted a country in crisis during his 2016 campaign for the presidency, Duterte assumed office at a time of promise for the Philippine economy. He will leave office with a legacy that includes, not least, a hapless inability to spare his countrymen from the impoverishment, heartache, and lasting dread of the Covid-19 pandemic.

Divining Duterte does more than simply inform the politics of the moment, or even of the past half-decade, however. It also relates the developments of that period to long-fundamental questions in the national life of the Philippines. It explores the tension between Duterte's plaintive populism and his country's need for effective social capital. Highlighting Duterte's reliance on soldiers to undertake not only peace-making in Muslim Mindanao but also the battle against the coronavirus, the book evokes the sinister dictatorship of Ferdinand Marcos. Situating Duterte in the regional elite of Cebuano-speaking Davao and diagnosing missed opportunities in the establishment of the Bangsamoro Autonomous Region in Muslim Mindanao, *Divining Duterte* is masterful in its treatment of Mindanao, the Philippines' southern "land of promise". Finally, de Jesus makes clear that Duterte's ongoing campaign against his country's decades-old communist insurgency may make the last year of his presidency as bloody as its first.

The generous liberal sensibility that Edilberto de Jesus brings to *Divining Duterte* will both appeal to and enlighten any reader, Filipino or foreigner, concerned with the future of one of Southeast Asia's largest and most dynamic societies.

—Michael Montesano, Ph.D.
ISEAS-Yusof Ishak Institute, Singapore

De Jesus divines why and how Duterte could get away with his contrarian, curse-filled, home-grown populism that defies everything taught to, and believed by, Filipinos—from good manners and right conduct reverence for constitutionalism and awe for God.

One can only passionately agree or passionately disagree with him. His arguments are provocative, his logic compelling and his conclusions inexorable. To disagree, one must match—nay, overcome—his arguments, logic and conclusions.

—Artemio V. Panganiban
Retired Chief Justice of the Philippines

De Jesus has long been one of the premiere public intellectuals of the Philippines. In *Divining Duterte*, he offers lucid and succinct sketches of the longue durée of the regimes of Duterte and his immediate predecessors. Ranging from corruption to the drug war, from Mindanao to the West Philippine Sea, from human rights to federalism, and from electoral reforms to the COVID pandemic, de Jesus offers us touchstones for thinking about a wide range of issues in the Philippines and the Global South. His book is a valuable addition to understanding the history of present.

—Vicente L. Rafael, Ph.D.
Professor of History, University of Washington
Author, *The Sovereign Trickster: Death and Laughter in the Age of Duterte*
(Duke Univ. Press, 2022)

This is a collection of column essays that noted intellectual D.J. de Jesus has published over the years from 2012 to 2021. As its title suggests, *Divining Duterte* dwells mainly on Philippine President Rodrigo Duterte, "a colorful and controversial character, passionately supported by his followers" and "passionately detested by his critics". In limpid prose, the author traces the development over four years of Duterte's policies and programs and offers an incisive portrait and critique of a strong man who has maintained high approval and trust ratings while enacting policies that the same opinion-poll respondents reject. The book also offers informed, wide-ranging discussions of such issues as pork barrel, political dynasties, intra-elite competition, corruption, and law and order, and their political implications. The book provides important sign posts for anyone who wants to look back at the recent history of the Philippines and understand who were on center stage and what policy issues were at stake in broader political and economic contexts. I strongly recommend the publication of this book manuscript.

—Takashi Shiraishi
Professor Emeritus, National Graduate Institute for Policy Studies, Tokyo Author, *Maritime Asia vs. Continental Asia: National Strategies in a Region of Change*

A year before the presidential elections of 2022 Philippine historian, past administrator and opinion maker Edilberto de Jesus looks back at the Duterte years. He presents a selection of earlier columns from the viewpoint of an active participant in various sectors of public affairs, still fairly weighing opportunities open to the president. Trying to seek a balance between his strong feelings of despair about the developments of the past five years he still gives Duterte considerable benefit of the doubt. The book, though "necessarily personal and subjective" gives the reader lively insight in forces at work and presents the contexts necessary to understand the movement of the Philippines away from a somewhat democratic towards a more authoritarian, top-down political system.

—Otto van den Muijzenberg, Ph.D.
Retired, University of Amsterdam, Sociology and Modern History of South and Southeast Asia University of Amsterdam

Divining Duterte is a welcome collection of pieces because as former Presidential Spokesperson Ernesto Abella once said, "If we follow his [Duterte's] style, let us not put a period at the end of his statements." As we approach the 2022 elections, the period is about to be placed in the long meandering paragraph that is Duterte's presidency. Time now to ask what the sentences meant, if they meant anything at all. Time now to begin figuring out which deliberate words and silences led to our nation being built or unbuilt.

Let this timely book by Dr. Edilberto de Jesus help us decide and elect who gets to write a better paragraph after his period.

—Jose Ramon T. Villarin, S.J., Ph.D.
Former President, Ateneo de Manila University
Intergovernmental Panel on Climate Change

Divining Duterte

Perspectives, Policies, Performance

Edilberto C. de Jesus

PENGUIN BOOKS
An imprint of Penguin Random House

PENGUIN BOOKS

USA | Canada | UK | Ireland | Australia
New Zealand | India | South Africa | China | Southeast Asia

Penguin Books is part of the Penguin Random House group of companies whose addresses can be found at global.penguinrandomhouse.com

Published by Penguin Random House SEA Pte Ltd
9, Changi South Street 3, Level 08-01,
Singapore 486361

Penguin Random House SEA

First published in Penguin Books by Penguin Random House SEA 2021

10 9 8 7 6 5 4 3 2 1

The views and opinions expressed in this book are the author's own and the facts are as reported by him which have been verified to the extent possible, and the publishers are not in any way liable for the same.

ISBN 9789814954747

Typeset in Adobe Garamond Pro by Manipal Technologies Limited, Manipal

www.penguin.sg

Contents

POLICY ISSUES

Foreword

I wrote my first opinion piece on Rodrigo Roa Duterte for the Makati Business Club (MBC) in January 2016. This was five years after I had accepted the MBC's invitation to join three other members in covering the weekly space that the *Philippine Daily Inquirer* had offered me in its Saturday issue. At this time, the Duterte campaign for presidency had just begun to gain traction. After his election in May, five months later, most of my editorial opinion pieces focused on him and his governance of the country.

Before the *Inquirer* assignment, I had written columns for the *Manila Bulletin* on a bi-weekly basis. Writing on the MBC schedule, it was more difficult to sustain coverage of an issue when the follow-up would come only after a month. The challenge was finding from month to month a subject of current interest to both MBC members and the general readership of the *Inquirer*. Writing on Duterte was a simple solution to the issue of timeliness and relevance. Duterte was the newly-elected president, presumably setting a new direction for the country. Especially in the early months of the administration, covering anything he said or did—or refrained from saying or doing—would likely make an impact on the public and would be timely and relevant.

Duterte was also a natural choice. Compared to his predecessor, Benigno Simeon (Noynoy) Aquino III and all other past presidents, Duterte was clearly cut from a different piece of cloth. He emerged on the national stage and came to power, relatively unknown outside Davao City in Mindanao, where he had served as mayor for over twenty-two years. He had made his mark in Davao during the troubled years of martial law, fighting communist insurgents and criminal elements with the support of the business community. In Davao, he became a colorful and controversial character, passionately supported by his followers and detested in equal measure, by his critics. There was truth both to the claim that he had brought law and order back to Davao and to the contention that he had done so at the cost of blatant human rights violations.

Periodically, the problems of Davao made ripples in the national media and provided Duterte with both positive and negative publicity. But it was not until his election campaign began picking up steam that he started to capture the fancy of crowds across the country. As a presidential candidate, he demonstrated a casual disregard for the courtesies even seasoned, powerful politicians were careful to observe, when courting the public. He made extravagant promises, for instance, to uphold the validation of Philippine claims to maritime boundaries by the UN International Court of Arbitration—he would jet-ski to plant the flag on the West Philippine Sea (WPS) territory. This tended to discount the gravity of threats to fatten the fish in Manila Bay with the bodies of executed drug dealers. Surely, both statements must have been spoken in jest.

We had to acknowledge early on the truth that we were not exactly sure how to deal with the person we had elected. Several of the early columns reflected on the conundrum that Duterte presented to the public, as he maintained high approval and trust ratings while pushing policies that the same opinion poll respondents rejected. Our understanding of the president improved, of course, as he began to reveal more and more of himself to the public in challenging political situations, particularly in the latest and most formidable threat of the COVID-19 pandemic.

The idea of collecting the Duterte columns published in the *Inquirer* and online, by *Rappler*, came from friends who suggested that others may benefit from my effort to gain a better understanding of this president and his presidency. With the Duterte administration coming to its close, Filipinos must also try to measure its impact on the country's political institutions and culture. Efforts towards such an assessment would help voters in the 2022 elections determine the directions they would like the country to take.

I considered different terms to describe the effort to understand the president: "analyze," "evaluate," "decipher," "decode." These sounded too academic and scientific, and suggested objectivity, precision and conclusiveness, to which I did not pretend to aspire. The columns were based on careful reading of texts and the best evidence available to me. But these were opinion pieces and therefore, necessarily personal and subjective.

Finally, I opted for "divining." Not to identify Mr. Duterte with divinity—though this may appeal to some of his supporters—but to suggest that the process of interpreting his intentions from his words and predicting their consequences was akin to the effort of soothsayers to anticipate future events, by dissecting the entrails of doves and goats. The term also aligned with the advice that Sec. Ernesto Abella, the first presidential spokesperson, gave to the media and the public: "If we follow his [Duterte's] style, let us not put a period at the end of his statements." Media was to "understand" the president instead of "taking him literally." He encouraged them to "use creative imagination" to reconcile confusing or conflicting presidential statements. With this caution, the spokesperson appeared to abdicate his role to communicate clearly to the country the meaning of the president's messages to the country. Abella's successors have not really offered better advice.

The Philippine Constitution limits the incumbent president to one six-year term. Those who will run in 2022 will have to evaluate whatever successes and failures the Duterte administration has recorded. They will then have to tell the voters how closely they want to follow the policies that administration pursued. The columns collected in this volume trace the development over four years, of key Duterte policies and programs.

If journalism offers a first draft of history, opinion pieces might serve as useful footnotes. They supply context, providing real-time reflections on the range of public sentiments prevailing at the time. Philippine media is remarkable for the number of columnists to whom mainstream publications allow space. In politically developed countries of the West, readers know the ideological or policy orientation of their national newspapers and subscribe to those whose views align with their own. In the Philippines, where political parties can seldom be accused of ideological or logical consistency, even the newspapers known to favor the ruling administration strive to demonstrate their impartiality by permitting a few token government critics to contribute opinion pieces.

My own academic training in History offered a safer occupation. After graduate studies, however, my job at the Asian Institute of Management involved conducting critical review of public management initiatives to address development concerns, with the goal of improving their performance. Add to the accidental mix of educational and employment background, my involvement in the opposition to martial law and unplanned service in government in the cabinets of Corazon Cojuangco Aquino and Gloria Macapagal-Arroyo; their convergence gave me information and opportunity to contribute to the discussion on public issues.

Historians coming after us, with the benefit of 20-20 hindsight, will have the luxury of ruling which views, however well-received in their day, misread the portents of the times and which proved prescient. Perhaps, they will also be able to determine the factors shaping the views which these columnists propounded, and why some of them turned out more accurate than others.

Opinion writers venturing to interpret contemporary issues inevitably become vulnerable to charges of ignorance, carelessness and bias—and must accept that risk. I tried to reduce the risk, as most academics reflexively do. The columns themselves have benefitted from the interaction with colleagues in the various institutions I have worked with, over the years. They shall remain nameless to spare them the problem of guilt by association.

Part of the risk-mitigation measures involved inflicting my views on the women in my life: my wife, Melinda, and our daughters Lara, Mariel and, via internet from Singapore, Noelle. They served as sounding boards for the writing of the original columns. In the period of pandemic lockdown, during which this book project was implemented, they were a captive audience at extended mealtime conversations. To them, I must express deep contrition and profound gratitude for their patience and love in enduring, on too many occasions, my stubborn insistence on disputing substantive issues and even grammatical points. They have responded with rolling of eyes, exasperated sighs and often with annoyingly pointed and persuasive arguments.

We all need people to call us out and cut us down to size when necessary. Even the emperor must welcome the warning, before he shows himself to the public, that he is venturing out without clothes. They have rescued me from more embarrassing errors than I have committed. To them, in humility and with much love, I dedicate this book.

Prologue

My original plan excluded from the collection the columns written before Duterte's launch of his presidential campaign. This plan changed for two reasons. First, as a matter of fairness, I needed to acknowledge that many of the country's problems predated Duterte and will survive after he has departed the scene. The columns that addressed these contentious problems provide context to what Duterte had to deal with, as well as to what the population might have expected from him.

A major concern of the voters focused precisely on how he would manage and decide on these issues. During the election campaign, for instance, he had already signaled his support for a hero's burial for Ferdinand Marcos and his reservations about asserting Philippine rights to its Exclusive Economic Zone (EEZ) in the South China Sea (SCS), confirmed by the United Nations Court of International Arbitration. But the majority of the public who disagreed with him on both issues still hoped that a presidential perspective would lead him to reconsider his views. The second reason stemmed from the obligation for complete transparency and full disclosure.

I disagreed with many of the policies he indicated he would pursue as president and I did not vote for him. Nevertheless, like most of the country, including the opposition, we accepted the results of the elections and welcomed, in particular, the quick and peaceful transition of political power.

On his election as president, an association of former senior government officials (FSGO) issued a statement that I had drafted. The statement began with a tribute to his "indisputable and impressive" victory. It ended thus:

> "Election results do not immediately erase the problems of peace and order, graft and corruption, hunger and poverty, climate change and environmental degradation that we continue to confront. President-elect Duterte has the privilege and the responsibility to unite and lead the nation to address these problems. Given the opportunity and in our respective areas of competence, we have the obligation to help him succeed in this task."

Mr. Duterte won about 39 percent of the votes for the presidency. FSGO felt it important to remind him that a greater number of the electorate wanted another person as president. He was elected to lead the nation, not just those who voted for him. He had the obligation to consider the views of the majority who did not vote for him as well as the views of other elected officials who had won their own mandate from the electorate.

Unfortunately, a better understanding of administration policies did not translate into their acceptance. In a democratic system, dissent is permitted and may even be an obligation. It is important, however, to demonstrate that the disagreement did not originate from bias. For this reason, I decided to include opinion pieces that were critical of other political leaders. These demonstrated that Mr. Duterte was not being held to stricter standards than his predecessors, but to the same measures of performance.

In all Philippine presidential elections, corruption figured as a standard campaign issue. As exemplified by "crony" and "booty capitalism," it reached world-class levels during the martial law regime, with Ferdinand Marcos ranking second in the top ten list of the most corrupt rulers in the world.[1] "People Power" did not stop corruption issues, which continued to plague the Ramos, Estrada and Arroyo administrations. Not surprising, then, that the Aquino theme—*Kung walang korup, walang mahirap* (no poor people without corrupt people)—resonated with the electorate, with the business sector mobilizing its own Integrity Initiative program to support the government.

Noynoy Aquino tried to deliver on his promise to push back against corruption. His administration saw a record number of high government officials being prosecuted on corruption charges, with some actually convicted. The list included the chief of the Supreme Court, Renato Corona, who was impeached and removed from office. Ombudsman

Merceditas Gutierrez was also impeached but resigned days before the start of her impeachment trial. The dragnet caught several senators, including Juan Ponce Enrile, who had presided over the impeachment trial of Chief Justice Corona. Joining the senators in the list were Gen. Alan Purisima, chief of the Philippine National Police (PNP); Jejomar Erwin "Junjun" Binay, Jr., mayor of Makati, the country's financial capital; Junjun's father, Jojo Binay, the incumbent vice president, for transactions during his own term as Makati mayor; and former President Gloria Arroyo.

If for nothing else, the case load generated during the Aquino administration underlined the issue of entrenched, systemic corruption that plagued the country and that the next administration would inherit.

Aquino probably achieved a world record; the government during his term managed to bring to the prosecution stage, charges against a former president, senate president, an incumbent Supreme Court chief justice and an incumbent vice president within its term.

But the millstones of the justice system in the Philippines grind exceedingly fine and exceedingly slow. Plaintiffs, especially those with financial and political resources, have multiple options to escape punishment, including the elevation of cases to the Supreme Court for reversal and the appeal for clemency and pardon from a more understanding president.

While many of the cases had not reached final judgment, they already made an impact on the 2016 presidential race. A dark horse winner in the 2010 vice-presidential race, beating Mar Roxas, Noynoy Aquino's running mate, Jojo Binay had the inside track from Day one for the 2016 presidential elections. The constitution did not define performance metrics for which the electorate could hold the vice president accountable. Binay could spend the six years of his term preparing the ground for the presidential run. But the televised hearings on corruption charges took their toll in eroding his political capital and contributed to his defeat.

Whether his case and those of the other officials would prosper or not during the 2016 presidential term was, therefore, a matter of significant interest to the electorate. The final decision on the cases would come from the judges—from the judicial, not the executive branch of government. They were the key actors in the drama. But the stage belonged to the president.

1

Thinking about Pork

(*PDI*, August 02, 2013)

Can Asians Think? Evasive statements from parties implicated in the alleged pork barrel scam recalled the question posed in his book by Kishore Mahbubani, former Singapore ambassador to the UN and dean of the Lee Kwan Yew (LKY) School of Public Policy. The alleged scammers apparently believe that Filipinos cannot think.

Responding to allegations that she distributed to fictitious beneficiary organizations grants from the Priority Development Assistance Fund (PDAF) entrusted to senators and congressmen, Janet Lim Napoles denied any wrongdoing. The Janet Lim Napoles (JLN) Corp., she claimed, had been doing business for many years, unblemished by any suspicion of fraud.

Napoles never addressed the basic questions even the casual reader would have liked answered: What is the business of JLN Corp.? What product or services does it offer its clients? How does it make a profit? She must explain her company's business model in a clear and credible way. A long business record is by itself no proof of virtue; a crook can successfully operate for a long time without being caught.

From the media accounts, the business appears to operate in the following manner. The company sets up non-government organizations (NGOs) to support pro-poor and priority government development programs that can be funded through the PDAF. It then secures funding support from legislators, who each receive a share of the PDAF budget (P200 million/year for the senators and P70 million/year for the congressmen).

NGOs compete for a share of a large but still limited pie. The challenge for Napoles and her staff is to market the projects of their NGOs to the politicians as superior to those offered by the others. One strategy is to get supporting endorsements of their projects from officials of local government units (LGUs).

Implementation of development projects is a function of the executive branch. Congress has the responsibility to evaluate the proposed programs and determine the budget executive agencies should receive. Wide discretion in deciding where PDAF funds go gives legislators a role in implementation.

The PDAF presumes that elected politicians know the urgent needs of their constituencies and should have some means of responding quickly to them. The backlog in development projects, the perennial shortage of funds, and the bureaucratic requirements that delay executive action, buttress the case for the PDAF.

Politicians are key to whatever business Napoles is operating. Those implicated in the alleged scam, such as Senators Lito Lapid, Ramon Revilla Jr., Juan Ponce Enrile, Jinggoy Estrada, Ferdinand Marcos Jr., Gregorio Honasan and Vicente Sotto, are not neophyte politicians. They are supposed to be intimately familiar with the challenges facing their constituencies. Why should they need the services of Napoles?

Surely, in a country where more than a third of the population lives below the poverty line and where thousands of NGOs are working to help the poor, politicians would not lack creditable NGOs and meritorious projects to fund. What makes the NGOs of JLN Corp. more deserving of support?

JLN's political clients have a lot to explain. So far, the explanations have not been persuasive, but indicate the defensive lines the politicians are preparing: 1) The allegations constitute black propaganda against "presidentiables." 2) They were responding to urgent, priority requests from local government officials. 3) Their trusted staff cleared the projects before they gave their approval. 4) Other executive government agencies, not they, are responsible for monitoring implementation and stopping fraud.

The first response is a pathetic evasion of the issue, as religious leaders have noted. The second requires investigation, as LGUs are disputing claims that they initiated the request. The third requires us to trust congressional staff on the mere say-so of their bosses, who can later conveniently throw them overboard. The fourth slides past the prior, prejudicial question: the decision of the congressman or senator to favor JLN NGOs with their PDAF.

The truth about the alleged pork barrel scam does not require expert rocket science research. It begins and can end with the basic question on the character of the NGOs organized by JLN Corp. LGU officials have reported that, even when their PDAF requests are granted, they still have to deal with the NGOs recommended by the legislators. What was the track record that recommended the JLN NGOs? What was their PDAF performance?

Congress has control of the purse. Its members are accountable to the public for their stewardship of the PDAF. The casual, careless and possibly corrupt handling of the PDAF program has brought disrepute to the entire institution.

Debates on whether to continue or scrap the PDAF should take place but should not distract from the task of getting to the bottom of the JLN business. The thorough investigation of the issue will inform debates and indicate policy directions. This and sanctions for the guilty will be necessary to rebuild public trust.

2

The "Peanut Butter Defense"

(*PDI*, October 05, 2013)

Sen. Jinggoy Estrada wasted few of the 6,000-plus words in his privilege speech on the Senate floor to refute the plunder charges filed against him in the Office of the Ombudsman. He forfeited, therefore, the chance—which he claimed he was denied—"to confront the evidence."

He did not explain why he decided to direct his PDAF resources to the Napoles NGOs. He did not detail the benefits that his projects delivered to the community. He took a different strategy, the essence of which the *Inquirer* banner headline on September 26 distilled as: "Jinggoy rats on colleagues."

Litigation lawyers, when confronted with damning evidence, joke that respondents seek shelter behind the "Peanut Butter Defense"—spreading the blame. One website condensed the thrust of this strategy thus: "I am a thief, but I am not the only one."

But Sen. Jinggoy spread the blame beyond personalities. After brushing his colleagues with the black paint of corruption, he generously excuses them and himself by blaming the system: "I believe that we are all victims of a flawed system, which is so ingrained that it has been institutionalized."

By casting all who work within the flawed system as "victims," he again suggests that all senators disposed of the PDAF as he did, even as he graciously covers them with the protective cloak of victimhood. But Sen. Jinggoy's assessment of the system as "flawed," even if self-serving, is one point in his speech few will dispute.

The spin recalls another old joke, morbid, cynical, and because factually accurate in its details, black-humor-funny: a young man not yet of legal age kills his father and mother to collect on their insurance benefits. He then appears before judge and jury and pleads for clemency—because he is a minor and an orphan.

Apart from the fact that he is no minor, Sen. Jinggoy takes an altogether too narrow a view of the "system." Thus, his concluding statement in Filipino—narrowly focused and innocuous—fails to rise to the challenge of changing what he acknowledges as an "ingrained" mentality: "We can only speak of a truly straight path once the rotten system has been changed, the corruption corrected and the wrong made right" (my free translation). The senator omitted the issue of punishment of the guilty—an element essential to excising a defect deeply embedded in the system.

Variants of the pork barrel system have been at play for many years. The pained response of various legislators to the proposed abolition of the PDAF suggests their familiarity with its uses for political purposes. Far from being surprised by the system, they looked forward to participating in it.

The Peanut Butter Defense is convenient because, sadly, prevailing laws still permit the lawmakers to receive pork barrel funds. Sen. Jinggoy did succeed in muddying the waters. The media have played up the question of whether the administration had the authority to channel budgetary savings to legislators through the Disbursement Acceleration Program (DAP). No one has so far surfaced any evidence of corruption in the use of DAP funds. But the issue that has provoked public outrage about PDAF is how the legislators used the funds entrusted to them.

Given his family background and track record in politics, can anyone believe that Sen. Jinggoy reached the Senate, virginally innocent of the potential pork barrel opportunities? Like the appeal of the orphaned young man in the joke, Sen. Jinggoy's self-portrayal as a "victim" strikes a discordant note.

The "Orphan Defense" is both weak and offensive, especially to those who voted for the accused legislators. Granting that the system was flawed, it begs the question of responsibility for creating the conditions that corrupted the system. Senators are not ordinary mortals helplessly caught in a web of structures that they are powerless to alter. They hold political positions of enormous powers. As movers and shakers at the center of the web, they cannot easily disclaim responsibility for cultivating and embedding the pork barrel mentality.

It was the individual and collective obligation of Senators Jinggoy, Ramon Revilla Jr. and Juan Ponce Enrile—as well as their colleagues in the legislature—to correct the flaws of the system, and not to institutionalize and exploit them for personal gain. With their potential involvement in crimes now exposed, they bemoan their plight as victims of the flawed system they helped to create and now promise to reform.

How many Filipinos truly benefited from the millions of pesos released from the senators' PDAF through the Napoles NGOs? How many lives might have been lost because funds were unjustly denied to the right programs and their rightful beneficiaries?

If people raging against the pork barrel corruption now appear bloodthirsty in their demand for justice, can they be blamed? They know they are the real victims.

3

DAP: Thinking in Time

(*PDI,* November 02, 2013)

Technology has given us wristwatches that tell time within a fraction of a second. This has not necessarily made us more punctual in our habits. Often, we still have to guess the duration of a given "Filipino time" or, more common regionally, "rubber time."

This casual attitude towards time, unfortunately, can lead to more than just missed appointments or mistakes in judgment. Take the case of the claim that the administration released additional pork barrel funds through the DAP to buy the impeachment of then Chief Justice Renato Corona. Why has this allegation appeared plausible despite its dubious source—a senator charged with plunder?

The administration has denied that DAP funds were given as pork barrel and dismissed any link between the release of these funds and the impeachment trial. This response, critics will say, was only to be expected.

But, second, no senator has come forward to admit that his or her vote had been bought. Even Jinggoy Estrada, who first raised the bribery issue, maintained that the pork, which he accepted, did not influence his decision; although he could not speak for his colleagues. No one confessed to voting on the basis of a bribe. Some senators who voted to acquit apparently received these funds, while others who voted to convict did not.

These factual considerations alone should have laid the bribery charge to rest. And yet, the suspicion persists, and it may be getting traction—not just from the parties desperately trying to divert public attention from the PDAF plunder cases against Janet Napoles and her partner-legislators. It lingers also, I suspect, because the diversion effort exploits how we naturally think about causality and time.

The Senate impeached Corona. And then—actually, about six months later—they received DAP funds. Therefore, they must have received these funds because they had agreed to impeach Corona. The premise that what happened before caused what happened after, appears plausible since the cause must come before the effect.

Our philosophy teacher used a favorite example of this fallacy that mistakes a temporal sequence for a causal relationship: roosters crow just before daybreak. Should we then believe that the crowing of the cocks causes the sun to rise?

Respecting the chronology of events would also help avoid unwarranted conclusions. Newspaper headlines, for instance, have called attention to the continuing irregularities in the use of PDAF and DAP funds in the PNoy administration. Whether intended or not, such headlines sell the spin that the administration already knew about the Napoles racket, but knowingly permitted it to continue. It insinuates administration complicity in the corruption.

Even the Commission on Audit (COA), however, only disclosed evidence of the PDAF scam at about the time that the Napoles staff started blowing the whistle. Why it took the COA so long to undertake the audit is an important side issue, but it bears stressing that the order to do so came only with the advent of the PNoy administration. Until that time, PDAF operations, whose origins preceded PNoy, enjoyed the presumption of legality.

Given this presumption, the administration, in implementing the DAP, allowed 9 percent of the funds to be treated like the PDAF, allowing legislators to recommend projects, as long as they met DAP guidelines. Unfortunately, some senators—the media has surfaced, among others, the names of Senators Vicente Sotto, Gregorio Honasan and Ferdinand Marcos Jr.—have allegedly managed to direct these funds to Napoles and, perhaps, other bogus NGOs.

It is disappointing that former Sen. Ping Lacson should ask why senators had to be consulted if the DAP targeted already approved projects. As he must know, very few legislators can be accused of doing the right thing only because it is the right thing to do. The project may be good, but the perennial question comes up: what is in it for me, or less crassly, for "my constituency?"

Legislators are politicians, and politics everywhere is a negotiations game. The executive branch would prefer cordial relations with Congress to keep the bargaining within the bounds of decency. The Napoles Scam, whether the funds came from the PDAF, DAP or Malampaya Fund, clearly breached ethical and legal boundaries.

The Supreme Court will rule on the constitutionality of the PDAF and of the DAP. These are two different mechanisms, neither invulnerable to corruption. But the constitutional issues are separate from the criminal charges filed and to be filed against those accused of plundering public funds.

In a recent national address, PNoy reassured the citizens, his "bosses," that he will pursue to its conclusion the investigation and prosecution of the pork barrel cases. The scale and brazenness of the corruption already exposed now, make imperative the accounting of the use of pork barrel funds by all legislators, whether from the opposition or the administration.

Hopefully, we will see this in Philippine Standard Time, not in rubber time.

4

Practicing Political Patronage

(*PDI*, December 06, 2013)

The Supreme Court decision declaring unconstitutional the PDAF and similar arrangements, paves the way for the radical restructuring of legislative-executive relations. Alas, it will not create a totally and permanently corruption-free government.

Any human system devised to determine the deployment of limited resources will remain vulnerable to inefficiency, ineffectiveness and abuse: because human beings are frail, fallible and subject to temptation. But we can begin with initiatives to reduce the gravity and scale of corruption and the damage that it brings.

Neither will ending the pork barrel system eradicate the practice of political patronage. Not for as long as we maintain a democratic system anchored on the separation of governmental powers.

Patronage originally focused on the power to make appointments to an office. It expanded to include the authority to approve and to allocate resources. The exercise of patronage is both a privilege and responsibility arising from authority.

The executive, legislative and judicial branches of government each have their own share of patronage powers but must respect the areas of competence and authority of the others. As coequal institutions, they have to bargain among themselves.

The abbot of a monastery derives his authority from the professed commitment of the members—as a matter of religious faith—to subordinate their will to the monastic rules he administers. He does not need to court the favor of the monks.

Mao Zedong, at the peak of his powers, could impose his will on the population. Control of the communist party, the bureaucracy and the armed forces, dispensed even with the need to consult with other political leaders.

Business establishments address the needs of their clients by delivering products and services at prices that leave them a margin of profit. They invest resources on market incentives—discounts, rebates, "mileage" points—to gain the loyalty, the patronage of their customers.

Voters do not vow obedience to the candidates they elect, or to their appointees. Leaders chosen in democratic elections receive a mandate to get things done but must do so with only limited access to market incentives or to command-and-control powers. They must supplement whatever formal authority their titles confer with skill in the exercise of patronage.

The sources of leverage—military, financial or spiritual/ideological—are not mutually exclusive; reliance on any one approach renders it less efficient. Even the absolute tyrant will not want to rely only on whip and gallows. Corrupt politicians have tainted the practice of politics, but politics and consequently, patronage, operate in business, among not-for-profit organizations as well as in the churches.

Some reform groups demand that legislators restrict themselves to enacting laws and leave the budget allocation and spending alone. But arguably the most important law Congress must pass each year is the General Appropriations Act that authorizes the national budget.

Congress has the duty to review and approve the budgets proposed by the other branches of government and to monitor their use. This mandate gives legislators the window to press for their pet projects and to push for the appointment of favored protégés to the bureaucracy.

Why should not a congressman push the appointment of a qualified school principal or district engineer who enjoys his confidence? Assuming the candidate has the required credentials and expertise to deliver the expected results, why not? The pressure is problematic only when the nominee is clearly an inferior choice because of professional or ethical considerations.

The conflict between a cabinet secretary and a legislator over projects is not necessarily a battle between good and evil. Resources and time constraints compel choices among objectively meritorious projects. Which deserves priority funding: a bridge or a university?

Different perspectives, arising from project timelines and constituency concerns, will understandably lead to conflicting preferences. Congressmen will want projects completed before their terms end. Cabinet secretaries may prefer projects expected to deliver national or regional benefits; the congressmen and their constituencies will favor projects that immediately benefit their districts.

Conflict over priorities becomes intractable, if the options remain restricted to just the bridge and the university. Expanding the discussion to cover more choices helps generate possibilities for accommodation. Secretary or legislator can yield ground on one issue, in return for assistance on some other problem, such as right-of-way for a road, land for a school building, or the redeployment of expert personnel.

Why should this kind of give-and-take be condemned as corrupt and corrupting "political patronage"? The problem is not the bargaining process, which takes place even between spouses and can often yield more productive results. The problem is the object of the bargaining.

We are not talking here about collusion to cook the procurement process or to fix elections. The charges against the parties allegedly behind the Napoles scam to divert public funds into private bank accounts, go beyond political patronage; they involve criminal conspiracy to plunder.

The public needs to distinguish between the two scenarios. And learn to elect politicians who understand the distinction and act accordingly.

5

Valuing Senators

(*PDI*, January 31, 2014)

Sen. Miriam Defensor-Santiago estimates that senators legally get P1.4 million a month in compensation and allowances. What does the public get? Lately, allegations that some senators get much, much more in criminal pork barrel scams, raise serious questions about the integrity of the institution.

Senators themselves have provoked the questions, as Sen. Ramon "Bong" Revilla Jr. recently did on the Senate floor. Coming six months after being implicated in the Napoles PDAF scam, the privilege speech did little to blunt the charges raised against him or to burnish the image of the Senate.

Less than 14 percent of his 4,500-word, 60-minute-speech dealt directly with the PDAF case and he only whitewashed any involvement with a comprehensive denial: "I have nothing to do with this scam, those whistle-blowers, nor Janet Lim Napoles. I have no dealings and transactions with them!"

In support of this assertion, he claimed that: 1) his signature on incriminating documents were forgeries; 2) the alleged recipient of funds, a Richard Cambe, identified by whistle-blower Benhur Luy as his chief-of-staff or political chief officer, held no such office; and 3) Cambe was abroad on the date Luy reported meeting with him.

Perhaps, Revilla Jr. did not sign the documents himself. Perhaps, someone else in his office, not Cambe, took money from Luy. These details are peripheral to the central issue of the senator's innocence or culpability.

The public needs a clear and credible accounting of: 1) who have been receiving his PDAF allocations; 2) the objectives or outcomes expected from the grants; and 3) the benefits actually delivered to the public.

The speech was silent on these critical points that bear on the senator's management of PDAF grants. That he apparently had more than one transaction with Napoles dummy organizations further underlined the issue of his stewardship over public funds entrusted to his care. Luy's claim, still to be verified, that Napoles counted then Sen. Ramon Revilla Sr. as a pork barrel source as early as 2003–2004, does not help Revilla Jr.'s situation.

Over 85 percent of the speech covered assorted issues not pertinent to the crime of which Revilla Jr. is accused. Wittingly or not, like a bull chasing the red cape that the toreador waves, media news coverage pursued the senator's diversionary directions. In the case of the impeachment bribery red herring, Malacañang unfortunately lent support to the senator's strategy.

It would be naive to believe—and unconvincing for the administration to pretend—that PNoy was a disinterested party in the case involving Renato Corona, the then chief justice. Even if he were, it would be an impossible, self-defeating task to try to prove that he had completely avoided any action or utterance that could have influenced the outcome of the trial.

The president cannot resort to force or bribery to secure the decisions he wants. But if he believed that the chief justice had abused his position and that the country's interest required his removal from office, he would be duty-bound to work within the law to achieve the objective.

As it turned out, enough senator-judges agreed with the president that the chief justice had to go. This inconvenient truth makes it difficult for senators who voted against the chief justice (against whom graft charges have now been filed) to accuse the administration of intimidation or bribery; any such accusation would be self-incriminating.

Sen. Jinggoy Estrada was the first to raise on the Senate floor, the issue of the DAP as a mechanism to buy the senators' votes. But while admitting he took the DAP funds, he insisted that he voted according to his conscience.

Notwithstanding his "weird" trip to Malacañang, Revilla Jr. did not appear to fear for his life or virtue, during his meeting with the president. He said he resisted presidential pressure for a Corona conviction, telling PNoy, "I will do what is right."

Regarding the votes of their colleagues in the Senate, Estrada and Revilla Jr., like the toreadors, must evade both horns of the bull. To affirm the integrity of their fellow senators would discredit the charge that the administration bought the ouster of Chief Justice Corona. To suggest that DAP funds determined the outcome of the impeachment trial, impales them on the horn that discredits the Senate itself.

Insinuations about a DAP-bought verdict erodes the credibility of an institution deeply tainted by the allegations of senatorial involvement in the Napoles scam. Are we now being told that we voted into power senators so craven and corrupt as to be so easily intimidated or bribed?

The question sharpens doubts about the costs, now being publicly disclosed and discussed, that we bear to maintain the Senate. The Senate has a legitimate governance role. But we need to focus more closely on that role and on what value, what benefits individual senators have really delivered to the country and the people.

6

"Politically Motivated"

(*PDI*, March 01, 2014)

Following Ruby Tuason's appearance at the Senate to speak on the Napoles pork barrel scam, Vice President Jejomar Binay questioned her enlistment in the government's Witness Protection Program, dismissing as a "dud," not a "slam dunk," the testimony she could provide.

Perhaps this was an instinctive response to a question launched in an "ambush." His political advisers would have cautioned him against stepping into the pork barrel muck—it was safer to continue flying below the radar and distancing himself from the sticky stain spreading from the scam.

Commenting on the case involving the PDAF exposes him to danger from two directions. It opens a potential, premature rift with the president, because the Napoles scam has emerged as the defining milestone in the administration's "*Daang Matuwid*" (Straight Path) campaign. It also risks raking up unproven charges of sustained and systemic corruption in Makati during the multiple terms of himself and his family members as mayor.

But the vice president's leadership over United Nationalist Alliance (UNA) does aggravate the public perception problems from the Binay terms in Makati. When this political coalition was launched, the branding focused on the leaders, projected as the Three Kings of Philippine Politics: Senate President Juan Ponce Enrile, former President Joseph Estrada, and Vice President Binay himself.

The alliance, obviously not based on ideology or governance programs, collects "strange bedfellows." Sen. Enrile and Vice President

Binay had been fierce antagonists: the architect of martial law and the street parliamentarian defending human rights. Senator Enrile's perceived involvement in the post-EDSA coup attempts squandered the merit gained at EDSA 1 and again placed him and Vice President Binay on opposite sides.

Now Manila mayor, Estrada was convicted of plunder and pardoned by President Gloria Macapagal-Arroyo, now also charged with plunder. Senator Enrile also faces plunder charges, together with UNA partner Sen. Jinggoy Estrada. People will wonder what kind of kingdom the UNA Three Kings control. Another cliché, "birds of a feather," comes to mind. This hurts the vice president, who has avoided being tarred and feathered by the Napoles Scam.

Those charged in the scam denounce the investigation as "politically motivated," connecting it to the alleged bribery of legislators to secure the conviction of the impeached Chief Justice Renato Corona. UNA Secretary General Tobias Tiangco demanded that the budget department disclose the congressional recipients of DAP funds.

SecGen Tiangco's fixation on who got what and for what reason, focuses him on the wrong end of the gift horse. The DAP differs from the PDAF, although some politicians illegally deployed the funds the same way. But even the PDAF, until revealed as a vehicle for plunder and ruled unconstitutional by the Supreme Court, enjoyed the presumption of legality.

The public is correctly more concerned about how politicians used the funds, a question SecGen Tiangco does not probe. He could set an example by disclosing to whom he entrusted his PDAF allocations, and urging his colleagues to do the same.

Neither have print and broadcast interviewers pressed the indicted senators on this question. For over six months, they have remained silent on where they put their PDAF allocations, for what reasons, and with what results.

In the same *Inquirer* report citing SecGen Tiangco, party-list congressman Terry Ridon maintained that the disbursement of DAP funds was "politically motivated." This phrase has become a shorthand formula to denounce behavior, policies and people as unworthy of support or belief.

Student activists do complain about "commercially motivated" education programs or liberals about "religiously motivated" demographic policies. It would be surprising for a businessman to condemn a venture as "commercially motivated," or a priest to dismiss projects as "religiously motivated."

Politicians themselves like to use "politically motivated," often to deny charges they find difficult to debate. But it is a retort that diminishes and discredits their chosen profession. Why are motives associated with politics seen by their practitioners as necessarily suspect? What should matter is not the source from which the motives spring, but their substance and validity.

Politics addresses issues of governance and citizenship. The movement to liberate the country from the Marcos regime and to impeach a president linked to illegal gambling were, undeniably, "politically motivated." Despite having been debased by many political leaders, politics remains an honorable and necessary calling. Politicians should want to celebrate—not demean—motives inspired by politics.

Citizens want officials who will protect, not plunder, the resources of the state, and will use these for the benefit of the public. They want a "strong state" that can ensure the rule of law and exact punishment for those who exploit their exalted offices to steal from the people. They want elections that will place in power, officials who will hold themselves accountable to the electorate.

To establish a strong state, ensure the rule of law and enforce public accountability are politically motivated objectives: legitimate and, in the view of political philosopher Francis Fukuyama, essential for the development of a mature, democratic community of citizens.

7

Political Persecution?

(*PDI*, July 05, 2014)

The week began with a front-page story in the *Inquirer* reporting the result of the Supreme Court investigation concerning Sandiganbayan Associate Justice Gregory Ong. Tasked with the inquiry, retired Supreme Court Justice Angelina Sandoval-Gutierrez recommended Ong's dismissal "for gross misconduct, dishonesty and impropriety."

Ong had chaired the division that acquitted Janet Lim Napoles in 2010 on the corruption case involving a P3.8-million contract in 1998, to supply Kevlar helmets to the Marines. The case tested the strategy later used for the scam involving the PDAF: exploiting connections with decision-makers to win fraudulent contracts for dubious companies headed by relatives. But the key element in the Napoles strategy was networking beyond the extended family to gain access to public officials.

Persistent tugging at the threads of the Napoles-Benhur Luy relationship eventually caused the entire fabric of her smoke-and-mirrors enterprise to unravel. Napoles was exposed as an inclusive, equal-opportunity corruptor. She has managed to ensnare in her web, officials from the executive branch, the House of Representatives, the Senate, local governments, and with Ong, the judiciary.

"Ensnare" is not the right term. Those who collaborated in the projects were not injured, innocent victims; they were partners, who also feasted on Napoles' prey. They did their part, busily weaving strands that expanded and strengthened the web and helped to protect the Queen Spider. Her various scams could not have worked without official collusion.

Without the exposure of the PDAF scam, it is unlikely that the Supreme Court could have reopened the Kevlar case. Hopefully, the pork barrel scam served as the heavy brick threatening to break the back of the camel—which had for so long borne the burden of corruption—that finally provokes it to strike back. We are now witnessing government initiatives to identify and prosecute criminals in public offices.

The same *Inquirer* issue that carried the Ong-Kevlar story also covered the case of Baguio Rep. Nicasio Aliping, Jr., who pushed a road building project through a protected watershed. The project destroyed grown trees and tree saplings, allegedly polluted a water source for the city, and endangered the stability of the Ibaloy burial caves.

Another story reported on the cases that Customs Commissioner John Philip Sevilla is launching against nearly a hundred agents. The cases involve suspected connivance with smugglers to misclassify and undervalue imported goods to avoid paying the correct taxes.

One retired employee tried to extort payment from a businessman for the release of his goods. The extortion target reported the attempt and helped an entrapment operation to catch the criminal. Such citizen cooperation requires confidence that the government will do the right thing.

We should be glad that the government is pursuing these cases and that the media are reporting on them. This will encourage the public to be more vigilant in exposing and combating corruption. Still, the narrative of how people, to whom we have entrusted power to protect our interests, have used it for so long to exploit and oppress us and to enrich themselves and their families, triggers both depression and rage.

The flood of corruption cases brings to mind a wooden plaque I had seen fastened to the wall of a Buddhist temple in Yangon. It carried a warning to the faithful to beware the ten "curses." Along with plagues and natural calamities, the list included the government as a curse on the people.

With corruption seemingly so pervasive and entrenched, it is tempting to interpret the Buddhist warning as a judgment on everyone in politics and every government as equally corrupt. We know that this is not the case. Without honest officials in government, we would not now witness so many corruption cases coming to light. But this is what those who have been caught want the public to believe.

The more dirt they can smear on PNoy and the administration officials who have brought them to justice, the easier to project their plight as the result merely of a change in the political weather—and themselves as victims of political persecution. We should now expect extreme efforts to equate the PDAF and the DAP.

But we must distinguish between the offenses attributed to officials of the executive branch and the offenses that have led to plunder charges. We must ask which caused the country the greater harm: the way the funds were sourced or the way the funds were used. And let us also be clear that legislators who used the DAP the way the indicted senators used the PDAF—as an opportunity for kickback—must also be held accountable.

The theme of political persecution as a ploy to solicit sympathy also offers the guilty the comforting hope that they can expect deliverance, when fickle political winds once again blow their way.

Which prompts another thought to cause depression and anger: with the 2016 elections just around the corner, who can say they are delusional?

8

Napoles Scam from a Distance

(*PDI*, June 07, 2014)

The Napoles scam will mark, hopefully, a historic milestone in the country's painful progress toward political maturity, with the righteous conviction and punishment of powerful, formerly untouchable, politicians.

When the dust has settled, when the principal protagonists, perhaps, have themselves turned to dust, some historians will revisit this landmark case. If they had only the information now available to us, how will they make sense of the evidence?

Their first task must be to determine what crime was committed. Spending pork barrel funds was not a crime, until the Supreme Court decision ruled it unconstitutional. Neither was using NGOs as channels for these funds. Nothing wrong, even, in coursing such funds to Janet Napoles' NGOs—if the NGOs actually received and used the funds for projects that actually benefited the intended recipients.

They would quickly dismiss the desperate attempt to implicate Budget Secretary Butch Abad as Napoles' "mentor." Tutoring Napoles on the budgetary process and the potential role of NGOs is not a crime. Academic institutions offer training programs on the budgetary process and how NGOs can avail themselves of public funds. Terrorists who kill with bombs cannot blame their crime on science teachers from whom they learned about explosives.

Even if such a personalized tutorial had transpired—which Abad has denied and Napoles has not proven—so what? Napoles would have to prove that Abad actively arranged the transactions with corrupt legislators and benefited from this assistance.

Conspiring with legislators to direct their pork barrel funds to bogus NGOs, defrauding the intended beneficiaries of most or all of the funds, and dividing the money between the legislators and the NGOs' architect—those constitute the crime.

Napoles has denied that she masterminded the scam, perhaps hoping to turn state's witness. Historians would find the denial worthless, because she did not identify the real mastermind who instructed her not on the pork barrel system, not on organizing NGOs, but on how to pinpoint the legislators willing to allocate their pork barrel funds to her "fake" NGOs and how to negotiate the "kickback" price.

While Napoles cannot escape culpability by claiming that she got the idea from someone else, she could not have succeeded without help. The assorted lists of conspirators coming out in the media will show historians that she had no lack of willing partners.

Sorting out the "Napolists" will be a major task. Historians would begin with official records, identifying the agencies or organizations to which the legislators assigned their pork barrel funds and the projects they were intended to support. Legislators who had nothing to fear about their pork barrel spending should have rushed to take this step. Not many have done so, despite the public demand for this accounting.

The legislators' list of pork barrel channels and intermediaries must then be compared with two other sets of lists: the "official" lists from the agencies of the executive branch and the lists originating from Napoles and the whistle-blowers, which reportedly recorded her collaborators. Suspicion would fall most heavily on the legislators appearing in all these lists.

Since the scam spanned several years and focused on different sectors, only a few hardworking legislators, if any, would appear in all lists. Those distinguishing themselves by appearing in the whistle-blowers' lists early, often and in a variety of sectors, would merit closer scrutiny.

Anyone who used a "ghost" NGO and squandered government funds on nonexistent projects would be fair game for the historians. They might cut some slack for someone who used the Napoles channels once or, perhaps, when she was just starting the scam. They would find more difficult to accept claims of innocence by repeat customers.

Given the number of people implicated in the scam, historians will want to distinguish different degrees of guilt. The amount of money stolen from the projects and the number of people victimized would factor into their judgment. But they will probably go beyond financial returns to determine which circle of Dante's *Inferno* each perpetrator should occupy.

Napoles may have gained more from the scam than any individual senator, and she should suffer commensurate punishment. But she is a private person, exercising no political powers, bound by no oath of public service or duty.

We entrust vast powers to the state and its officials to prevent people from taking advantage of each other. We expect and trust the government to look after our collective interests and to protect us from people like Napoles.

Historians will document how the politicians we elected not only failed in this duty but directly participated in plundering the public to enrich themselves.

We cannot accuse Napoles of betraying our trust, since we never gave it to her. Betrayal of public trust is the other crime for which historians will indict the politicians who partnered with her. In Filipino, the description for guardians turned oppressors is *bantay-salakay* (sentries who attack).

9

Guarding the Guards

(*PDI*, September 06, 2014)

The appearance of former Makati officials before the Senate Blue Ribbon Committee investigating the city's allegedly overpriced parking building has perked up public interest in the hearings. Their revelations recall a classic problem the ancient Romans recognized and, like their successors, never entirely resolved: who will guard the guards?

Because those given power to ensure honest governance can use it to facilitate and conceal corruption, we introduce more and stricter rules and procedures, such as the public bidding process, to prevent abuse of authority. Nonetheless, Mario Hechanova, who headed Makati's General Services Department and served in the Bids and Awards Committee (BAC), related how routinely the process was fixed to favor preselected bidders. He denied taking a kickback from winning contractors, but admitted to receiving a monthly BAC allowance of P200,000, allegedly from the then mayor, Jejomar Binay. Ernesto Mercado, then vice mayor and Mayor Binay's chief operating officer, also acknowledged that "he had benefited" (*may pakinabang*) from the Makati system.

Both men accepted inclusion in the Witness Protection Program, with Mercado publicly announcing that any harm he may subsequently suffer would come only from the Binay family. The first threat the two men are facing is legal prosecution. By their testimony, both have incriminated themselves in illegal acts: Mercado for gaining personal benefit from questionable official transactions and Hechanova for his role in rigging the bidding process. Both spoke out before securing immunity for themselves.

The risk they took has enhanced their credibility. Few corruption cases are successfully prosecuted without an insider blowing the whistle.

Serving as guards against corruption, they were also the mayor's subordinates; as Hechanova declared, he was just a soldier following orders. Another guard, the COA, should be less vulnerable to pressure than employees reporting to the mayor. COA resident auditors deployed in major government offices report to their agency. Under Sen. Alan Peter Cayetano's intense questioning, however, the COA auditors reviewing the parking building showed unfamiliarity with standard tools that individual home builders and businesses use to check that construction costs are within the reasonable range of expected values.

At the session she attended, COA Chair Grace Pulido Tan confessed embarrassment that her staff had not done a better job in auditing the Makati project. The confession elicited soothing words of comfort from Sen. Cayetano, who acknowledged the work she was doing to strengthen the agency. Clearly, a lot remains to be done.

COA resident auditors enjoy discretionary powers to make things easier or more difficult for implementing agencies. They can "work to rule," demanding strict compliance with every procedural point, thereby causing unnecessary bureaucratic delays. Or, they can relax requirements—to expedite implementation, but possibly, to extract personal gain. Their job is neither simple nor safe, especially if they are deployed in offices controlled by people of influence and power.

Which is why the COA must take steps to tighten recruitment criteria and to provide training and support to its field people. Providing them the construction reference and manuals identified by Sen. Cayetano would be a start, as well as on-the-job training on the technical aspects of the specific sectors they are assigned to oversee.

Mercado's testimony has provoked Vice President Binay into an angry denial that he profited from the building's construction. Both whistle-blowers have expressed their belief that the then mayor knew the details of the parking building's contract and costs, and may have taken a kickback. The senators have mainly and properly focused on the prior issue of whether the building was, in fact, overpriced.

In the last hearing, Sen. Cayetano picked apart the reasons offered for the high cost of the building: its "world-class," "green" character; the surge in the cost of steel; and the need for reinforced foundations. Rogelio Peig, vice president of Hilmarc, the general contractor for the project, denied that the company had ever represented the building as world-class or green. Unable to provide the Blue Ribbon Committee with cost information, he was also forced to withdraw any categorical conclusion that the building was not overpriced. The next hearing, to which the Hilmarc board was invited, should help clarify the issue.

The Makati government has used clearances from the COA as a shield against the overpricing allegation. The COA chair's own discomfort about the quality of the agency's project oversight makes this defense unconvincing.

Moreover, the COA still has to present its conclusions on the project. Appealing to COA clearances becomes an even slimmer reed behind which to seek cover when members of the COA resident staff are also included in the investigation. Collusion among the guards is always a danger.

The issue that perplexed the Romans continues to concern us: what is the recourse when the guards expected to protect the public coffers are incompetent, poorly trained, or easily prey to corruption or coercion? But we are relearning the lesson that much depends on the leader governing the guards.

10

Inclusive Corruption

(*PDI*, November 01, 2014)

Inclusive growth is the mantra of the moment, echoed by a chorus of development experts and social activists, and even by some politicians. We remain some distance away from this cherished goal. But if Makati whistle-blowers are to be believed, the country's richest and most developed city is apparently achieving inclusive corruption.

The Binay family allegedly appropriated 13 percent of the revenue from city contracts awarded through a rigged bidding system. This kind of systematic plunder of Makati's coffers, carried out for more than twenty-five years, could have been directed from the top but could not have been implemented without the collaboration of officials at lower levels. The *tongpats* (kickback) had to trickle down.

On top of the Binays' 13 percent share, an additional 12 percent allegedly went to Makati City officials: 6 percent to the vice mayor, sixteen councilors, two sector representatives, the council secretary and the commissioner; 3.5 percent to the engineering department; 1.5 percent to the BAC and the technical working group; and 1 percent to the budget, accounting and treasury heads.

That took care of the city officials, some of whom have already admitted to their take. Auditors of the COA deployed in Makati to prevent corruption also had to be managed. Hence, 2 percent was reportedly reserved for the resident auditor and 1 percent for the technical audit specialist.

Former Vice Mayor Ernesto Mercado, the key insider witness, noted that one resident auditor, Celia Cagaanan, declined her share for signing off on the Makati City Hall Building II (MCHBII). Her restraint was salutary and commendable, but the revelations about the MCHBII cast doubts on her decision to sign the clearance. To resist a conspiracy involving the city officialdom requires not just honesty but also heroism.

The hearings conducted by the Senate Blue Ribbon Subcommittee have also revealed that the crime did not involve only government officials. The overprice also required the participation of private business corporations in a perverse form of public-private partnership. The scam needed the assistance of a Hilmarc Corp., the construction company that built the MCHBII and nine other Makati buildings in the last ten years.

The link between the MCHBII and "Hacienda Binay" was the allegation that Hilmarc needed to collect from the Makati building, the bill for its work on "Hacienda Binay" and other advances it had made to the Binay family. To justify the billings, Hilmarc reportedly charged for work that was not necessary or should not go on the government's account. Hilmarc is also suspected of complicity in the rigged bidding process.

A small item discussed in the October 22 hearing illustrated the key role of contractors. Businessman Antonio Tiu denied that his firm had ever participated in any bid to supply Makati with hospital beds. The firm did sell Taiwanese-made hospital beds to Apollo Medical Equipment, which in turn sold the beds to Makati as US imports. How much the Tiu firm sold the beds to Apollo for, was not disclosed. But Makati paid P36 million, when import documents recorded the cost at under P2.5 million.

The contract between Apollo and Makati needs investigation. It is not clear that Tiu committed any crime in his transaction with Apollo—unless he also benefited from the second transaction. Perhaps, like his professed disinterest in who actually owned the "Hacienda Binay" he bought, he was unconcerned about Apollo's business dealings with Makati.

In the modern world, however, collusion between contractors and government officials is not sufficient for systemic, large-scale graft to succeed. Anti-graft experts in the West have documented the emergence of a corruption industry that includes the participation of realtors, lawyers, accountants, investment bankers and tax experts. Professionals in these fields contribute their expertise to conceal assets, evade taxes and avoid their appearance in the statements of assets, liabilities and net worth, required of government officials.

From the parade of witnesses summoned before the Senate Blue Ribbon Subcommittee, we appear to be catching up with the West on the best practices for managing corrupt transactions. The public is getting an education on the construction of corporate shells and the appointment of dummies in the board of directors so that the owners can retain control over assets while keeping their identity hidden from the public and the tax collectors.

It takes an entire village to raise a child, we are told. It turns out that it also takes virtually a whole village to prosper a crook. With the large cast of characters involved in running business operations, while also cooking the books, it is not surprising that someone will accidentally or deliberately let pieces of the truth slip out. What is surprising is how the scam has remained a secret for so long.

If Vice President Jejomar Binay is innocent of the charges raised against him, he must still explain how corruption, allegedly abetted by practically the entire city bureaucracy, has flourished in Makati over the twenty-eight years he and his family have controlled the city.

11

Water Torture

(*PDI*, December 06, 2014)

A statue on a bridge in Bruges honors the martyr John Nepomucene, ordered drowned by King Wenceslaus—according to one narrative, after his tongue was torn out because he would not disclose what the queen had confessed—serves as a reminder that neither the government nor the general public has any right to know what transpired between Vice President Jejomar Binay and the Catholic Bishops' Conference of the Philippines (CBCP), if the vice president had gone to the bishops for confession.

But, protesting that he was being "crucified," the vice president did not appear to be in a penitential mood when he appeared before the CBCP in his Boy Scout uniform. The reference to the crucifixion, recalling the charges raised against him, seems to border on blasphemous. The CBCP executive secretary, Fr. Edu Gariquez, told the press, after hearing the VP's "unconvincing" presentation, that the prospect of a Binay presidency "scared" him. A personal, perhaps imprudent comment, but no breach of the confessional seal.

The VP's torment is really not the relatively quick Roman capital punishment of crucifixion, but the exquisitely extended water torture credited to the Chinese. It's no big deal to splash some water on a person. But, drop after drop, hitting the same spot on a person's body over a sustained period, reportedly inflicts unbearable pain.

Since August, the drops have been falling one after another: a contractor, falsely recorded as officially bidding for contracts in which he did not qualify and was not qualified to participate; a businessman confirming being trapped in an elevator to delay his submission of a bid; the contractor for MCHBII admitting that it was neither "world-class" nor "green," as proclaimed.

Some drops, produced by whistle-blower research, have come from directions distant from the MCHBII—documents reflecting the purchase of overpriced hospital equipment for Makati; an old woman wondering, on camera, why the land she had sold to Mayor Binay remained under her name; electricity bills for "Hacienda Binay" still paid by a firm linked to VP Binay; allegations about dollar accounts undisclosed in Statement of Assets, Liabilities and Net worth (SALN) submissions; a COA report questioning the 2012–2013 financial reports of the Boy Scouts, which the VP has headed as president for decades.

Other drops have come from unexpected sources, causing self-inflicted pain: a 2010 videotaped interview of VP Binay talking about his Batangas property; an Instagram post by a Binay daughter claiming ownership of "Hacienda Binay;" Department of Environment and Natural Resources (DENR) permits for exotic animals for the "Hacienda Binay" zoo issued to Sen. Nancy Binay.

The drops continue to come, the latest being the VP's alleged ownership of condominium units extorted from building projects in Makati. The VP's defenders dismiss each drop that falls as mere allegation, lacking probative value. Coming in a steady stream, they gain progressively greater weight not easily deflected by defiant denials.

Objective observers initially sympathized with the VP's plight: how does he prove the negative; that he, for instance, did not own the condo units reportedly belonging to him? But the testimony given at the Senate hearings shifted on him the burden of refuting the documentary evidence presented by whistle-blowers.

VP Binay has thus far declined to address the substance of the charges raised against him. He first tried the political card: the investigation was a political demolition job. He has also claimed that his opponents were against him because of his "*Nognog*" (implying unfashionably dark and small) appearance, or because they were rich and he was poor.

The counter-charges of corruption filed against former Vice Mayor Ernesto Mercado and against Sen. Alan Peter Cayetano and Taguig

Mayor Lani Cayetano for assorted anomalies (overpriced multi-cabs, ghost employees, fraudulent SALN) take another tack: to blur any difference between the VP and his accusers, showing that every politician is vulnerable to unproven, politically-motivated charges. This is a risky strategy. Corruption charges, even when unproven, cast doubt on the fitness of a candidate to hold the presidency. But Mercado and the Cayetanos are not 2016 presidential contenders.

UNA appears convinced that the assault against the VP has run its course and failed. While approval ratings did drop, the core support for the VP's candidacy remained firm enough to keep him in the lead. Supporters are betting that with other issues on the horizon, such as the investigation of more politicians implicated in the P1.5 billion Malampaya–PDAF scam, the public will tire of the Binay hearings and switch channels.

The Senate Blue Ribbon Subcommittee has indicated that its Binay investigation could last till mid-2015. It claims that whistle-blowers have much more evidence to show how the Binays have exploited political office for private gain. It seems likely that the VP will continue to stall and stonewall.

The senators are betting that, as water wears down rocks, the flow of evidence, drop by drop, will erode the foundations of the VP's credibility—and that they have enough time.

12

Unmasking "Robin Hood"

(*PDI*, July 04, 2015)

Vice President Jejomar Binay can present proof of his ability to solve the problem of poverty, reportedly the central pitch of his presidential campaign. From self-described, abject poverty, he has brought the Binay family to fabulous wealth.

Rags-to-riches stories resonate with Filipinos and contribute to Binay's popularity with the *masa* (general public). Periodic allegations of massive corruption punctuating the Binay family's twenty-nine-year reign in Makati have eroded, but not erased the populist appeal.

The Senate investigation of the MCHBII was not the first time Binay had to face corruption charges. In 1988, former Makati Vice Mayor Roberto Brillante accused Binay, only three years in office, of payroll padding, illegal disbursement, overpricing, ghost delivery, misappropriation of public funds and falsification of public documents.

By 1992, some members of Makati's business elite whom Binay brought into the city government had turned against him on the issue of corruption. In 2001, *Newsbreak* reported corruption allegations against Binay, then gearing up for another mayoralty campaign. Benefiting from his populist programs, including birthday cakes and cash gifts for Makati's senior citizens and the protection of informal settlers against eviction, voters ignored the charges and reelected him to office.

With the political cover provided by constituency support, even critics from the A and B classes, who believed he was probably guilty, tended to shrug off these earlier cases and give him the benefit of the doubt; first, because these were never proven in court.

Second, even granting that Binay might be profiting from corruption, at least Makati was moving forward. Binay claimed the development of Makati as his achievement, never mind that private sector initiatives largely accounted for the city's transformation into the country's premier business center.

In those days, defenders attributed elite hostility to Binay as stemming from the increased city taxes he had imposed, suggesting that he was only redistributing the wealth. They projected Binay as a Filipino version of Robin Hood, the fourteenth-century English folk hero who stole from the rich to give to the poor.

In the romanticized ballads and books, and in Hollywood films, Robin Hood figured as the rebel fighting feudal, religious and secular authorities, including the corrupt Sheriff of Nottingham, the King's deputy, who was privatizing the communal lands and the forest resources on which the livelihood of Nottinghamshire peasants depended. But Binay was not an outsider; *Newsbreak* identified him as the "Lord of Makati," making him not Robin Hood, but the Sheriff of Nottingham.

The Senate hearings showed no evidence of Binay battling "Big Business" abuses in Makati, but also no complaints that he tried to put the squeeze on them in any obvious ways; it's hard to imagine their executives being trapped in an elevator to prevent their participation in a bidding process.

Three possible explanations for the silence of the big business guns: 1) they had no need to do business with Makati; 2) they were big enough to take "fast-track facilitation fees" as a business cost that could be passed on to consumers or to bargain for other benefits; and 3) they were simply too big for Binay to bully.

What has provoked damaging comments on social media against Binay is the list of social sectors apparently victimized by graft. As the senators diligently pulled on the threads of the alleged overpricing of the parking building, the whole governance fabric began unraveling to reveal a pattern of Makati misgovernance.

We now have the cases of overpriced garbage disposal services; overpriced hospital beds; overpriced school building construction;

overpriced, because privatized, tuition for nursing students; and possible fraud committed against the Boy Scouts of the Philippines. It was Binay's duty to protect these funds that he is, instead, being accused of pilfering.

Even wealthy Makati will not have all of the resources required to provide the sanitation, health, education and social services that the city needs.

Diversion of public funds into private pockets that curtail the coverage or the quality of essential public services, disproportionately burdens the poor. The rich can always engage private providers.

The Senate investigations thus badly tarnished the Robin Hood image, revealing the crime as not robbing the rich, but stealing from the poor. Binay's trust ratings plunged during the period of Senate hearings, only rebounding when the Senate shifted public attention from Makati to Mamasapano.

In resigning from the Aquino Cabinet, in resisting Junjun Binay's preventive suspension, Binay continued to play the persecuted underdog card, hoping to divert attention from the corruption cases that made the resignation and his son's suspension necessary. But the ombudsman's decision to pursue these cases makes it difficult for Binay to dismiss them as mere election-inspired mud-slinging.

To recover the Robin Hood aura and give credibility to his presidential candidacy, Binay has to deal directly and decisively with the charges lodged against him. This is what voters are waiting for him to do.

13

Ends and Means

(*PDI*, August 02, 2014)

Security forces have recaptured a convicted terrorist with possible intelligence about an imminent suicide bombing attack. Can you torture the terrorist's child to extract information to avert the attack?

A runaway train, nearing a diversion track, will crash into the railway station, killing scores of people. You can prevent the disaster by pushing a bystander onto the path of the train to alter its direction. Can you sacrifice one life to save many?

Ethics professors pose these situations to probe the principle that the end does not justify the means, which, in both examples, violate the fundamental rights of blameless victims. Anti-administration moralists invoking and trivializing the principle, proclaim that the noble ends of the DAP do not justify its evil means.

What is inherently evil about interpreting "savings" to allow moving funds from stalled projects early enough to complete other projects beneficial to the public? Considering the nuanced Supreme Court decision declaring only certain acts and practices unconstitutional and the many dissenting/concurring opinions it provoked, the DAP definition does not appear unreasonable or unlawful.

That some legislators treated additional DAP allocations like the PDAF, which had been ruled unconstitutional, is a separate issue. In giving their DAP funds to ghost NGOs, legislators defrauded rightful beneficiaries, for which they and their partners should be held accountable.

The budget is a management tool. Corporate CEOs exercise considerable flexibility in deploying the budget—means authorized by the board to achieve organizational ends. Beyond lofty mission/vision proclamations, where the money goes more truly reflects the organization's priorities. It has become a Hollywood cliché, but the injunction to "follow the money" remains sound advice.

Reforming the government budget process, a complex, technical, tedious undertaking vulnerable to corruption, was thus crucial as a means to reach the administration's "Daang Matuwid". Who opposed or were even aware of the games that could be played with reenacted budgets? Critics demanding impeachment should ask which administration has worked harder to promote budget transparency, accountability and efficiency in achieving development goals.

Separation of powers, designed to maintain a system of checks and balances, also serves as a means to curb corruption. As rightly stressed by the Supreme Court in the PDAF and DAP cases, this principle must be reinforced to control arbitrary and self-serving decision-making by government officials.

The three branches of government must also work together to achieve other ends, including political stability and inclusive economic growth. More than in other countries, however, citizens look to the president as ultimately responsible for government performance.

A thousand fathers lay claim to government achievements. Paternity for failure is blamed on the president. The COA and the Commission on Elections (COMELEC) are independent bodies constitutionally separate from the executive branch. But the public assumes that the president, if he only wants to, can prevent the COA delays in investigating plunder cases or the COMELEC fiascoes in managing elections.

By interpreting rules liberally to accelerate development, the administration risked legal censure. Is the country better off enforcing more stringent budget rules to reduce the risk of corruption? This approach, taken during the first two years of the administration, as the World Bank noted, came at the cost of growth. Critics then complained that the "Daang Matuwid" must also deliver tangible benefits to the people.

In his televised defense of the DAP, PNoy shared a friendly tweet comparing his plight to someone who parks in a restricted zone to assist a sick person and gets a traffic violation ticket. PNoy quipped that the zone was not even clearly marked “No Parking.”

The analogy recalls Matthew’s Gospel account of the Pharisees challenging Jesus on the lawfulness of healing on the Sabbath. Jesus responded by asking who among them would refuse because it was the Sabbath, to rescue a sheep fallen into a pit. He did not instruct the people in the synagogue on Jewish laws. But his audience understood the spirit in which these laws should govern and continued to seek and to receive healing.

Flexibility in budget management allows a good president to deploy scarce financial resources where they are most urgently needed. People suffer real loss when funds lie idle instead of supporting the completion of more roads, the care of more patients, the education of more children. The country also suffers real loss when a bad president exploits budget flexibility for political and personal profit.

The choice appears stark: less development or less corruption, pick your poison. We should not allow ourselves to be impaled on the horns of this false dilemma.

Deliberations on the 2015 P2.606-trillion budget present a timely opportunity for Congress and the executive branch to clarify the concept of “savings.” None of the three branches can claim unblemished infallibility or integrity.

Working together with greater consciousness of common ends, they may yet craft a definition of savings and their legitimate uses that will better benefit the public.

PERSPECTIVES

President Duterte

Presidential candidate Rodrigo Roa Duterte was a largely unknown entity to most of the electorate who cast their vote for him in 2016. But he had clearly tapped into the rich sources of public dissatisfaction and his handlers conducted a clever, media-savvy campaign that exploited the reach of social media platforms to convert that discontent into votes.

My early columns on candidate Duterte tried to make sense of his public appeal, but also convey my doubts as to the directions into which he might try to lead the country. His first State of the Nation Address (SONA) as president offered hopes that he might use his popularity, as reflected in trust and approval ratings in public opinion polls, to maintain the development momentum generated by the previous administration.

Social Weather Stations (SWS) opinion polls at the point of the PNoy turnover to Duterte noted that public morale in the country had never been higher. The country's economic fundamentals were sound, the political environment reasonably placid. Winning the election from among a field of six candidates, Duterte was, inevitably, a minority president. Although more people wanted a different president to lead the country, no one disputed Duterte's mandate to govern. His closest opponents were quick to concede defeat and the passage from one administration to the next was a model for the democratic transition of power through elections.

Three years of the administration did not diminish in any large measure, the doubts of those who disagreed with government policies and their trajectory. And the administration offered few avenues for the discussion of their concerns.

1

The Duterte Dilemma

(*PDI*, January 02, 2016)

I remember first reading the story in Tagalog, probably in *Pilipino Komiks*. A colony of fiercely independent frogs fought bitterly among themselves because no one was willing to give way to another. Unable to agree on anything, the colony could not progress. Finally, they appealed to *Bathala* (God) to send them a leader to establish law and order and consensus. Bathala responded by sending them a log.

Initially impressed by the size and weight of the log, the frogs quickly discovered that it was also inert and incapable of controlling conflict and violence. They pleaded with Bathala to send them a more proactive leader. Bathala sent them a crocodile, which decisively imposed consensus by devouring those who disagreed with its decrees. The frogs rushed back to Bathala, begging him to recall the crocodile. But Bathala made them live with what they had prayed for.

This tale came from the collection of fables attributed to Aesop, a Greek storyteller of the seventh century BC, who used them to teach moral lessons. The fable of the crocodile king acknowledged that without a leader, unbridled individualism can block a community's progress and prosperity.

But submitting to a leader without regard for individual autonomy risked the loss of their rights and their lives. Since Aesop's time, humanity has been trying to strike the right balance between individual autonomy and social order. The issue confronts us again.

Mayor Rodrigo Duterte brings to the presidential race a reputation as a "strong" leader, quick to apprehend, judge and "neutralize" drug dealers.

Many voters, wearied and worried by the pattern of criminals prospering unpunished, have found Duterte's "decisiveness" admirable. Who wants a weak, indecisive leader?

Here is our Duterte dilemma: to control impunity, should we entrust power to someone suspected of abusing official powers with impunity? Former Commission on Human Rights (CHR) Chair Leila de Lima had conducted investigations on the extrajudicial killing of criminals by "death squads" linked to Mayor Duterte.

Unfortunately, the accusations never resulted in indictments. Duterte, therefore, was never compelled to address conclusively suspicions that he had violated legal and constitutional processes to achieve swift justice.

Duterte has projected the image of an action-oriented, results-driven executive who can address people's fears about an environment perceived as dominated by criminal elements. In the process, he has broadly, almost boastfully, hinted that he had indeed ignored human rights and legal norms, enforcing the law by violating the law.

Because he is now a presidential candidate, Duterte's self-incriminating statements increase the pressures on the CHR, the Ombudsman's office and the Department of Justice (DOJ) to fulfill their mandate. How can these agencies ignore hints of capital crimes gone unpunished, committed by one aspiring to lead the country? Especially when, according to de Lima, a whistle-blower has surfaced.

The CHR/Ombudsman/DOJ dilemma is that people do not seem repelled by, or even anxious about, the violations of human rights Duterte might have committed. Political operatives will try to discredit their investigations as efforts to influence the elections. Most people are not drug dealers and cannot imagine that they would ever contend with Duterte. But we should consider the implications of past impunity on his potential exercise of presidential powers.

Perhaps, Duterte might not have done any killing himself, though he may suggest even this to burnish the Dirty Harry brand. But as mayor, he had people ready and eager to follow his orders. As president, he would have even more people to do his bidding.

According to a newspaper report, Duterte said that as president, he would allow policemen on duty to kill criminals and would protect them against charges of human rights violations. He also said that the policemen would "go first, should they commit wrongdoings." He referred to three rogue policemen who had recently been killed, but "did not directly respond to the question if he was the one who killed the police officers."

Duterte is not infallible. Neither are the subordinates on whose information he depends. The execution of policemen who make mistakes offers small comfort to families of the victims. People will make mistakes, but these should not lead to irreversible consequences. Summary executions permit no room to appeal possibly erroneous decisions.

The issue is whether the police should have the power to execute people they arrest on the basis of their suspicions, without due process of law, and whether mayor or president should have the power—by direct order or by insinuation and promise of protection—to conduct these executions. A future president accustomed to act with impunity places everyone on a slippery slope. Where would Duterte draw the line on crimes he can punish without regard for constitutionally-guaranteed human rights?

Aesop's fable of the frogs cautions us against submitting ourselves to the judicious judgment of the crocodile.

2

Documenting Duterte

(*PDI*, April 16, 2016)

People remain ambivalent about Mayor Rodrigo Duterte. He wants to jail Vice President Jejomar Binay for plunder; Binay wants to jail him for his "death squad." Sen. Grace Poe wants to make him Crime Czar (Mar Roxas supporters say, "Elect Roxas and nail two for the price of one.")

Given Duterte's current lead in the election surveys, however, people should begin considering what a Duterte presidency might mean. Not so easy to do—he has performed as a one-note musician, trumpeting his law-and-order credentials in Davao City.

His political opponents have questioned his record, citing police data (2010–15) documenting Davao as third highest in the number of robbery cases, second in rape cases and first in murder cases. Then there is the "death squad" issue—that whatever the achievements, the Duterte approach to controlling crime had come at the high cost of other crimes, involving extrajudicial executions that allowed no appeal.

Duterte has repeatedly pledged to end criminality in the country within three to six months or give up the presidency. Perhaps it's just empty talk, although his official running mate, Sen. Alan Cayetano, is now echoing the six-month schedule. To be fair, Duterte had warned the public to be careful about what it asked for in "forcing" him to run: blood will have to flow for him to keep his promise.

But he should now expect more rigorous research on his past record and policy-related statements. He had been quite ready to speak his mind, even on delicate political issues—as when he addressed the Davao Trade

Expo on October 29, 2013, at the SMX Convention Center. (*Davao Today*'s report appeared on its website and on that of *Bulatlat*, but neither link is still functioning.)

In that speech, Duterte tackled the issue of the "revolutionary taxation" imposed by the New People's Army (NPA) in Region 11. *Davao Today* headlined his typically blunt advice to businessmen confronted by NPA tax collectors: "NPA taxation a reality, just pay them." The actual quote: "If you pay to the [Bureau of Internal Revenue], you prepare also for the NPA."

In December 2012, Duterte was quoted as admitting to paying revolutionary taxes amounting to P125 million a year. He later explained that he had spoken at a Communist Party of the Philippines (CPP) anniversary celebration in an area that Typhoon Pablo had devastated. The money he gave, he said, was not a revolutionary tax payment, but donations he had solicited for disaster victims. In the absence of any *barangay* (village) captain, he entrusted the money to the NPA.

He also lauded the NPA for offering to pay compensation to all the victims of its grenade attack on a gym in Paquibato. "When they informed me they will pay P5,000, I said, 'Good.' When I asked where they will get the money, they said they will get it from banana planters," he quipped.

The quip meant that businessmen will have to pay for the violence that the NPA had inflicted on undeserving victims. This did not seem to bother Duterte, who pointed out that the CPP had been the victim of "historical injustice." Sadly, he is not as concerned about the "historical injustice" dealt to the victims of martial law.

According to the survey agencies, Duterte draws support from the A, B, C sectors from which would come the investors with money to risk in Mindanao. Did they give this support knowing of the Duterte prescription on revolutionary taxes?

Duterte has admitted that his experience was in dealing with criminals, conceding that the national government must handle revolutionary groups. But the prospect of assuming the presidency has already tempted him to make unilateral policy pronouncements on the longest-running insurgency in the world.

Many in the business sector, and even among the military, would support the PNoy administration's plan to engage in talks with the CPP/

National Democratic Front (NDF), which Duterte also favors. But without careful preparation to arrive at mutually acceptable terms of engagement, such talks are unlikely to bear fruit. And yet, Duterte has already announced that he would invite "[Jose Maria] Sison and other communist leaders" to join his cabinet. He further declared that he would give the CPP/NPA three cabinet portfolios: agrarian reform, social welfare and development, and environment and natural resources.

His supporters applaud Duterte's decisiveness and his readiness to act. As mayor, he has probably not encountered much resistance from the city council to any of his initiatives. He will find the legislature and the Supreme Court more challenging governance partners, and Malacañang a more complex environment.

The NDF was more realistic in its assessment of the Duterte offer. Luis Jalandoni, chair of the NDF peace panel, courteously declined the invitation to take appointments in the Duterte Cabinet. Even the NDF recognized that the issue of peace required more than a private understanding between Sison and the Philippine president, even if he happens to be Duterte.

3

Betting on the Future: What If?

(*PDI*, May 07, 2016)

By this time, you may already have decided on your presidential candidate. Business schools recommend asking one final question to confirm or counter a decision: what if I am wrong? What if recent revelations about my candidate are true? What are the risks of electing this candidate?

Following his charges of unreported income and misdeclared SALN, Sen. Antonio Trillanes has filed a plunder case against Mayor Rodrigo Duterte for ghost employees. Rejecting laws against extrajudicial executions, Duterte now invokes laws that protect the privacy of his bank accounts. This advances the narrative that Duterte may be a human rights violator and also just another corrupt politician. Unusually, Sen. Alan Cayetano, who has pursued Vice President Jejomar Binay for corruption, is silent, finding himself now paired with the patriarch of "the Binays of Davao."

The last presidential debate, held in Dagupan, added little information on Duterte's plans for realizing his extravagant promises. Adversaries spared him further grilling on his "*Dapat ang mayor ang mauna*" (The mayor should be first) comment on the rape of an Australian missionary, which did say something about his views on the perks of public office.

But it exposed personality and character traits consistent with the diagnosis of Dr. Natividad Dayan, former president of the International Council of Psychologists, and with Duterte's way of dismissing accusations leveled at him. He applies laws selectively because his ends justify his means.

The medical assessment, reported by Aaron Lozada of ABS-CBN News, came from documents presented for the civil annulment of Duterte's marriage with his first wife. It concluded that he suffered from "antisocial narcissistic personality disorder," a condition characterized by "gross indifference, insensitivity and self-centeredness," "grandiose sense of self-entitlement and manipulative behaviors" and "pervasive tendency to demean, humiliate others and violate their rights and feelings."

The biggest damage Duterte suffered in Dagupan was inflicted by his statements giving credence to the psychological diagnosis. He said he would copy ideas from his opponents; he was used to "copying" (i.e. cheating) since he was in Grade one. The retort to the Mar Roxas offer of data on PhilHealth did sound like something from a grade school playground: without providing any data of his own, Duterte roughly responded with "I don't believe you." And then there was his plan to invite martyrdom by jet skiing to the nearest Chinese reclamation area in the WPS to plant the Philippine flag, because he wanted to do something heroic.

The debate raised serious issues that Duterte himself had emphasized. First was security, but beyond protection from criminal elements, on which he has focused. It also includes economic security and workers' need for better-paying, more secure jobs that will enable them to support their families.

Pangasinan fishermen, appealing for assistance against Chinese ships barring them from traditional fishing grounds in the WPS, underlined the link between national and economic security. Climate change, felt by the Kidapawan farmers suffering from the drought triggered by El Niño, has elevated security to the planetary level. On both issues, we need the diplomatic support of allies, whom Duterte has disrespected.

Force cannot be the main response to all aspects of security, nor to the electorate's concern for inclusive economic development. We have made progress in expanding economic opportunities, improving the delivery of social services and controlling corruption. Much remains to be done; the gains have left the lives of many people untouched. But compare the record of the last six years with the preceding twelve years of the Estrada-Arroyo administrations.

History shows no shortcut to secure, inclusive prosperity. Its achievement depends on enduring commitment to the rule of law and democratic values, and on leaders who can be trusted not to reverse the policies that have made a measure of success possible, so that we can build on what has been achieved.

"Daang Matuwid" has helped enable the country's economic performance. Granting that many more deserve prosecution, when have we seen so many "big fish" brought before the courts? What if, on the pretext of promoting unity, Duterte's intent is to bury, with Ferdinand Marcos' body in the Libingan ng mga Bayani (National Heroes' Cemetery), the cases against the Napoles plunderers, the recovery of the wealth plundered during martial law, the assorted scams during the Arroyo administration and the prosecution of those responsible for the Ampatuan massacre?

Will a Duterte presidency unite the nation? Consider his take-no-prisoner orientation and his Lone Ranger approach to contentious national issues, including negotiations with the NDF and with China. What if, now armed with the powers of the presidency, he continues this management style and policy thrust? What if, as Sen. Miriam Santiago declared, he is the NPA's candidate? The Skype consultations with the NDF demonstrated Duterte giving greater respect to Joma Sison than he showed to Pope Francis.

The results of this election will maintain or diminish the momentum for progress. Voters must consider what risks they are taking with their candidate. Can they risk the future on this decision?

4

Voter Education

(*PDI*, June 04, 2016)

Whether the presidential race was a referendum on the performance of the PNoy administration remains a disputed point among political analysts. That the vice-presidential contest became a referendum on the historical record of Ferdinand Marcos seems clearer.

Bongbong Marcos made it so by: 1) insisting that his father receive a hero's burial at the Libingan ng mga Bayani, 2) dismissing the claims of human rights victims of martial law as motivated by greed, and 3) denying his and his family's complicity in concealing the resources that the dictator had plundered from the country.

The strategy nearly worked. It cost the Robredo Team and the Silent Majority much time and effort to debunk the glorification of Ferdinand Marcos' World War II record and the assertion that the country achieved a "golden age" during his fourteen-year (1972–85) autocratic regime.

The Bongbong Marcos campaign initially benefited from three factors: the frustration among the A, B and C economic sectors with the government's inability to relieve the security and traffic problems in the cities; the nostalgia for the more tranquil time that the early years of "smiling martial law" as it appeared to those not directly involved in the struggle against the Marcos regime; and the general ignorance of the electorate about the context, causes and consequences of martial law in the Philippines.

But the strategy suffered from a fatal flaw: it lacked a foundation in reality. The evidence for the Marcos medals was a piece of fiction authored by Marcos himself and authoritatively exposed to the world over thirty years ago as fraudulent. The "golden age" was a myth that could be sustained by propaganda only over the short-term, until it shattered against hard data, such as the SWS files on Self-Rated Poverty (SRP) from 114 surveys stretching over more than three decades.

The latest SWS survey based on interviews completed in April 2016 reported that 46 percent of households considered themselves "poor." Though sadly still too high, the 2016 SRP was lower than the full-year 2015 rate of 50 percent and approached the best we have ever recorded: 43 percent in March 1987 and in March 2010, and 45 percent in December 2011. The lowest SRP rate came during the Cory Aquino administration and the next best three under PNoy.

The first SRP national survey, conducted in April 1983, before the crisis sparked by the airport assassination of Ninoy Aquino, recorded a 55 percent poverty rate. By July 1985, the accumulating burden of the assassination, cronyism and Marcos plunder had plunged nearly three of every four Filipinos into poverty, with the record SRP low of 74 percent.

The Bongbong Marcos campaign miscalculated in two ways: first, in projecting the competing narrative of the martial law "golden age" and the 1986 People Power Revolution as a contest that concerned only the Marcos and the Aquino families; and second, in allowing enough time for the victims of martial law to mobilize for the telling of their own stories.

But the blade-thin margin of Leni Robredo's victory demonstrated that the education of the electorate remains an urgent task. The College Editors Guild of the Philippines is correctly concerned about the elimination in the new Department of Education (DepEd) curriculum, of a separate Philippine history course after Junior High School. This denies 60 percent of the youth who do not reach college, the chance to understand the forces that shaped the course of modern Philippine political and economic history.

The Commission on Higher Education (CHED) has recognized the vulnerability of a history-free basic education curriculum to politically-based historical revisionism. The issue is important because nation-building remains a work in progress. We remain a collection of tribes, choosing leaders because they come from the same clan or region or language grouping. The Philippines, as an imagined community for which

Filipinos willingly offer loyalty and life, cannot consolidate if people tell conflicting stories about so critical an event as martial law.

The choice of the narrative must be dictated, not by political fiat, but by historical research that, once validated, must transcend personal or political preferences. Further research will add nuance, but the main contours of the martial law experience are already as clear as those of the Holocaust in Europe, where Holocaust-deniers can be brought to court.

A pope can insist that the sun orbits around the earth and order dissenters to be burned at the stake. A president may behave like a pope and canonize Ferdinand Marcos a hero—but to what purpose and at what cost? National unity cannot be based on a blatant lie, and on a lie that sides with the criminals against their victims.

President-elect Rodrigo Duterte has spoken about permitting Marcos' burial at the Libingan. Perhaps, recognizing how this decision can perpetuate the miseducation of the public, he can consign his declaration among those "preposterous statements" he has warned the public not to believe.

5

High Hopes

(*PDI*, July 02, 2016)

Has the worm truly turned into a butterfly? The speech at the presidential inauguration hopefully heralds the beginning of the transformation: the candidate is working to become more presidential.

President Rodrigo Duterte's election strategists had tapped into the rage repressed over decades of government failure to address basic needs. They stoked and fanned this anger to fever pitch by a campaign of calculated crudeness and verbal violence and turned it against political rivals—especially those in power—as the presumed sources of the current public misery, whose roots were actually planted well before their term.

The strategy succeeded brilliantly, mobilizing anonymous and unverified social media speculation to trump more rigorously vetted social science research and projecting a sense of national crisis that demanded decisive, strongman rule. This narrative baffled followers of SWS surveys, which reported positive approval scores for the overall performance of the administration and public morale never higher at the end of a presidential term.

The trash-talking, scorched-earth strategy, we were told, was devised only for the campaign. The authors recognized that what had proven emotionally effective for exciting and engaging voters can impede rational problem-solving, the crafting of public policies and the pursuit of good governance.

Now that he has claimed the big prize, Mr. Duterte can afford to manifest magnanimity; he no longer needs to carry such a big chip on his shoulder. Even those who have expressed grave reservations about a Duterte presidency fervently hope he will succeed. They know that the country can ill afford six years of drift or a risky rush into contentious political commitments.

Mr. Duterte assumes the presidency armed with advantages no president in recent memory has enjoyed. The broad popular support, reflected in the wide margin of victory, gives him an undisputed mandate to govern. This has also facilitated the formation of a compliant supermajority in Congress, with politicians taking the huge lead as the justification to switch parties.

Few in the incoming administration emphasize a third crucial advantage that Sonny Dominguez, appointed finance secretary, has recognized: Mr. Duterte is taking over a going concern. He inherits an economy that has averaged an annual GDP growth of 6.2 percent during the previous administration, the best performance in the region after China.

Much remains to be done, but objective observers acknowledge that the PNoy administration made a start in addressing the concerns over systemic corruption in the bureaucracy that delayed the implementation of public-private projects. The public expects the Duterte administration to hit the ground running, especially since it does not lack projects that should gain the support of even the 60 percent of the electorate that did not vote for him.

The Duterte administration will have enough on its plate, after dealing with the inevitable complications of managing the transition period and getting its own bureaucracy up to speed. Electoral campaigns necessarily project black-and-white differences between candidates to distinguish more sharply one's strengths from the frailties of the others. But there is enough convergence on governance goals between outgoing and incoming administrations. This should encourage Mr. Duterte to use whatever successes the previous administration may have achieved as a platform to accelerate the completion of what it had not been able to accomplish.

After six years of preparation, the K12 program, a key advocacy of the PNoy administration, needs continuing support. Whatever his initial misgivings, Mr. Duterte has accepted, after conducting consultations with its proponents and with the appointed education secretary, Leonor

Briones, that K12 may advance his own vision of how to improve the education sector. He now has the opportunity to bring behind him the Education Nation that persuaded PNoy to pursue the K12 program. SWS surveys during the latter years of the PNoy administration showed the areas where the "bosses" gave it a poor performance rating. An unfulfilled promise, for instance, was the enactment of a Freedom of Information Act, a law which should strengthen Mr. Duterte's expressed advocacy for transparency and his campaign against corruption.

SWS respondents were also critical of the glacial pace in the prosecution of the Ampatuan massacre judicial proceedings. In a recent speech at the turnover of the PNP command in Davao City, Mr. Duterte showed himself well-versed in the problems of local government officials who use their positions, especially their control of police and security forces, for criminal purposes.

There should be other issues that those who voted for Mr. Duterte and those who did not can identify as common concerns. These include the strengthening of the Reproductive Health Law and the prosecution of the Napoles and Makati City cases. It may be prudent for the new president to seek the harvest of low-hanging fruit around which the voters can rally, rather than target controversial goals over which they can be expected to divide.

6

Decoding Duterte

(*PDI*, August 06, 2016)

It is not easy to reconcile seeming discrepancies among statements made by President Rodrigo Roa Duterte (PRRD)—between what he says and what he does. But the task should not take the skills required to read tea leaves or chicken entrails. Five weeks after he assumed office, we begin to get a sense of the presidential style.

First, prepared scripts do not sit well with PRRD, as demonstrated not only by his casual treatment of the SONA prompter, but also by his undisguised surprise at portions of his text. After reading the plan to accelerate commuter train speed from 40 to 60 kilometers per hour, he commented: "*Huwag kayong maniwala dito.*" (Don't believe this.) He then talked about the risk of raising speed limits with dilapidated train tracks.

He softened this warning by addressing Transportation Secretary Arturo Tugade: "*Art, ambisyoso ka, ah. Kaya mo kaya ito*?" (Art, you are ambitious. Can you really do this?) The possibility of being publicly disavowed may make PRRD's executives more modest in their claims. It may also lead the public to wonder which of the prepared texts issued under his name PRRD takes seriously.

Second, the remarks probably reflect PRRD's limited time and patience with protracted planning processes. Management consultants would prescribe a system for approving speeches or, for instance, critical personnel appointments. The latter would involve several steps, including preparing a short list of candidates and the metrics to evaluate each one's fitness for the job. This was not the process PRRD described in appointing Environment Secretary Gina Lopez.

PRRD acts decisively, guided by a quick read on people and a gut feel sharpened by personal experience. In the Lopez case, he explained his judgment: "I would not be appointing somebody who is alien to my thinking. I would take in somebody who shares my horizons in life."

This spontaneity can become problematic, as in the reported offer of the CHED chairmanship to Jose David Lapuz, PRRD's former professor at Lyceum. The post was not vacant, as the fixed term of the current chair, Patricia Licuanan, had not expired. Lapuz apparently also lacked the earned doctorate required for this position.

PRRD's experience, his "horizons," came mainly from twenty-three years as a mayor. Elected as a local government executive, brought him closer to his constituency and, perhaps, reinforced the tendency toward action more than analysis and the emphasis on service delivery. In the SONA, he pushed for facilitating the processes of obtaining driver's licenses, passports, business permits, even train tickets.

These were low-hanging fruit, perhaps, but these addressed issues that directly touched the majority of people who lack the money or the connections to ease the oppressive irritants of daily life. He understood—and empathized with—the plight of those who have to camp on city streets overnight to secure a place in the queue: "I do not want to see people lining up under the heat of the sun. I do not want people lining up in the rain."

While sensitive to the concerns of the marginalized, PRRD's passionate crusade against the drug trade leads to some dissonance. Addressing the issue of the communist insurgency, he waxed emotional, speaking of feeling the pain and grief of the widows and orphans left behind by slain government soldiers and rebels. But he has no sympathy to waste on those widowed and orphaned by the action of police or vigilante groups.

Surely, whatever the circumstances of their loss, those widows and orphans also feel pain and grief. His dismissal as "drama-drama" of the Pieta-like photograph of the grieving woman cradling her dead, alleged drug-pusher partner, which the *New York Times* reprinted, thus appears uncharacteristically callous.

Many rely on PRRD's assurance that his "adherence to due process and the rule of law is uncompromising." Not "belief," not "commitment," but "adherence," which is validated in action. He has already proven that he can deal death to drug dealers. He still has to demonstrate that he can act as decisively in punishing those who practice extrajudicial executions in violation of the rule of law.

A third point has become obvious: PRRD is not afraid to change his mind. After initially finding reasons for their actions, he has come around to characterize the Abu Sayyaf as terrorists and criminals. He has agreed that a basic law for Bangsamoro autonomy should not have to wait for a federal system. He switched from supporting a constitutional commission to a constitutional assembly as the mechanism for political change. This willingness to change course gives hope to those who believe in a legal basis for denying Ferdinand Marcos burial in the Libingan ng mga Bayani.

The president's presumed "transparency" has rightly drawn much favorable comment. We just need to remember that "transparent" does not necessarily mean "consistent," much less "predictable." We still need to understand what role messengers or messages play in persuading PRRD to change his mind.

7

Insulting God

(*PDI*, July 07, 2018)

In countries where many religions coexist, governments view with apprehension public statements on religious beliefs, icons and customs. Such statements can spark internal communal violence and complicate international relations. Recall the editorial cartoons ridiculing Mohammad in the Danish and French media that triggered diplomatic protests against Denmark and riots in several Muslim countries in 2005, and the Al-Qaeda attack on the Paris newspaper *Charlie Hebdo* that killed twelve people in 2015.

Where faith communities also divide along ethnic lines, religion becomes an even more sensitive topic. Well before the European incidents, governments facing this challenge imposed limits on freedom of expression, prohibiting speech likely to offend the faithful. They followed the same logic that punishes pranksters who endanger the public by shouting "Fire!" or "Bomb!" in a crowded theater.

Not particularly praised for its liberal values, the Duterte administration has become an ally of the most fervent Western defenders of free speech. President Duterte has ridiculed as "stupid" the God of the Christian Bible, which Muslims also regard as holy. In one statement, Mr. Duterte seemed to demean the majority of the people, forcing his minions to invoke his right to free speech—a defense that, in some ASEAN (Association of Southeast Asian Nations) countries, would not save him from sanctions.

Mr. Duterte is free to worship whichever god he chooses to create in his own image and likeness. But it is offensive, if not unconstitutional, when he uses the bully pulpit of the presidency to peddle his views on religion. Even worse is when he hurls, from this elevated platform, gratuitous insults on the faith of his compatriots.

Many Filipinos did find Mr. Duterte's comments on Christian religion offensive. He has declared that he will not issue an apology for his insulting statements. The God we worship suffers no damage from any insult coming from someone like Mr. Duterte and has no need for his apology. It may not even restrain Duterte followers, who have used the controversy to spew more fake news and insults against Church and clergy.

Many, perhaps, welcomed suggestions from the Palace that he would be open to a dialogue with the Church hierarchy. This may have value, if it focused less on Mr. Duterte's insults than on his policies. I suspect our God would feel less aggrieved and angered being called "stupid" than being confronted with the continuing killing of His people in the administration's drug war.

The evidence-based study on the anti-drug campaign by a consortium composed of Ateneo de Manila University, Columbia University's Stabile Center for Investigative Journalism, De La Salle University and the University of the Philippines would provide a rich subject for this dialogue. Unfortunately, it met with a muted response from Malacañang, which paid more attention to Mr. Duterte's "God is stupid" comment.

Clarifying facts would serve as a useful starting point for the dialogue. The consortium study counted 5,021 drug-related deaths between May 10, 2016 and September 29, 2017. The PNP offered lower figures for a longer time frame: 2,235 drug-related deaths from July 2016 to January 2018. Surely, it can supply the numbers for the same time frame. Then, it can perhaps explain why the study was wrong in counting 2,753 killed by policemen during police operations.

Presidential Spokesperson Harry Roque questions the study because it relies on media reports. But both print and broadcast reports draw from police sources, including police blotters. He accepts that the victims were mostly the poor, but asks for independent verification that they were killed because of the anti-drug war. If Roque has doubts on this issue, he should ask the police who did the killing, to explain their action.

The consortium has declared its eagerness to collaborate with the government in the analysis of the count and context of the drug war deaths.

Otherwise, how can we proclaim the government's anti-drug campaign a success? And the rising death count will remain a continuing insult and offense to God and our Christian values—a proper issue for the Church and the president to pursue.

8

Trusting Duterte?

(*PDI*, March 02, 2019)

Political observers have viewed, with delight or despair, survey reports on the extended "honeymoon period" enjoyed by President Duterte. SWS Chair Mahar Mangahas cautions readers to take these reports in historical context. Every president after Ferdinand Marcos has maintained a net satisfaction score of at least +30 for a year, except for Gloria Macapagal-Arroyo who got no honeymoon rating and no positive performance score in her nine years in office.

Duterte's honeymoon now extends over ten quarters, approaching PNoy's fifteen honeymoon quarters, which attracted little notice. Different in many respects, both presidents enjoyed the people's trust. But what is the source, significance and consequence of this "trust" in the president? Can it be bought or "engineered" through social media and propaganda? Does it drive people's beliefs and behavior? Is this trust transferable, as many electoral candidates, busily currying the president's favor, clearly believe?

We value the judgment of people we trust; we follow the prescriptions of our trusted doctor. The quality of people's trust in President Duterte seems of a different character. Duterte spews venom against the UN, the US and the Church. But these insults have not affected the public's perception of his targets.

54 percent of survey respondents were aware of the complaints against the drug war presented to the International Criminal Court (ICC); 40 percent knew about Duterte's decision to leave the ICC. But the ICC's

trust rating rose from +20 to +30 in 2018. The UN had a net trust rating of +61, followed by the US at +60.

China, upon which Duterte has heaped lavish praise ("I simply love Xi Jinping!") rated a -7 trust rating. By the September 2018 survey, all respondents were aware of the conflict with China in the WPS, including the confiscation by the Chinese Coast Guard of the catch of Filipino fishermen and the inability of the government to prevent the Chinese from encroaching on our exclusive fishing grounds. Ninety-nine percent knew that China was using reclaimed islands as military bases.

Hearing Presidential Spokesperson Salvador Panelo interpret Duterte's policies on the WPS, people might wonder who the president represents.

The December 2018 survey showed that 89 percent of respondents considered regaining control of the islands very important or somewhat important and favored a more proactive policy posture. Eighty-eight percent believed it was wrong to ignore China's construction activities in areas claimed by the Philippines. Ninety-three percent sought the strengthening of the country's military and especially, naval capabilities. Seventy-seven percent favored mobilizing international support for our diplomatic objectives.

On the federalism issue, net support for a new level of local government was 8 percent. SWS flatly denies any alleged popular "cry for federalism." In the war against drugs, the number who believed the police narrative that they killed suspects in self-defense was lower than the number who dismissed this *kwento* (story) as a lie, 27 to 28 percent. Eighty-nine percent considered it important that the police capture, not kill, the suspects.

The surveys also show that most of the respondents recognize the vulgarity of the language Mr. Duterte directs at his critics and at women, and respondents likewise considered vulgar, his pressure on a married Overseas Filipino Worker (OFW) in Seoul for a kiss on the lips. Like unwanted policies, however, vulgarity has not reduced their regard for Mr. Duterte. Hence, this curious "puzzlement"—this disconnect between the trust people express for Mr. Duterte and their strong disagreement with his behavior and his policies.

We need a deeper probe into the meaning and source of people's trust in their leaders, and how it is won or lost, to understand its potential for helping or harming the country. Good survey grades may deceive Mr. Duterte into believing he must persist in what he is doing because he is following the people's will—which a more comprehensive reading of survey results contradicts.

But how long will the people continue to reward him with high marks for pursuing policies they reject and for violating values they hold dear?

9

Writing Contracts on Water

(*Rappler*, January 06, 2020)

We enjoy no 20-20 vision on the ultimate consequences of the water concession controversy ignited late last year by President Duterte. The trigger was his order reported on December 4, 2019 to file charges that may include economic sabotage and plunder against those involved in the original 1997 contracts that privatized water services in Metro Manila and in their fifteen-year extension in 2009.

Within a week, Justice Secretary Menardo Guevarra condemned provisions of the government contracts with Manila Water and Maynilad as "onerous and disadvantageous to the government and the consuming public." The Metropolitan Waterworks and Sewerage System (MWSS) cancelled the contract extension from 2022 to 2037, fueling speculation that other players might take over the Ayala and Metro Pacific concessions. By then, the concessionaires had decided to waive the international arbitration court judgment, awarding them nearly P11 billion compensation and to explore the renegotiation of their contracts.

Another week later, both Guevarra and Finance Secretary Carlos Dominguez disclaimed any thought of canceling the contracts, despite Presidential Spokesperson Salvador Panelo's allegation that, guided by public officials, the concessionaires "raped the economy for their own personal aggrandizement," bleeding the country dry "to the outrageous detriment of the Filipinos." Both justice and finance departments support renegotiation with the alleged rapists.

MWSS has announced no plans for managing its responsibilities following the imminent termination of the concessions. Claims that contract provisions prevent the state from intervening in fixing contract fees are misleading. Regular review of rate adjustments that Mr. Dominguez advocated is already provided in the original agreements.

Never powerless

Government is never powerless against the private sector, which cannot compel the enforcement of contracts. Their recourse is international arbitration, permitted in the agreements, but also lacking both police powers and popular appeal, especially when the battle is waged in the arena of bureaucratic rules, populist politics and social media. Where 40 percent of families consider themselves poor, even mendacious accusations trump reasonable contracts when they promise lower consumer costs.

Still, no charges have been filed and the dispute might be arguably dismissed as a tempest in a teapot that did produce some good. High-profile hearings focused attention on the water services business, thus exposing the complaints of the COA and water districts against PrimeWater Infrastructure Corp. for high costs, poor service and failure to pay franchise taxes. These may also add pressure on transport and communications companies to improve their services.

But the furor also caused continuing, real-world consequences.

The concessionaires and their investors have not recovered from the P128-billion hit on the value of their shares. Banks have reportedly suspended releases on approved loans and new loan approvals, inflicting collateral damage on concessionaire contractors and consultants. The issue also clouds prospects for mobilizing the substantial, long-term funding to build and sustain the infrastructure for reliable, affordable water and sewage services.

Increased risk

The controversy cautions private business on the increased risk of ventures into highly-regulated projects covering public utilities. The field is sufficiently fraught and complex, demanding massive investments over an extended period and rarely promising quick recovery of capital and profits.

Hence, the Philippine privatization of water services in 1997, at a time of severe shortage, gained international notice. One concessionaire dropped the project, an indication that the contract was no sweetheart deal. Manila Water persisted and leveraged the expertise it acquired to emerge as the largest direct foreign investor in Vietnam's water sector, delivering half of the bulk water requirements of Ho Chi Minh City.

But it was government, assisted by international financial and legal advisers, that crafted the terms of the concession contracts. Offered to the private sector on a take-it-or-leave-it basis, the contracts went to the lowest bidders. If public officials are now deemed liable for onerous provisions in the agreements, two presidents, several of their cabinet members and the MWSS boards can face charges.

Over the concession period, such projects will encounter changes in technology, market conditions, and even in the natural resource environment that may lead to unforeseen, disastrous losses or spectacular profits. Agreements must provide against such contingencies to protect the public interest—without denying the rights of the concessionaires. What is their recourse against a successor administration unilaterally revising the covenants of an earlier government to negate rights granted them in the original agreements?

This is the critical question raised by the current water dispute. Without provisions for a credible process to negotiate protection from what is sometimes cited as Material Adverse Government Action, agreements might as well be written on water. This issue now threatens not just the water concessionaires, but other current and potential public-private partnership projects.

10

Babies and Bathwater

(*PDI*, January 11, 2020)

How did water concessionaires unjustly exploit the onerous provisions the Duterte administration discovered in their agreements? The original contracts, crafted by the Ramos administration, had been in force for over two decades, overseen by the MWSS, a government regulatory agency. Also unclear is why their extension by the Arroyo administration was deemed "irregular" enough to deserve cancellation.

President Duterte now tells Maynilad and Manila Water they must accept new contracts or lose the business. They may welcome pre-termination; but will the government that rejected the adverse judgment of an international arbitration court honor liabilities defined in the agreements for this step?

Concessionaires must also worry that the contract they must accept has not yet been drafted. When Marlon Brando, as the Godfather, makes an offer that cannot be refused, he spells out the terms. And presents a clear quid pro quo. But even if they submit to an unseen contract, the concessionaires, according to the government, can still be indicted on the non-bailable crime of plunder. Government can then detain the accused for however long it chooses to drag out the investigation and trial. Witness the plight of Sen. Leila de Lima.

The president has also declared open season for customers to sue the companies holding the concessions. Never mind if the government approach is moral or just or wise; is it even lawful? Our law schools should describe for us the legal vestments in which the emperor is attired.

Business might worry about how the handling of the case might impact the international appetite for Philippine investments. Justice Secretary Menardo Guevarra "couldn't care less about this concern," disdaining mere profit-seekers in favor of foreign investors imbued with a sense of corporate social responsibility. Perhaps, he might suggest who among the People's Republic of China (PRC) companies entering the country, might serve as model investors.

Another problem is not so casually dismissed: meeting the public need for safe, affordable and reliable water supply. Water levels at Angat and La Mesa dams, Manila's main water sources, dropped last March below the operating level of 180 meters to a crisis low of 160 meters. Reduced supply due to climate change and the increased demand of a growing population forced Manila Water to do rotational rationing, infuriating 1.2 million customers.

Public complaints exposed the company to government scrutiny and almost P1 billion in MWSS fines and its self-imposed penalty. By September, restored water levels permitted the resumption of regular services. December rains raised the Angat level to 204 meters, still short of the year-end level of 214 meters needed to moderate the anticipated summer shortage and the anger of even more unhappy customers.

While pursuing the current concessionaires, government might give a thought to how the public will continue to get water. Who will assume the responsibility, not just for operating the delivery system, but for investing in the development of new water sources? Will other bidders find attractive the contract that the government is forcing upon the concessionaires on a take-or-leave basis? Can the terms be lawfully modified for new bidders?

Mr. Duterte has threatened to nationalize the sector. How will it source the capital expenditures and operating funds required, and who will manage the system? Privatization happened precisely because the MWSS proved unable to meet the challenge. A frequent Duterte default might offer an alternative: delegate the job to the military. This option is likely to encounter resistance from both the military and civilian sectors.

Another not-uncommonly recommended recourse would be to outsource the program to PRC companies. MWSS already awarded in 2018 a contract for the Kaliwa Dam to China Energy Engineering Co. Ltd. (CEEC). But the concerns raised about onerous contracts have given new force to complaints against the CEEC award by human rights and environmental activists, policy think tanks and even the COA.

Correcting any flaws in the water agreements is necessary. Billionaires (and presidents) should be jailed, if justly convicted of crimes. But beyond punishing guilty billionaires, the end goal of assuring water supply should not be forgotten. The danger is discarding the baby with the bathwater: pursuing a course of action considered beneficial but ultimately causing greater harm to many more people, to institutions and to the environment.

POLICY ISSUES

I

The Marcos Baggage

Part of Noynoy Aquino's drive against corruption was a renewed effort to recover the billions plundered by the Marcos family from the country during the period of authoritarian rule. The second-place finish of Ferdinand "Bongbong" Marcos, Jr. in the 2016 vice-presidential race on the ticket of Miriam Defensor Santiago, the predictable charges of electoral fraud against the victory of Leni Robredo, and the expressed preference of Duterte for Bongbong over Alan Cayetano as his running mate raised fears that Filipinos would permanently lose these stolen billions during the incumbency of the Duterte administration.

Even this concern, however, took second place to the issue of the internment of Ferdinand Marcos in the Libingan ng mga Bayani. This had become an election issue as well. Candidate Duterte was on record that he favored this advocacy of the Marcos family, because it had given him financial support for his presidential campaign. Still, surveys showed that a majority of respondents opposed this posthumous proclamation as a national hero of a person globally disgraced, not just for the plunder but for the egregious violation of human rights and betrayal of the country's democratic legacy.

The decision on the issue technically rested with the Supreme Court, an independent branch of government co-equal with the president. This and the public opinion polls gave a glimmer of hope that the justices of the Supreme Court would render a judgment that would honor the lofty position they were privileged to occupy.

1

Immortalizing Impunity

(*PDI*, June 10, 2011)

It seemed like an eminently Solomonic resolution of a contentious issue. Assigned to resolve the controversy sparked by the lobby for the interment of Ferdinand Marcos in the Libingan ng mga Bayani, Vice President Jojo Binay proposed a compromise: denial of interment in the Libingan ng mga Bayani, but burial with full military honors.

Although apparently acceptable to the Marcos family itself, as well as to Marcos' friends and political allies, the proposal met with fierce opposition from those who had fought and suffered during the Marcos regime. Even those from generations who only remember Marcos for the legacy of violence and corruption left by authoritarian rule and for fabricating a record of heroic guerrilla exploits, regarded a hero's burial as distorting the historical record and dishonoring authentic heroes.

Binay's search for consensus probably was doomed to fail. He had reportedly sought the opinion of various sectors, including the political parties, and launched a broad text and e-mail survey on the issue. But none of the thirteen COMELEC-accredited political parties, according to the vice president, submitted an official response. We do not know the outcome of the Binay survey, but an earlier SWS poll showed respondents split down the middle. But is a survey really the proper instrument for this issue?

The question of the proper resting place for the mortal remains of Marcos enfolds many layers of concern. It is a friction point between the Marcos and the Aquino families, and, therefore, has obvious political implications. It requires judgment on historical truth. It also interrogates our principles and values: what should we teach our children about leadership, heroism and patriotism? A survey provides substantive input to the calculation of political costs and benefits. Are ethical norms completely relative and mutable to be governed by this calculus?

Given this multi-layered interment issue, the burden of leadership demands the determination of the hierarchy of pertinent values and of the competing claims of affected stakeholders. Which should matter more, the length of the presidential term or the manner of securing and retaining power and what was done during the period of rule? Who should receive greater consideration, the victims or the victimizers?

Like other authoritarian regimes of the period, Marcos used the military to capture and retain state power. In Argentina, the estimates of the extrajudicially killed and "disappeared" during the "Dirty War" (1973–86), ranged from 9,000 to 30,000. Atrocities on this scale, after the collapse of the regimes they served, left the military a demoralized, damaged, disgraced institution.

Alfred McCoy noted in *A Question of Torture: CIA Interrogation, from the Cold War to the War on Terror* (2006), how movies like *Missing*, *State of Siege* and *Kiss of the Spider Woman* dramatized the ruthlessness of Latin American military regimes. But even matched against its contemporaries, the Marcos government owned a record that was comparably lethal.

The Brazilian junta, in its most brutal period (1964–79), caused 266 people to die or disappear. Gen. Augusto Pinochet in Chile (1973–90) had a record of 2,115 extrajudicial deaths. Human rights activists counted against the Marcos government 35,000 cases of torture and 3,257 casualties, including 2,520 "salvaged" victims—those who were tortured, killed and the remains dumped for display.

The EDSA People Power Revolution provided the military a measure of redemption, which was quickly squandered by the coup attempts against the Cory Aquino government. To require the armed forces now to render full military honors at the interment ceremonies for Marcos, even if the site is in Ilocos, imposes an unjust burden on an institution still struggling with issues of systemic corruption and cases of impunity during and beyond the period of martial law.

We cannot deny family and friends their desire to give a final tribute to Marcos. Ilocano friends tell me that they do not consider Marcos a hero. But let us grant that many Ilocanos continue to acclaim him for the benefits the province received from his government. The apparently sensible approach of allowing them to honor Marcos as they see fit also has a cost. It reinforces the country's ethnic and linguistic divides that time and national leadership have thus far failed to bridge.

National unity will clearly need a longer, generational process. But history has already rendered its verdict on Marcos and the responsibility he bears for the corruption, torture and murders committed during his rule. It is cause enough for regret and, for many, even rage, that Marcos did not have to account for these crimes in a court of law. Especially when neither he nor his family has ever acknowledged any guilt or expressed any sorrow or sought forgiveness for the harm done to people and to the country.

Marcos managed to remain immune to the consequences of wrongdoing during his lifetime. For the government now to render him full military honors, immortalizes impunity.

2

The Luck of Bongbong Marcos

(*PDI*, October 17, 2015)

"I am the luckiest person that I know and being a Marcos is part of that and I am very happy that I was born into the Marcos family," said Bongbong Marcos. Obvious, *ba* (isn't it)? Did Bongbong really have to rub this in?

When he was born in 1957, his father, Ferdinand Marcos, was already completing a third term in Congress. Two years later, Ferdinand won a seat in the Senate, from where he launched two successful presidential campaigns. Faced with term limits, he then imposed a martial law regime that enabled him to retain supreme power for another fourteen years. There were few disadvantages for the only son of the Philippines' most powerful politician.

It was not Bongbong's fault to be born into wealth and power, and it is an act of virtue to express gratitude for the benefits received from his parents. But his filial piety becomes suspect when he suggests that the blessings he enjoyed also spread to the rest of the population. It becomes delusional when he asserts that Ferdinand was the best leader the country has ever had.

Bongbong is aware of the issues raised in the past against the "conjugal dictatorship" of Ferdinand and Imelda Marcos. He argues that "history should be left to analysts," but believes that the Marcos "legacy" would boost his bid in the 2016 vice-presidential race. Bongbong and his family refuse to recognize that the "analysts" have already rendered a verdict on the Marcos legacy.

Take the myth of Maharlika, the guerrilla unit that Ferdinand supposedly organized and led from 1942 to 1944 in operations all over

Luzon, whose exploits earned for him thirty-two medals for heroism. There is adequate documentation for three medals, which we should commend. But the other awards, from Alfred W. McCoy's archival research, were figments of Ferdinand's imagination, invented to support a scam. Investigations conducted by the Pentagon concluded that his Maharlika unit roster was a fabrication to support claims for American back-pay benefits. Its proclaimed achievements were "fraudulent," "preposterous," and advancing them is a "malicious, criminal act."

On human rights violations during the Marcos regime, McCoy recorded a figure of 3,257 extrajudicial killings (EJKs)—compared to 2,115 under Pinochet in Chile and 266 under the military junta in Brazil—and over 2,500 "salvaged" victims. In September 1992, the US District Court in Honolulu found Ferdinand Marcos guilty of systematic torture and held his estate liable for damages to all 9,541 victims, later awarding nearly US$2 billion in damages—the biggest personal injury verdict until then in legal history.

Regarding plundered wealth, the 2004 Global Transparency Report listed Marcos second (behind Suharto of Indonesia) in its list of the World's Most Corrupt Leaders. Lee Kuan Yew of Singapore, often cited as a model authoritarian ruler that Marcos could have emulated, distanced himself from Ferdinand: "Only in the Philippines could a leader like Ferdinand Marcos, who pillaged his country for over twenty years, still be considered for a national burial. Insignificant amounts of the loot have been recovered, yet his wife and children were allowed to return and engage in politics."

Bongbong would prefer to leave the past behind and to address today's problems. He asks: "Why is the distribution of wealth not happening?" He should ask his mother. Speaking to the *Inquirer* in 1998, Imelda Marcos said: "We practically own everything in the Philippines—from electricity, telecommunications, banking, beer and tobacco, newspaper publishing, television stations, shipping, the airline, oil and mining, hotels and beach resorts, down to coconut milling, small farms, real estate and insurance." She was then planning to sue the cronies holding the family's properties.

The Supreme Court estimated the total legal income of the Marcoses, earned from 1965 to 1986, at over US$304,000. The Presidential Commission on Good Government (PCGG) tasked to recover the Marcos plunder, pegged what had been looted from the country at US$10 billion, less than half of which has been recovered. Might kleptocracy help explain the inequitable wealth distribution that so concerns Bongbong?

"Why is our education sector miserable?" Bongbong asks. Recent research has shown that from the Magsaysay administration (1954–57) to the two presidential terms of Ferdinand Marcos (1965–1971), education received the biggest share of the national budget, maintaining close to 28 percent. During the rest of the Marcos regime (1972–1985), education's share dropped to an average of 11.6 percent of the budget, even while basic education enrollment was growing at about 2.4 percent a year. During the period when Marcos could determine budget allocations, he chose to cut down support for education. An educated population, of course, poses a threat to dictators.

The judgment on the Marcos record is clear, but we have not fully plumbed the depths of the damage inflicted by the Marcos regime on the country.

How do we quantify the cost of leaders killed or suppressed during martial law? Bongbong's gratuitous celebration of the Marcos legacy challenges us to pursue the research effort.

3

Marcos: Dead, Not Gone

(*PDI*, November 28, 2015)

"Past is past, Bongbong says of dark Marcos years." This *Inquirer* headline (October 22, 2015) recalls novelist William Faulkner's oft-quoted statement: "The past is not dead. It is not even past."

The announcement early this week by Christie's, the jewelry auction house, illustrated Faulkner's point. Christie's discovered that an item described as "loose crystal" among over 700 pieces of jewelry left behind by the Marcoses in their flight to Hawaii, was actually an "extremely rare" pink diamond believed to belong to a Mogul emperor. The entire Marcos jewelry collection was initially valued in 1991 at between US$5 million and US$8 million. Christie's estimated the Mogul diamond alone, as worth US$5 million.

This reminder of martial law plunder rebuts Sen. Bongbong Marcos' insistence that Filipinos should just leave the Marcos legacy to discussions among "historical analysts." Current concerns, such as the deterioration of the educational system, domestic insurgencies and impunity, have deep roots in the Marcos' past. Historians will study the past to illuminate the problems of the present and the options for the future.

US President Barack Obama used the Faulkner quote to remind Americans that the current crises in the black community can be traced back to inequalities suffered by earlier generations under the brutal legacy of slavery. The current violence in the US arising from race relations cannot be understood or effectively addressed without understanding its historical context. The history of human rights violations during the Marcos regime is not of the same scale and duration as those suffered by the American black community, but it requires the same comprehension of context.

Millennials may have forgotten, if they ever learned, the costs and consequences of martial law. Their elders, who lived through this not-so-distant historical period, have not. Bongbong still has to deal with living victims of the Marcos legacy, whose demand for justice remains unfulfilled.

I do not believe that the sins of the father should necessarily and permanently burden the son. Bongbong could have unloaded the weight of the martial law legacy off his back. There were two conditions. The first is if he had quietly retired from public life, if he had stayed in Honolulu and mastered, say, surfing skills or whatever, instead of pursuing political office and lobbying for the interment of his father at the Libingan ng mga Bayani.

The second, more onerous condition, requires a public act of contrition for the damage done by martial law to the Filipinos and the Philippines.

Bongbong could probably have mustered the right words for this purpose, if he so wished. But confession and contrition will not be credible without compensation. Atonement must include the return of the plundered wealth.

The recently released autobiography of Jose Almonte, a key figure in the failed Reform the Armed Forces Movement (RAM) coup attempt against Ferdinand Marcos in 1986 and the national security adviser during the Ramos administration, renewed public interest in martial law issues. But the focus centered on whether the RAM plan envisioned the killing of Marcos and the members of his family.

Almonte's involvement in what he called the "Great Chase" for the wealth plundered by the Marcoses drew little attention then. In the course of this chase, Almonte visited the Marcoses in Honolulu. By his account, it was Bongbong Marcos who conducted the conversations, on payphones (to avoid "bugging"), with the Marcos Swiss bank liaison. Bongbong provided him with the identity of the account manager of the Marcos deposits, a senior vice president of Credit Suisse; a letter of authorization to deal with the transfer of funds from Switzerland to a bank in Vienna; and US$300,000. In traveler's checks.

Almonte's account is rich in details that the Marcoses have not contested. Bongbong's advice to leave the past to historians and move on is sickeningly self-serving in evading the issue of restitution. He has to justify why Filipinos should allow his family to keep US$6 billion or more in plundered wealth. For Filipino voters, this should be an election issue.

Bongbong's prescription of "forget and move on"—not "forgive and forget," because he has never asked for forgiveness—becomes deeply divisive because it exploits ethnic fault lines. He is counting on the family's Ilocano connections in the allegedly solid Ilocano North to ignore the past. Although the region clearly benefited from martial law, its list of victims also includes ethnic Ilocanos from all over the country.

Forgetting the past is not a healing strategy that can unify countries which have experienced extended violent communal conflicts, especially those provoked by religious, ethnic or ideological divisions. The protagonists nurture the memory of their grievances. The conflict between Catholics and Protestants in Northern Ireland had roots in the seventeenth century.

The historical experience of Ireland, South Africa, Chile and Argentina tells us that reconciliation—the key to national unity—requires truth-telling, contrition and reparation. Amnesia is not the antidote.

4

Deadlocked over the Dead

(*PDI*, April 02, 2016)

At their second debate, the presidential candidates had to declare their stand on a policy issue—silently, by a simultaneous show of hands. On permitting the burial of Ferdinand Marcos at the Libingan ng mga Bayani, Jojo Binay and Digong Duterte raised their hands in approval. Mar Roxas and Grace Poe did not.

The outcome was not surprising. Roxas probably shared and would respect PNoy's opposition to a Libingan interment for Marcos. After the backlash against the suggestion that she was open to the idea, Poe backtracked and issued a clarification. Duterte had been open to taking Bongbong Marcos as his running mate.

Vice President Binay's position requires some explanation. In 2011, PNoy asked Binay to make a recommendation on the issue. Binay said he surveyed the views of various sectors, including the political parties. None of the 130 parties accredited by the COMELEC responded.

Binay did not reveal the results of the text and e-mail survey but offered a compromise: burial with full military honors, but not at the Libingan.

Not surprisingly, the compromise met with resistance. The historical record argued against burial with full military honors. In 1986, based on previously classified documents, the *New York Times* exposed Marcos' claims of wartime heroism as "fraudulent," "preposterous," and "a malicious criminal act." Marcos himself declined to respond to the story.

Marcos had sought the US' recognition of his Maharlika guerrilla unit—allegedly counting as many as 8,300 members—to qualify him and his men for back pay and benefits. US Army Captain Ray C. Hunt, who directed guerrilla operations in the province of Pangasinan, dismissed Marcos' account of Maharlika exploits throughout Luzon as "a cock-and-bull story." Investigators further concluded that a number of people claiming Maharlika membership engaged, not in combat, but in black-market sale of war commodities to the Japanese.

What, then, changed Binay's mind in 2016? Forget the plunder charges against Binay, which precluded using Marcos' own record of plunder as a reason against a Libingan burial. Prescind from calculations the votes of Marcos followers. Allowed to explain his new stand, Binay would likely have echoed Duterte's rationale: the need to move beyond the Libingan issue to promote peace and unity in the country.

But elections magnify the cleavages created by conflicting political loyalties. Because of Bongbong Marcos' attempt in his vice-presidential campaign to burnish the Marcos legacy, a Libingan burial will more likely divide than unite people. Bongbong had aggravated an already deep fracture in Philippine society, arising from the martial law experience.

This fracture needs healing. But it cannot be mended by the band-aid of a lie. As in other countries devastated by periods of brutal authoritarian regimes, healing requires truth-telling. After seven years of military rule (1976–83), a restored democracy in Argentina established the National Commission on the Disappearance of Persons (CONADEP). Its 1984 report, "Nunca Mas" (Never Again), documented the abduction, torture and death of over 7,000 individuals and estimated that nearly 9,000 of the disappeared had yet to be found.

The 1991 Rettig Report of Chile's National Commission for Truth and Reconciliation reviewed nearly 3,000 cases of human rights violations during the military dictatorship of Augusto Pinochet (1973–90). It recorded over a thousand known to have been killed outright by the regime and nearly an equal number arrested and "disappeared."

These commissions of Chile and Argentina gave priority to truth-seeking. The Rettig Report affirmed that Chile's "moral conscience" demanded the truth about the grave violations of human rights perpetrated by the military dictatorship as the necessary foundation "to meet the basic demands of justice and create the necessary conditions for achieving true national reconciliation."

For Argentina, the truth was "an absolute, unrenounceable value." To ensure that the country would not repeat the tragedy it had suffered, the people must clearly know what had happened and must never happen again. While the truth will not necessarily secure justice, it may end for many, the continued injustice of "an anguishing, endless search" for the disappeared.

Marcos' acclamation as a national hero with a Libingan burial would perpetuate the lies about the Marcos war exploits and martial law legacy that Bongbong Marcos now wants written into our history. The casualty count of martial law compares with the number lost in Chile and Argentina. But we have thus far failed to establish our own Truth Commission—and, arguably, allowed an environment that tolerated continued human rights violations beyond martial law.

Bongbong Marcos has unwittingly performed a public service in compelling us to confront our past: to acknowledge that we have not yet really recognized the injustice suffered by the victims of martial law. Their bodies, and not only that of Ferdinand Marcos, also await proper burial.

5

Between a Rock and a Hard Place . . .

(*PDI*, November 05, 2016)

. . . is where the Supreme Court justices find themselves. Expected in September to rule on the interment of Ferdinand Marcos' remains in the Libingan ng mga Bayani, they set the issuance of their ruling to October and then to November 8.

Shortly after assuming power, PRRD directed the military to prepare for the Marcos burial in the Libingan, an order forestalled by an appeal lodged at the Supreme Court. He has since said he would accept the high court's verdict.

Notwithstanding this assurance, it is imprudent, even for members of a coequal branch of government, who presumably know the law as well as PRRD, to defy the decision of a popular president. But can they render, in deference to the president, a judgment whose wisdom future generations of lawyers will question and that will indelibly mark their respective places in the history books?

The agreement that allowed the Marcos family's return to the Philippines included the condition that Marcos' remains stay in his region. PRRD believes he can rescind this agreement, arguing that the Libingan, which had been established for soldiers and presidents, should make room for Marcos, who had served as both.

Will the Supreme Court now affirm that anyone who served in the military can demand Libingan interment as a right? Given the costs of dying these days, every soldier should make a bid for Libingan real estate. But surely, the Libingan was meant for those who had served the country with distinction. Or, at least, had not caused it injury and shame. Declining entry to infamous criminals should be reasonable.

That Marcos should be considered innocent of the crimes alleged against him because he had not been convicted in a Philippine court, should carry little weight with PRRD. Risking extrajudicial executions, he has unleashed the police against drug offenders he feared the courts could not touch. But a US court has convicted Marcos for martial law atrocities and plunder. Filipino and foreign historians have also exposed to the world his fraudulent claims of heroism. Can the Supreme Court turn a blind eye to this public record?

PRRD has virtually admitted that a Libingan interment was part of the price for the Marcoses' electoral support. Nevertheless, the justices must still evaluate his claim that the bargain he made will also bury the controversies over martial law, unite the country and allow it to move forward.

How many living today know about the 1906 US massacre of Muslim rebels at Bud Dajo from a contemporary of the victims? But PRRD, who has shown a commendable sense of history, has neither forgotten nor forgiven the Americans for this century-old atrocity. Dredging out of the blue an incident that had not surfaced as a public policy issue, PRRD denounced the Americans for never having expressed remorse over the historical injustice committed at Bud Dajo.

Martial law is not just a historical issue. Its living victims feel as a present reality the injustice they suffered that has not been redressed. But PRRD, who feels the historical injustice of Bud Dajo so keenly, now wants these martial law survivors to forget the injustice they continue to suffer, for which the Marcoses have never offered restitution as authentic remorse. The victims include the country whose plundered wealth the government continues to seek and from which the Marcoses continue to benefit.

A Libingan burial for Marcos will reinforce attempts to revise history: to persuade the people that Marcos ushered in a golden age of progress and prosperity. If so, his overthrow at EDSA, which the world celebrated with the Philippines and which we annually commemorate, was a misfortune and a mistake. How will propagating this narrative unify the country?

The Supreme Court justices, by their ruling, will make a judgment on our history. In turn, history will make a judgment on their decision and its reflection on their wisdom, their integrity, their courage.

6

Low Ball in the High Court

(*PDI*, November 12, 2016)

Will the justices of the Supreme Court be "liberal or literal?" Former Chief Justice Artemio Panganiban posed the question on the eve of the high court's decision, already twice postponed, that the nation had breathlessly awaited. The mountain mightily labored and produced a mouse.

Fate had given the justices the chance to write a judgment that might have resounded as a ringing affirmation of that moment in history when the world marveled at what the Filipinos had done—defy a dictator and overthrow, with a minimum of bloodshed, a regime built on blood. Invited to reap the recognition of posterity, ten justices flinched and fled.

Justice Bienvenido Reyes recused himself from the case. He had served in a company established by Benigno Aquino III, who had also named him to the Supreme Court. He was also the fraternity brother who administered President Duterte's oath of office. Links to both parties might have qualified him as ideal for the case, and recusal cause for unhappiness on both sides.

Nine justices carried the decision: Diosdado Peralta, Presbitero Velasco Jr., Teresita Leonardo-de Castro, Arturo Brion, Lucas Bersamin, Mariano del Castillo, Jose Perez, Jose Mendoza and Estela Perlas-Bernabe. The initial brief on the decision evoked a gasp of incredulity, so breathtaking was its base, pedestrian character. The highest arbiter of the law set for a deposed president the lowest bar for posthumous honors.

They declared: that Mr. Duterte had complete power to decide how public lands should be used (the Libingan ng mga Bayani, the resting place of national heroes, as a pet cemetery?); that no law barred a Libingan burial for Ferdinand Marcos, who deserved it because of the offices he had occupied, regardless of how effectively and ethically he discharged their responsibilities; that the military rebellion against him did not constitute "dishonorable discharge" because he was not then in active service.

The cases against Marcos, decided with finality here and abroad, were irrelevant, the justices said, because these were "merely civil in nature [and] do not establish moral turpitude." Consider the crimes judged "contrary to community standards of justice, honesty or good morals" that moral turpitude encompassed. How could the plunder, torture and murder committed during martial law escape its ambit?

Rejection of Marcos' burial in the Libingan could have reinforced the struggle for justice by the victims of martial law, the government's efforts to recover plundered wealth, the Philippines' sense of its history and identity. But, binding itself with "judicial restraint," the Supreme Court dismissed the issue as a political matter beyond its purview. It thus sanctioned the president's perfunctory treatment of the Marcos burial as a triviality that could be bartered for political favors.

Blind to the symbolic impact of Mr. Duterte's decision, the justices issued a verdict seemingly based on a finger-in-the-air reading of the political wind. They interpreted the votes for Bongbong Marcos as proof that Filipinos had forgiven his father, and Mr. Duterte's election as support for his Libingan decision.

People had hoped that the justices, in their collective wisdom, would see as simplistic or duplicitous the claim that a Libingan burial would bridge the sharp divide among Filipinos, bury the issue of martial law, and allow the nation to move forward. Protests against the decision, spontaneously erupting across the nation, disproved this view.

Evaluating Marcos "in his totality as a person," the justices concluded that he deserved Libingan interment because "he was not pure evil . . . just a human who erred like us." By this standard, who could be excluded from the Libingan? Even the most depraved serial killer must have sometimes shown kindness to his mother or his dog.

Facing a dangerous choice, the justices, perhaps, set a low-ball norm that might equally serve as the measure by which their decision would be judged.

They also were not pure evil, just human beings, vulnerable to human frailties, fears and temptations.

II

Duterte Drug War

Administration problems partly arose from the presidential communication style. While the presidential staff presumably drafted coherent statements for him to deliver, Duterte was impatient with reading prepared papers and, not bothering to conceal this impatience, often lapsed into adlibs.

Departing from the text indulged habits that made it difficult for listeners to grasp the message. He tended to speak in tongues, blending Tagalog, Cebuano and English in one verbal flow. He was generous in his use of digressions and parenthetical phrases, often of a distractingly profane or scurrilous nature. On the other hand, he was parsimonious in his use of punctuation marks or verbal equivalent to indicate the completion of a sentence or a thought.

On one point, he was crystal clear: drug users deserved to die. He dismissed the objections of those appalled by the mounting body count of casualties in the Duterte war against drugs. The voters elected him, after all, when he had made clear during the campaign that he would wage the war without mercy and fatten the fish in Manila Bay with the corpses of drug criminals.

The voters supported a vigorous effort to suppress the drug trade. But those repelled by the human cost of the war wanted to understand the logic of the policy: the scale of the problem, as reflected in credible estimates of drug user numbers; the effectiveness of the mailed fist approach in dealing with drug addiction, looking, for instance, at the experience of other countries; the protection of human rights in the prosecution of the war; the balance of costs and benefits.

Evaluating the proportionality of the ends and means of the drug war required looking at the issue of its impact on the security forces of the state and their relations with the civilian government in a democratic society.

Among the most damaging, debilitating costs of martial law was the erosion of public trust in the police and the military establishments, when human rights violations escaped punishment and bred the enduring problem of impunity.

Their role in EDSA I helped in rebuilding this trust, a process that took a step back with the series of coup attempts between 1986 and 1989 against the government of Cory Aquino. With the election in 1992 of Gen. Fidel V. Ramos, one of the leaders of EDSA I, the military embarked on an institutional reform process that enabled it to survive the political complications of EDSA II, when its leadership once again played a crucial role in determining the presidential transition without entirely losing its credibility. But impunity remained a problem.

Other countries afflicted by drug addiction have learned that approaching it as a war, to be prosecuted mainly by the security forces of the state, was costly in terms of both financial resources and human lives and ineffective in eliminating the problem. Moreover, it ran the risk of undermining the professional cohesion and integrity of the security forces themselves. The arrest in October 2020 of Gen. Salvador Cienfuegos, former defense minister of Mexico as the inside man of the drug cartel provided the most recent egregious example of the danger.

The military has thus far escaped entanglement in the drug war, a fate that the police could not avoid. But already, police officials have been involved in drug-related crimes or plain vanilla extortion and murder, masked as part of the war against drugs.

1

"If I Had a Hammer . . ."

(*PDI*, September 03, 2016)

Someone with only a hammer for a tool may be tempted to treat every problem as a nail. His election as president provides PRRD with many hammers. But the presidency offers many more instruments beyond the hammer to address the complex task of nation-building.

Because it seems to have worked in Davao, the hammer strategy of "shoot to kill" remains PRRD's favored device for dealing with the drug menace. But other cities have reportedly managed to control criminality while observing constitutional rights to due process. The summary killing of suspects by government forces arguably undermines the rule of law and contributes to a climate conducive to vigilante murders.

No one questions the need to dismantle the drug trade and demolish the network of narco-criminals among politicians, bureaucrats, judges and security forces who have profited from promoting its expansion. The public's growing uneasiness about the means employed to achieve the laudable ends of the war on drugs is not without basis. No country has eradicated the drug problem simply through the ruthless application of violence.

In a poor country, the drug trade partly stems from the problem of poverty. The poor apparently resort to low-dose, low-cost "*shabu*" (methamphetamine hydrochloride) sachets to dull hunger pangs and boost energy for physical labor. Their need creates a shadow economy yielding princely profits to those who organize and finance the trade, while luring the poor into serving as drug pushers.

As in other countries, the "shock and awe" impact of the hammer strategy initially produced encouraging results. But even the death of drug lords barely shakes the business. Two months after the killing of Jeffrey "Jaguar" Diaz by Las Piñas Police, according to the Philippine Drug Enforcement Agency (PDEA) in the Central Visayas, his drug syndicate was back supplying consumers in the Cebu City Jail. Violence directed at replaceable, penny-ante addicts at the street level is even less likely to threaten the trade.

Frustration with the weaknesses of the justice system has muted resistance to the hammer strategy, justified as required by the epidemic spread of the addiction to dangerous drugs. Are those who reject the shoot-to-kill strategy underestimating the scale and the gravity of the drug threat?

Since 1986, SWS has included in its regular surveys perceptions of public safety as a critical quality-of-life measure. Monitored quarterly since 1992, one module inquires into the respondents' actual experience of crime (burglary of the home and robbery outside the home; theft of motor vehicle; physical violence). A second looks at anxiety about the safety of the home and the neighborhood.

In 2005, SWS added a third module, asking whether respondents believed there were already "too many people addicted to banned drugs" in their neighborhood. This first survey elicited a 37 percent agreement with the statement. Agreement rose to the 40s in 2006–08, dropped back to the 30s in 2009, before climbing back to the 40s in 2012 and recently exceeding 60 percent.

The upward trend is cause for concern, though the drug war itself might have contributed to the perception of rising drug addiction prevalence. But it should also be assessed in the context of the movement in the other two public safety modules.

The government has not achieved much success in alleviating people's apprehensions about home and neighborhood security. Over the last three decades, some 50 percent and, more recently, over 60 percent of the respondents reported that they feared to walk around the neighborhood at night and were concerned about criminals breaking into their homes.

On the actual experience of crime, however, the numbers have been running in the opposite direction. During the Cory Aquino administration,

23 to 38 percent of families reported that they were crime victims. The numbers progressively improved until they reached the lowest figure of 6 percent in mid-2015 but crept back during the period of the presidential electoral campaign to 11 percent.

The trend lines on the three modules of public safety do not appear to move in synchronized, lock-step fashion. Despite lower public concern about the drug problem, the feeling of insecurity stayed at high levels. While the number actually victimized by crime has been going down, anxiety about security and the incidence of addiction has prevailed.

These numbers need validation and assessment before we can accept the contention that the country confronts a "crisis." This narrative of a society in crisis that needed an iron fist at the helm worked effectively during the electoral campaign. The same script now seeks to strengthen the hammer strategy by a 300 percent increase in the confidential and intelligence budget from P500 million to P2 billion.

The financial and human costs of the strategy call for subjecting the script to a thorough review and analysis.

2

Learning from Mistakes

(*PDI*, October 01, 2016)

Preferably, from mistakes committed and paid for by others. We should thus thank *Bangkok Post* deputy editor Nopporn Wong-Anan, who suggested that "Duterte should learn from Thai drug policy" in his article I caught during a Bangkok visit, last month. In Manila, recently for a media conference, Nopporn found similarities in the anti-drug policies followed by PRRD and former Thai Prime Minister Thaksin Shinawatra.

The parallels were obvious. Thaksin was equally disdainful of the UN, which had expressed concerns about the conduct of the "war on drugs" he had launched in 2003: "The UN is not my father." The rhetoric was comparable: "We have to be as ruthless with drug dealers as they are with our children." Drug dealers "deserved" to be shot dead. The war claimed 2,800 deaths in the first three months of the campaign.

Nopporn cited an official investigation, after Thaksin's ouster, which revealed that more than half of those killed had no drug connections. Many were victims of envious neighbors suspicious of their wealth, or of existing feuds with police officers. Nopporn reported that "despite a decades-long campaign, narcotic drugs use shows no signs of abating in Thailand."

Thai Justice Minister Paiboon Kumchaya also concluded that the war on drugs had failed. Imprisonment did not seem effective in curing addiction. Despite jailing some 250,000 of an estimated 1.3 million addicts, 70 percent of drug offenders remained in prison, and people still complained about drugs in their communities. Addressing drug abuse as mainly a criminal problem also compromised Thailand's campaign against HIV. Fear of arrest and imprisonment prevented drug users from essential, harm-reduction treatment services.

At a recent forum, Thailand's Drug Policy Revisited, convened by the Institute of Justice, Paiboon focused on drug abuse as a health issue, enlisting support from the Ministry of Health. Dr. Sophon Mekthon, Permanent Secretary of Public Health, cited plans to implement three measures on the drug problem: 1) amending laws to encourage addicts to undergo rehabilitation; 2) improving the screening and rehabilitation of drug abusers; and 3) increasing the number of service points at *tambon* (village) level, where "*yaba*" (their equivalent of *shabu*) users can seek help.

As part of the policy shift, Paiboon is coordinating with the Ministry of Health for the downgrading of yaba to Category 2 in the dangerous narcotics list. Private possession and use would still be illegal but would be subjected to reduced penalties. The reclassification would also permit the government—instead of destroying confiscated yaba—to use it for treatment under medical supervision.

A lucrative market for illegal drugs makes the trade difficult to stop. According to the Office of the Narcotics Control Board (ONCB), nearly 2 million Thais consume up to 4 billion yaba tablets a year. A manufacturing base in a neighboring country could produce at least 1 billion tablets a year—half of which were smuggled into Thailand, with about 20 percent or some 100 million pills seized by authorities.

Thus, Paiboon also wants to deploy an economic weapon in the drug war. He is proposing that the Food and Drug Administration (FDA) produce the non-narcotic wakefulness-promoting agents modafinil and armodafinil as part of "harm reduction" measures. These substances would cost only 34 baht (US$1) per pill compared to the yaba pill, that costs 200 baht (US$5.88) in the illegal market. Competition could further reduce amphetamine prices to 5–10 baht per pill. Paiboon believes that this drop would make the illegal drug business unprofitable. He is also prepared to consider removing marijuana and cannabis from the narcotics list, as they could be classified as medicinal herbs.

PRRD has already acknowledged the international dimensions of the drug problem. Thailand and the Philippines differ in language, religion, institutions and culture. These differences should not prevent our learning from each other's experiences in confronting a common drug problem.

The lessons drawn from Thaksin's anti-drug policy come from sources that PRRD should find credible. A career military man, General Paiboon had been a candidate to head the Thai Army and had also faced criticism for alleged violation of human rights. He had supported the junta's zero-tolerance policy on drug offenders, until responsibility for dealing with the drug issue apparently prompted a change of strategy.

It was Thaksin's popularly elected, civilian government that launched a violent war on drug criminals. With vastly greater weapons for that war, a military junta is now deliberately moderating the use of violence and shifting the drug policy from a mainly police perspective. Its pragmatic approach to the problem, calculating the costs and benefits of conducting the war, has led it to a more holistic approach that recognizes drugs as a health and social problem.

PRRD should have no qualms about learning from Thailand's failed drug policy.

3

Duterte's Holy War

(*PDI*, December 03, 2016)

Why are Filipinos across the country's breadth and beyond back in the streets?

PRRD assumed power at a time of great hope, with public morale at a record high. The economy was robust. Crime and poverty rates were trending down. The campaign against corruption among the powerful was proceeding. The Permanent Court of Arbitration in The Hague recognized our rights in the WPS, vindicating our commitment to the rule of law, for which we had won the respect of democratic nations.

A contentious presidential election notwithstanding, the succession proceeded peacefully. PRRD's decisive victory delivered Congress into his hands and the political levers to accelerate the growth momentum. The public gave him a great deal of slack, accepting without much comment appointments awarded to classmates, province-mates and friends—despite the questionable credentials of some appointees and the people's general unfamiliarity with the track record of many others.

PRRD was blessed at the starting gate with advantages none of his predecessors enjoyed. But these clashed with his campaign premise that depicted the Philippines as a country in crisis and himself as the appointed savior. Post-election pronouncements and policies reinforced and validated the campaign narrative.

His core messages have remained the same. He won without the support of any political or business group. He owed no one favors to be repaid, excepting so far only the Marcoses. Having placed him in power, voters must be presumed to support whatever policies he chose to pursue—on the Marcos burial, on foreign policy, on the drug menace.

His speeches continue to denounce drug addiction as the existential threat, corrupting the powerful, destroying the weak, turning the country into a narcostate. Habitual drug use dissolves the brain, producing demented addicts beyond redemption. He repeatedly shares personal stories of *shabu*-crazed addicts killing parents and raping children to justify ruthless measures to jail or kill them. He repeatedly asserts the need for additional powers to cope with "the crisis in this country involving drugs, extrajudicial killings and . . . an environment of lawless violence."

But we are not told how many addicts have committed fratricide and child rape, the evidence against politicians implicated in drugs, the definition of a narcostate. Incredibly, officials responsible for crafting public policy, like Sen. Vicente Sotto, have dismissed data as unimportant, justifying exaggeration to legitimize the drug war. Administration minions have used another country's photographs to depict Philippine drug crimes.

The war on drugs has assumed the character of a crusade, a holy war founded on faith, on dogma, not data. But its deadly consequences demand evidence on the balance between ends and means.

Prudence warns us against committing to a cure potentially worse than the disease, in promoting, for instance, an arbitrary manipulation of the law and a culture of lawless violence.

When he chooses, PRRD sticks narrowly to the letter, as in the Libingan ng mga Bayani case. He is not equally strict on enforcing the law on due process. Official figures estimate about 2,000 deaths in the course of police operations since he took office, as well as another 2,500 unresolved, drug-related murders.

Critics have attributed these murders to the police themselves or their subcontracted killers—to meet PNP performance targets or eliminate whistle-blowers. PRRD has repeatedly disclaimed vigilante killings as administration policy. Accept this denial and the possibility that the murders stem from warring drug lords, but also continue to hold the government accountable for stopping these vigilante criminals.

A crusade condones no criticism. Critics raising questions are insulted as *buang* (crazy), *unggoy* (monkey), imperialist idiots, SOBs. On the altar of this holy war, PRRD dramatically declares he would sacrifice his presidency and his life. Fine.

But, before that, he would sacrifice the rule of law, the regard of nations, constitutional guarantees, human rights, moral principles, Filipino values and however many lives it may cost.

Did we buy into this bargain?

4

Drawing the Line

(*PDI*, March 04, 2017)

"Kellyandanar" was coined to suggest that Martin Andanar, head of President Duterte's Communications Operations Office, and Kellyanne Conway, counselor to US President Donald Trump, played comparable roles. The comparison was not complimentary.

Conway, Class 1989 of Trinity Washington University (TWU), is arguably the most prominent alumna today of this small (2,200 students) Catholic women's institution. It was thus surprising that TWU president Patricia McGuire should publicly rebuke Conway for her "large role in facilitating the manipulation of facts . . ." Responding to critics of the US administration's immigration policies, Conway had defended Trump with "alternative facts" that others would commonly call lies.

Universities are happy enough to acclaim alumni who ascend to positions of power and to bask in the honor they bring. They are less ready to acknowledge their black sheep. But what should universities expect from alumni who reach the highest ranks of government and can presumably influence its directions?

It would be unrealistic for universities to expect alumni to take senior appointments only in those administrations whose policies they support. Once appointed, alumni must place their talent and resources at the service of the president. It becomes their duty to advance their president's policies, however repugnant these may be to their universities.

The role of projecting a president's messages to the public implicates officials like Conway and Andanar in all presidential statements and actions. TWU drew the line; faithful service cannot be at the cost of betraying its bedrock values: "People can agree or disagree around national policy or domestic policy . . . But when you lie so consistently as this administration does, that's a moral issue. We are teachers . . . We believe deeply in upholding the value of truth . . . It's urgent not to be shy about it."

Other senior officials covering more specific, functional areas can closet themselves within the boundaries of their professional mandate, concentrating on goals supported by their constituencies. They can try to distance themselves from other aspects of governance that are not their direct concern and that they may privately oppose.

The silo strategy works—up to a point. Sectoral concerns will inevitably collide with each other. Policy decisions on environmental protection measures affect business operations and must concern economic ministers. Agencies responsible for health, education and the economy must consider the impact of the peace process or the law-and-order environment on their own goals.

Mr. Duterte's war on drugs has been pursued mainly as a police and security issue. From the outset, the strategy had provoked public anxiety because it was anchored on a police force with a record marred by inefficiency and corruption. The killing of Mayor Rolando Espinosa in his jail cell, the brazen murder of Jee Ick-joo in Camp Crame, both perpetrated by police officers, have confirmed fears that the strategy would promote a climate of impunity.

Apart from expert and loyal service, senior government officials have a duty that presidents do not always appreciate: to caution them when policies threaten the violation of laws and fundamental constitutional and human rights. Raising the alarm on potential threats emerging from issues beyond their specific departmental responsibility is also their duty to the country and the people. At some point, inaction becomes complicity in these violations.

Determining the point where that line must be drawn is the difficult, personal decision each official must make. Despite the confessions of Matobato and Lascañas and close to 8,000 casualties in eight months, has any cabinet member acknowledged the reality of extrajudicial killings and the risks of the war on drugs?

Universities that proclaim adherence to moral principles, must also make their own judgment call on when to warn alumni, as TWU did, that they have crossed the line. Their willingness to do so may help the leaders they have educated locate the lines they must draw for themselves and renew their moral core.

5

2017: Searching for Common Ground

(*PDI*, January 07, 2017)

In 2017, national interest requires an honest effort to find common ground between critics and supporters of President Duterte. On the drug policy, surely they can all agree that: 1) we have a drug problem requiring action; 2) law enforcement is part of the solution; and 3) enforcing laws may lead to casualties.

Shouldn't they also agree that: 1) an informed strategy must guide policy; 2) drug addiction afflicts many countries; and 3) we can benefit from the global experience with addressing drug addiction? Unfortunately, Mr. Duterte has shown little inclination to accept the global lessons learned at great cost over centuries, preferring to go by his thirty-year experience in Davao City.

While repeatedly rejecting US influence, Mr. Duterte has come up with a strategy that follows the war on drugs that America waged at home and exported abroad in the 1970s and '80s. This policy, anchored on police action and punitive sanctions, arguably helped push the death penalty for drug offenses from ten countries in 1979 to thirty-six by 2000.

This approach has now fallen into disfavor. By 1977, sixteen countries had abolished the death penalty and 140 have done so today. And thirty-three countries rarely impose the death penalty they prescribe for drug offenses. Since 2010, only seven countries have conducted executions for drug offenses, according to a report by the International Drug Policy Consortium (IDPC).

China, Iran and Saudi Arabia, described by Harm Reduction International as aggressive executioners at the "extreme fringe of the international community," raised the number of drug executions in 2014 to about 600. With the fatalities in Mr. Duterte's war on drugs at over ten times that number, the Philippines now stands at the extreme end of the fringe.

A moral basis drives the trend against the death penalty, despite the "eye for an eye" policy practiced for centuries. As humanity progressed toward higher stages of political and economic development, the understanding of what it means to be human and what constitutes humane behavior also evolved.

We no longer throw widows into the fires that cremate their husbands. No country now permits the profitable business of slavery.

Other governments have waged a war on drugs even more vigorously than Mr. Duterte. They abandoned the mailed-fist strategy even when it still enjoyed popular support. They did not miraculously acquire "*pusong mamon*" (marshmallow hearts), becoming suddenly overwhelmed by guilt over human rights violations. They changed course because the war approach did not pay off. The costs, which included damage to their international standing, loss of economic benefits and the escalation of domestic violence, exceeded the gains.

Consider Mexico, where drug trafficking had flourished since the 1960s. Elected in 2006, President Felipe Calderón made its suppression his top priority and unleashed the military against the drug cartels—an approach Mr. Duterte wants to follow. By the time Calderón left office in 2012, more than 60,000 Mexicans were dead and another 25,000 missing. Meanwhile, official sources reported that heroin addiction increased by nearly 83 percent between 2007 and 2013.

Calderón's successor Enrique Peña Nieto scaled back the war, and the killings declined from over 21,500 in 2012 to 17,000 in 2014. But the first ten months of 2016 registered over 17,000 deaths, the highest since 2012.

Accompanying the surge in violence, drug trafficking continued to prosper. Rather than resolving the underlying causes of addiction, the state-sponsored war promoted criminal violence and contributed to eroding the rule of law.

Colombia has also experienced decades of narcopolitics and drug war violence. Addressing the UN General Assembly's Special Session on the

World Drug Problem last April, President Juan Manuel Santos shared Colombia's painfully learned insight: "If something is not working for more than forty years, logic and common sense tell you that it must be changed."

Cast aside moral convictions—logic and common sense should teach us to avoid failed policies. Must we wait for six years and Mr. Duterte's 3 million casualties?

6

Common Ground on EJKs?

(*PDI*, February 04, 2017)

That remains difficult to find, as the angry government response to Amnesty International (AI) criticism demonstrated. But the blowback from the murder of Korean businessman Jee Ick-joo in Camp Crame by Anti-Illegal Drugs Group Police has opened space for constructive dialogue. Still, logic, language and policy issues abound.

Assistant Interior Secretary Epimaco Densing III argued that, without a death penalty, there is no judicial killing: "If a country has no judicial killing, there's no extrajudicial killing." Should we not instead conclude that if there is no judicial killing, then all killings by state authorities are extrajudicial?

Speaker Pantaleon Alvarez believes EJKs will decline with the death penalty. Will it rather not rationalize EJKs? Why postpone execution through an expensive, time-consuming court process, when the expected verdict is death? Anyway, the DOJ's mandate, Secretary Vitaliano Aguirre II apparently believes, extends to determining who is fully human and deserves human rights. Seriously?

Reviewing fifty-one drug-related incidents between June and December in 2016, Reuters reported the police kill ratio at 97 percent. The figure between 2013 and 2015 for Rio de Janeiro police, also accused of EJKs, was 80 percent. National Capital Region (NCR) Police Office Chief Oscar Albayalde disputed Reuters' figure as "probably not true," and quoted a 5–6 percent kill ratio.

Albayalde was calculating the number of suspects killed against the total number of suspects targeted in NCR police operations. Reuters was looking at fifty-one incidents when police fired their weapons, killing 100 out of 103 targets. For PDEA Spokesman Derrick Carreon, this showed that police were "good at shooting."

Alternatively, the kill ratio suggested that police were good at shooting unarmed suspects, like the three survivors in the fifty-one incidents. This would also explain the PNP's low casualty rate in the war on drugs. In Rio, one policeman died for every twenty-five suspects, against 118 suspects for every slain PNP officer. Investigative reports say guns found near suspects in distinct cases carried the same registration number, suggesting the planting of evidence.

On the Jee abduction, Malacañang spokesman Ernesto Abella said: "It's a matter of concern, but it's not alarming because police scalawags are already existing." Isn't the reverse more accurate? Any human institution will have its share of scalawags—always a matter of concern. That the scalawags are committing heinous crimes is alarming.

The Jee murder confirmed conclusions to which even the PNP admitted. "*Tokhang*," the police strategy to make a direct appeal through house calls on suspected drug addicts, has become a tool for extortion. More cases following the Jee murder playbook have surfaced. Sen. Panfilo Lacson has shown dismaying video evidence of plainclothes cops planting evidence for uniformed colleagues to discover.

But has President Duterte's blanket assurance of pardon for police who kill in the line of duty perhaps encouraged the expansion of extortion activities? Might police have committed EJKs? The administration has not conceded to either point. It will not count the Jee murder as an EJK, because the police were committing a crime, not performing official duties. Nevertheless, it makes AI's report of "unlawful and deliberate killings carried out by government order or with its complicity or acquiescence" more believable.

Mr. Duterte has repeatedly ridiculed the notion that bodies wrapped in masking tape could be the work of state authorities—because "government is not in the mummifying business." This argument now cannot stick, with the tape police used in the Jee murder. Cops murdering for profit would not shrink from EJKs to gain points and, if AI is correct, bonuses from superiors. The danger is that those accustomed to EJKs will escalate to murdering for profit.

Suspending Tokhang to probe rogue police is a necessary step. Completing the investigation of killings done by cops in the line of duty advances this process. So would addressing the cases of over 4,000 “vigilante killings.” Even if police were not involved, these are crimes that the government is responsible for solving and stopping. Bringing their perpetrators to justice would clear the PNP’s reputation and help in purging its ranks of rogues.

7

Pardon for the Albuera 19?

(*PDI*, April 01, 2017)

Two events last week raised extrajudicial killing as an urgent concern for our political leaders and the public. No April Fool's joke.

On March 27, PNP Director General "Bato" dela Rosa launched his personal drive to "disprove" claims of 7,000 EJKs. On March 29 in Oriental Mindoro, Duterte said he would advise the policemen charged with the killing of Albuera Mayor Rolando Espinosa to plead guilty, and then grant them absolute pardon.

The government has tried various ways to counter claims about EJKs in the country. One attempt was to redefine it away. Assistant Interior Secretary Epimaco Densing III argued that, without a death penalty, there is no judicial killing: "If a country has no judicial killing, there's no extrajudicial killing." Another approach was to refuse to search for evidence of its existence.

Whistle-blowers Edgar Matobato and Arturo Lascañas offered testimony on EJKs based on personal knowledge, under oath and against self-interest.

Detecting mistakes in details, the Senate inquiry dismissed Matobato's veracity; EJK victims, for instance, were wrapped in "packaging," and not "masking," tape, as he had claimed. But masking tape was the common generic term in the region, the way Colgate once stood for toothpaste.

Senators deemed Lascañas untrustworthy. He had fooled them once in denying that "death squads" operated in Davao; they refused to be fooled a second time. As appropriate reflection for Holy Week, one wonders if our

Bible thumpers in the Senate would disqualify Peter as a witness because he thrice-lied about knowing Christ.

Dela Rosa took a slightly different track. That over 7,000 killings have taken place under PRRD's watch was not really under dispute. The controversy was over the classification of these killings. Which ones were EJK?

From dela Rosa's perspective, none of them. At a Camp Crame briefing, he asked the media to "forget about EJK, don't use that term," challenging them to cite any instance when the PNP used it. For him, EJK meant "state-sponsored killing." But a meaningful response to EJK allegations must take the term as it is generally understood.

The essential element of EJK is not state-sponsorship but the participation of state security forces or their agents in the killing of any person without sanction of a judicial or legal process. Rogue police can commit EJK. Both dela Rosa and Duterte have publicly denounced widespread police corruption that required the suspension of Tokhang operations.

To assert that the government has not ordered, has opposed and has punished EJK is not sufficient. International law binds states to "take effective action to prevent, combat and eliminate [EJK] . . . in all its forms and manifestations."

As dela Rosa intended, the criterion of state sponsorship for EJK sets a high bar for proof. But Duterte has undermined his intent by intervening in the case that comes closest to meeting the standard: the killing of Albuera Mayor Espinosa. In the dark of dawn, avoiding security cameras and keeping eyewitnesses at bay, nineteen police agents, including high-ranking officers, killed Espinosa in his jail cell. A confessed drug criminal and father of a drug lord, Espinosa had surrendered to dela Rosa, believing that he would be safe in prison.

The National Bureau of Investigation and several senators concluded that Espinosa's death was a "rubout." No official, written order for the Espinosa killing has yet surfaced. But the careful planning and the involvement of so many PNP and state agents give the case the odor of a premeditated state operation. Duterte's insistence from the beginning that the killing was justified and that he would give them absolute pardon may supply the final stamp of state sponsorship of the murder.

Many may believe that Espinosa deserved to die because he was a drug-addict bastard. But Duterte has a rather broad list of bastards he considers deserving of death. Who is to say who will land on that list?

Senators Antonio Trillanes, Panfilo Lacson, Grace Poe and Bam Aquino have opposed Duterte's plan, which would effectively transform the police into a private presidential force vested with impunity. They need the support of their colleagues in the government and of the public.

8

How Many Filipino Druggies?

(*PDI*, May 27, 2017)

In 2015, there were 1.8 million drug addicts, according to the Dangerous Drugs Board (DDB). "Wrong," pronounced President Duterte, who had been saying "4 million" even before his election, and summarily sacked DDB Chair Benjamin Reyes without explaining why 4 million was the correct number.

Actually, according to PDEA Director General Isidro Lapeña, the real number by May 2017 had already climbed to 4.7 million. The update provoked the inevitable question: how did they surpass even Duterte's estimate after ten months of a drug war that allegedly drove the surrender of over a million drug abusers and killed off thousands of them?

Through the letter of Deputy Director General Ricardo Quinto, PDEA ventured to explain the "exact science" behind its figures. It pointed out that DDB based its estimate on a nationwide survey of 5,000 respondents 10–69 years old. In contrast, PDEA relied on the PNP's "*Oplan Tokhang*" visits to nearly 7.8 million households, about 34 percent of the total number nationwide.

Tokhang compelled the surrender of about 1.27 million "drug personalities," or at least one drug user/pusher in 16 percent of the households visited. The large number of households covered by the PNP and the resulting harvest of surrenders apparently gave PDEA the confidence to project from the Tokhang sample, the incidence of drug abuse nationwide at 4.7 million.

How valid is the conclusion that the drug abuse in the country mirrors the proportions discovered among the Tokhang households? The validity depends on how well the Tokhang sample represents the larger population. More critical than sample size is the rigor of the random selection process, which ensures that the sample and the findings from it are representative of the larger community. Were the Tokhang households selected at random, so that any household in the country had an equal chance of being chosen?

Much controversy has surrounded the issue of how households were selected for inclusion in the Tokhang visits and what registration in the "surrender" list means. What is clear is that the PDEA sample was neither random, nor representative. The target Tokhang households were apparently already suspected of harboring drug addicts. Stressing the accuracy of its information, PDEA noted that those who surrendered "have actual faces and profiles stored in the PNP's databases."

These databases may serve legitimate police purposes, but the Tokhang sample cannot provide a scientific basis for estimating nationwide drug addiction. A projection of the cancer incidence in the Philippines would be similarly flawed if we selected the respondents only from the population of hospital patients or, even worse, of clinics focused on cancers.

Other unsupported PDEA statements are unhelpful, such as the claim that 47 percent of Philippine barangays are "affected" by illegal drugs. What does "affect" mean and how do we measure its intensity? The failure of government authorities to distinguish between drug user, addict and pusher is also problematic. There are different levels of addiction, and the laws themselves make a distinction between using and trafficking drugs. Without a clarification of these terms, drug addiction numbers will remain questionable.

We need more explanation of the numbers from DDB, President Duterte and PDEA. For an issue with life-and-death implications, this is hardly academic nitpicking. A credible estimate of gross numbers is critical to the validation of the Duterte war on drugs. Is the country truly a narcostate in the grip of an existential drug crisis? Experts agree that we face a drug problem but nowhere near the scale confronting countries commonly branded narcostates.

Our response to the drug problem must be proportional to its scale, lest the cure inflict more damage than the disease. The same principle should apply to the declaration of martial law throughout Mindanao.

PDEA deserves credit for declaring its willingness to "submit to any Senate or congressional probe . . . to clarify the 'real' statistics." We urgently need this clarification to begin a sober assessment of the rationale, context and consequences of the Duterte war on drugs.

9

Hate Speech for Free?

(*PDI*, June 24, 2017)

The capacity for speech and the power it gives to express and receive ideas differentiate the human person from other animals and privileges freedom of expression as a basic human right deserving of constitutional protection. But this fundamental right provides no license to shout "Fire" in a crowded movie theater.

Can purveyors of hate speech directed against people of different ethnic origin, language, religion, political persuasion or sexual orientation escape culpability for the violence they provoke by invoking their right to free speech? Or should government subject them to the penalties prescribed for the provocateur in the movie theater? What if government agents themselves indulge in hate speech? One study claimed 65–77 percent more killings in Rwandan villages reached by a radio station urging the extermination of the Tutsis it dehumanized as "cockroaches."

These questions, at a time of more violent civilizational clashes, demonstrate that much work remains for International Freedom of Expression Exchange (IFEX). Celebrating its twenty-fifth anniversary, IFEX convened in Montreal, last week, a panel of international resource speakers led by Agnes Callamard and Oxford University Professor Timothy Garton Ash to explore the global challenges facing free speech and human rights.

Callamard served nine years as executive director of Article 19, the international NGO named after the article on freedom of expression in the Universal Declaration of Human Rights. Her mission continues as Director of Columbia University's initiative for Global Freedom of Expression. But Callamard became better known in the Philippines as UN special rapporteur on extrajudicial executions, especially after critical comments on the Duterte war on drugs at a human rights conference in Manila last month, triggered a pro-Duterte troll attack.

Filipinos should know more about Professor Ash and his recent book, *Free Speech: Ten Principles for a Connected World.* Ash argues that globalizing forces have made critically urgent a global consensus on the principles to govern the exercise of this right, as immigration constructs increasingly more physically connected but more culturally diverse communities. More people now live not in small homogenous villages, but in global megacities for which Ash has coined the term "cosmopolis."

Over 50 percent of Toronto's population are foreign-born (Filipinos make up the third largest immigrant group.) The third most spoken foreign language in Montreal is Arabic.

In the cosmopolis, ethnically distinct communities, empowered by different languages and comforted by different deities, share common national frontiers and submit to a common political governance system. By collapsing the boundaries of both space and time, the internet has made it possible for immigrants to maintain their connections to the homeland and preserve their cultural identity, thus sharpening and strengthening the differences between them and their host communities.

Some governments would restrain public discussion and debate over religious or racial issues that have historically provoked protracted, violent conflict. But the attempt in the US to kill legislators, apparently because they belonged to the Republican Party, demonstrates how political color and identities can produce as much violence as skin color and ethnic identities.

Despite the dangers posed by the diversity in the cosmopolis, selectively suppressing dialogue on contentious issues will not promote its long-term health and survival. Ash argues that all human beings, whatever their community, must be free and able to express themselves and "to seek, receive and impart information and ideas, regardless of frontiers." The majority of the world's countries that have signed on Article 19 should similarly respond to the question of how free should speech be.

But the effective practice of Article 19 depends also on the response to a second question: "how free speech should be." How should people exercise the right of free speech? The conduct and the quality of the political discourse, in social media and among government leaders, can raise or reduce the risk of partisan violence. The right of free speech does not demand a duty to be crudely, discreditably disagreeable.

The leaders of the cosmopolis must model the practice of vigorous disagreement without vicious offensiveness.

10

The Parojinog Provocation

(*PDI*, August 19, 2017)

Frustration with a judicial system that did not deliver justice drove many to support Rodrigo Duterte's presidential bid. But many have recoiled at the post-election surge in unresolved killings by police forces and freelance vigilantes. As in the Aesop's fable, the frogs who accepted a crocodile king to discipline their divided and dysfunctional colony discovered that a ruler's unrestrained power to exterminate the guilty also risked extinguishing the innocent.

The government's predawn assault on the homes of Ozamiz City Mayor Reynaldo Parojinog on July 30 produced sixteen fatalities (including the mayor and his wife, sister, brother and nephew) and sharpened the dilemma that President Duterte posed for many voters. Those vulnerable to the clan's power probably felt liberated and relieved, even if they objected in principle to EJK. Reflective of this dilemma was Sen. Panfilo Lacson's ambivalence on whether to conduct a Senate inquiry into the matter.

Octavio Parojinog rose to power in the 1980s as the founder of the Kuratong Baleleng, a government-backed anticommunist militia group. Tolerated as a vigilante group, the Kuratong turned to extortion, armed robbery and kidnapping for ransom, provoking criminal charges and armed clashes with the police. Octavio was killed in 1990 while resisting arrest; charges against his sons, Renato, Ricardo and Reynaldo, were dismissed for lack of evidence.

Whether admired as Robin Hood figures or feared as a Mafia family, the Parojinogs remained dominant in their province and easily diversified into politics, also a potentially lucrative undertaking. In 2001, Renato won a provincial board seat and Reynaldo became the mayor of Ozamiz. Third-generation descendants subsequently won city and provincial elections. Mayor Reynaldo and his daughter, Vice Mayor Nova Princess, were charged with corruption in 2008 and ordered arrested in 2016. The charges were dismissed only a year later.

As chief superintendent and head of the Presidential Anti-Crime Commission (PACC), Lacson led Task Force Habagat that engaged and killed eleven Kuratong gang members in 1991. The victims' families denounced the operation as a "rubout." Charges filed against Lacson and his men reached the Supreme Court, but were dismissed in 2002.

Despite the similarities with the killing of Albuera Mayor Rolando Espinosa—operations conducted in the dead of night, missing or non-functioning surveillance cameras—Lacson was inclined to see the action against the Parojinogs as aboveboard. But he was categorical in condemning the killing of Espinosa as premeditated murder and the downgrading to homicide of the charges filed against Supt. Marvin Marcos and his men. Mayor Parojinog, he observed, was not killed in a jail cell.

Mayor Parojinog reportedly had the inside track for the governor's seat in the next election. Even those concerned about EJK recognized that further consolidation of the family's grip on provincial politics would likely doom any criminal case lodged against its members. This pragmatic assessment argued for quietly accepting the summary execution of notorious criminals, rather than depending for justice on our fragile legal institutions. But who will make the call on who deserves EJK? As Joaquin Bernas, SJ used to say, "The King should have this power—if I am King."

Senior administration officials appear recently to have rediscovered the Constitution. Defending Superintendent Marcos, Presidential Legal Counsel Salvador Panelo admonished critics to observe "the constitutional presumption of innocence," a line also taken by the PNP Chief Ronald dela Rosa. Allegations of Davao City Mayor Paolo Duterte's involvement in Bureau of Customs corruption involving drugs did not prompt Mr. Duterte to call for the investigation of the case; he asked to see the evidence proving his son's guilt.

We should welcome the administration's appeal to constitutional rights, due process and credible evidence. It has not been as zealous about meeting these standards before executing suspects in drug crimes. It has insisted that it must privilege the rights of the innocent over those of criminals. But, as pointed out with greater eloquence by St. Thomas More, rejecting the laws that protect the rights of the guilty deprives the innocent of their protection.

Granting the government the power to choose whose rights deserve respect, slides us back to square one: an unjust judicial system giving impunity to the powerful—the problem that voters had hoped the Duterte presidency would correct.

11

EJK: Policy and Practice

(*PDI*, September 23, 2017)

The messages in the September 21 "Day of Protest" at the University of the Philippines Chapel Mass and the unveiling of the Jose "Pepe" Diokno statue at the CHR headquarters inevitably focused on EJK. The issue remains cloudy, despite the precious time Senate hearings spent fruitlessly debating what has become almost an academic issue: is there a government policy to kill drug offenders?

PNP Chief "Bato" dela Rosa insisted that President Duterte has never issued a policy statement or direct order instructing the police to kill drug addicts. Mr. Duterte has maintained the same point. Although he has explicitly warned addicts, "I will kill you if you are destroying my country," he tirelessly repeats that no law prohibits him from threatening to kill criminals.

Until someone miraculously discovers documentary evidence of high officials prescribing EJK, government authorities can simply stand on their denials. Debating the issue only served to inflict on the public, dela Rosa's tearful defense of his misunderstood, unappreciated policemen. But, whether explicitly mandated or not, EJK is undeniably taking place, raising legitimate questions about unresolved killings done during police operations or by unnamed vigilantes.

The issue is not policy, but practice. Threats to kill addicts would not themselves be alarming, except that suspects actually end up dead without benefit of due process. The administration has made little progress investigating these thousands of deaths, let alone delivering justice to the victims.

The corollary question revolves around the extent to which Duterte's statements contributed to justifying and promoting the practice of EJK. Both BBC and the *New York Times* have collected some choice items:

"Forget the laws on human rights . . . You drug pushers, holdup men and do-nothings, you better go out. Because . . . I'll dump all of you into Manila Bay, and fatten all the fish there."

"[As mayor] I'd go around in Davao with a motorcycle . . . and I would just patrol the streets, looking for trouble . . . I was really looking for a confrontation, so I could kill."

"Hitler massacred 3 million Jews. Now, there are 3 million drug addicts . . . I'd be happy to slaughter them."

He stood by the police charged with the killing of Albuera Mayor Rolando Espinosa, "because they might have really followed my order (*Kasi baka nga talaga sinunod yung utos ko*)."

Presidential apologists twist their tongues and turn cartwheels to interpret the intent of these statements on EJK and impunity as histrionic, hyperbolic or humorous. But presidential words matter. At the minimum, the death count in the drug war clearly causes the president little concern. He rejoiced at the one-day record of thirty-two drug-war deaths established in August: "That's beautiful (*Maganda yun*). If we can just kill thirty-two every day, then maybe we can reduce what ails this country." At that rate, journalist Vergel Santos calculated, it would take Mr. Duterte over thirty-four years to eliminate his estimated 4 million drug addicts.

We are also familiar with policies and regulations that are routinely violated because they are not enforced and violations go unpunished. We now discover examples critical to the drug war.

Within a year, two shipments totaling nearly 1,500 kilos of *shabu* went through the Bureau of Customs. Sen. Franklin Drilon and Sen. Panfilo Lacson noted that the laws prescribe detailed guidelines on the disposal of captured drug materials and the prosecution of suspects implicated in the capital, non-bailable crime of drug trafficking. Sen. Richard Gordon joined them in denouncing the lax implementation of policy that allowed massive quantities of drugs to flood the country—while the police vigorously hunted down possible peddlers of *shabu* sachets.

We see, on one hand, clear policies validated by successful anti-drug campaigns in other countries that interdicted the flow of drugs from overseas and targeted the big drug lords, which are not being faithfully enforced. On the other hand, we see piling up suspected and unresolved EJK cases. The administration denies that this is the result of policy, but the suspicious deaths are daily happening in practice, without visible government intervention.

It is a curious and outrageous predicament that has not provoked, but might have justified, the usual presidential expletives.

12

Is EJK OK?

(*PDI*, November 11, 2017)

Two basic elements define EJK, as it is globally understood: 1) the killers are agents of the state or acting for them; and 2) the killing takes place without benefit of judicial proceedings.

The PNP and the DOJ insist that no EJK has happened during the Duterte administration, citing Administrative Order (AO) No. 35, issued when EJK apparently targeted specific groups of victims: political dissidents, cause-oriented activists, investigative journalists. Even by AO 35 criteria, the killing of Zenaida Luz, Oriental Mindoro anti-crime crusader, must qualify as EJK. Nevertheless, her killers, Sr. Insp. Magdalino Pimentel, Jr. and Insp. Markson Almeranez, were allowed to post bail, and are now back on the PNP payroll.

But AO 35 was meant to focus government efforts on stopping crimes against the most prominent EJK targets at the time, not to exclude other classes of victims. To argue that Kian delos Santos was not an EJK victim because he was not an activist, journalist, or dissident, insults the common sense of the public. Even if Kian were only a drug pusher, his execution, while on his knees begging for mercy, was not justified, as even President Duterte has conceded.

Denying the reality of EJK simplifies matters for the PNP. To acknowledge even one case of unlawful EJK opens up the possibility of similar cases in its inventory of "deaths under investigation." But the blanket denial of EJK undermines government credibility and is self-defeating, since not all EJKs are illegal.

Without capital punishment, there is no judicially sanctioned killing. By definition, all killings done by state agents are extrajudicial, but not all such killings are unlawful. Self-defense against clear and mortal danger justifies killings committed by law enforcement agents while performing their duties. But the claim requires proof. Hence, law enforcement agencies themselves must investigate all EJK cases to determine that these were not summary executions that violated constitutional and human rights.

The "presumption of regularity," when deaths result from legitimate police operations, provides a necessary but not sufficient condition to excuse the killings; these must still undergo investigation. Despite patient coaching by Sen. Panfilo Lacson in the Senate hearings, PNP Chief Ronald dela Rosa refused to accept this point.

When law enforcement agencies prove unwilling or unable to complete credible investigations, the CHR must intervene. The CHR has neither the resources nor the mandate to investigate all cases of violence inflicted on the public. This is the task of law enforcement agencies and the CHR must focus on their performance.

CHR oversight is important to ensure public trust in these agencies, given the resources and the license to apply lethal force against citizens. The government needs police and military forces to protect the public. But the key question, especially in democratic states, remains: who will guard the guards?

Recent surveys on EJK are troubling because they deliver an ambiguous message. Seventy-three percent of respondents believe that unlawful EJK is taking place, doubting claims that police were compelled to kill suspects in self-defense. Sixty-five percent reject the notion of a cash bounty for drug war kills. Ninety-five percent believe that drug suspects should be apprehended alive. But 88 percent support the Duterte war on drugs. This support and the president's good approval and trust ratings lead his spokesperson Harry Roque to speculate that people are OK with the killings.

Do Filipinos really believe there is nothing wrong with summary executions? The question must be asked, though we may not like what the responses might reveal about the depth of people's faith values, the formation of their conscience, and their regard for the moral order and the rule of law.

The question must also be carefully formulated and explained.

Respondents must understand that the question critically measures their confidence in the police forces. To tolerate summary executions means to entrust to police officers the authority to decide whom to spare and whom to kill.

President Duterte has effectively delivered this power to the police, despite his suspicion that 40 percent of the force are complicit in corruption. Is this responsibility a burden police officers want to embrace? Is this a right that the public is prepared to yield to them?

13

Trick or Treat

(*PDI*, December 07, 2019)

Good governance practice calls for periodically reviewing major and controversial programs. Modifying the structure of the Inter-Agency Committee on Anti-illegal Drugs (ICAD) offered an occasion for such a review. Daring Vice President Leni Robredo to act as ICAD co-chair also seemed a clever political move. Why the ploy failed—and the consequences of the failure—will continue to unfold.

The initial offer was surprisingly generous. To prove sincerity, explained Presidential Spokesperson Salvador Panelo, the appointment would place "all offices, bureaus, agencies or government instrumentalities involved in the enforcement of the law on prohibited drugs . . . under [Robredo's] command and supervision with a cabinet secretary portfolio" and would be coterminous with the president's term. Political rivals, starting with those Robredo defeated in 2016, had no reason to cheer her success, which would strengthen her as a competitor in future elections. Add to the list those who had been responsible for driving the drug war and may fear that Robredo might inadvertently stumble over buried bones and expose incompetence or corruption.

For Mr. Duterte himself, however, it was a low-risk gambit. By his own admission, the drug war needed "tweaking." It had aggravated the problems of the justice system, adding to the congestion of the courts and the prisons, some already holding four to five times their capacity. Concern over a public health crisis in the prisons was not surprising. With limited health care facilities, detention could become a death sentence even for suspects not yet convicted.

Public opposition, not to the drive against drugs, but to the killing of mainly low-level suspects, had not abated. Prosecution of the campaign relied mainly on the police, but too many officers had been implicated in extortion, graft involving the recycling of drugs and suspected EJKs. The president had also admitted to this problem, even talking about taking over the PNP because he had difficulty finding an honest officer for the position.

But a campaign to clean up a weaponized agency he had empowered was risky. It made sense to enlist a dupe to draw the fire and distance the presidency from potential flak. If Robredo fails, she loses credibility as an opposition leader. Alternatively, any semblance of success would give Mr. Duterte credit for his "out-of-the-box" appointment. He controlled all the cards, including the initiative in setting Robredo's performance standards.

This fail-safe scenario depended on a clear government good-faith effort to give Robredo realistic goals and commensurate authority and resources. It must convince the public that it had not stacked the deck to ensure failure or risk a backfire. Robredo did not make this easy. She sought clarification on the scope of her authority; a presidential meeting for this purpose never came. She accepted the restrictions to the original offer, including the withdrawal of the cabinet post and denial of access to the drug list. She prudently declined to intervene in operational issues, limiting herself to seeking and reviewing data needed for proposing evidence-based policies. She tried to keep the president informed about her initiatives through reports that he never read.

Hence, the reasons offered to justify her unceremonious dismissal from the post were unconvincing and contradicted the public rationale for her appointment. While communists were considered capable of serving national interests in the cabinet, an elected vice president was deemed not deserving of equal trust.

Although denied the time to effect meaningful change in the prosecution of the drug war, Robredo focused attention on strategic elements: the drug trade as a global challenge that requires international collaboration; addressing addiction as both a police and health concern, demanding a serious and visible rehabilitation program; holding erring police officers to account as indispensable to the restoration of public confidence in the PNP. It did not take long to expose the ICAD Halloween appointment as a trick, not an early Christmas treat.

Mr. Duterte never intended to empower Robredo and probably never expected her to call the bluff. But the issues Robredo flagged remain crucial and, along with the report she promised to share with the public, should not be forgotten.

14

Wasting Opportunities

(*PDI*, February 01, 2020)

Media reports and independent research, using government and police records, had earlier flagged many of the key issues raised in Vice President Leni Robredo's ICAD report on the drug war. They bear repeating. Still unsettled after three years, they explain why a task initially promised for completion in six months cannot be delivered, as President Duterte has admitted, even after six years.

These issues touch upon structure, policy and implementation: 1) lack of reliable figures on the extent of the country's drug problem and an objective, transparent way of measuring the progress toward its resolution; 2) disproportionate focus on street-level enforcement of drug laws that deemphasized rehabilitation and reintegration; 3) damage done, not least to the PNP itself, by the *Tokhang* (knock and plead) strategy perceived as abetting abuses, impunity and police corruption; 4) continuing flow of drugs and the recycling of captured contraband; 5) impact on the country's congested courts and prisons.

The Robredo report organized available information into a coherent framework, correlated data, and identified missing and conflicting figures. It is neither exhaustive nor definitive—an unreasonable expectation, given her unceremonious firing by Mr. Duterte after only nineteen days in office. The government did not dispute the relevance of the report. It attacked the unfavorable performance evaluation of the drug war, making it appear even more negative than intended to project the judgment as unreasonable and unfair.

The report rated government control of drug supply a "dismal failure," calculating that it captured only 1/100 or 1 percent of the estimated total *shabu* consumption. Onion-skinned officials rejected the 1 percent "grade," but how would the PDEA (or Presidential Spokesperson Salvador Panelo) rate this performance? They can contest their own data, but the math is not a "wild assumption." Countering the 1 percent score with surveys showing 80 percent satisfaction with the anti-drug campaign makes no sense; opinion polls cannot provide an accurate tally of drugs captured.

But, whatever the true figures, the report gave the grade only to the goal of supply interdiction, not to the entire anti-drug campaign. The administration can easily evaluate and grade itself by publicly responding, with the suitable explanation, to yes-or-no questions posed by the report.

Has it implemented provisions to guide the drug war as mandated by Executive Order (EO) No. 15 (2017)? These included the formation of a National Anti-Drug Task Force and the promulgation of a uniform manual of regulations for the conduct of all anti-illegal drug operations. Did it conduct a nationwide survey in 2018 on drug prevalence in the country (EO 66)? Has the government established and rigorously followed a system for distinguishing drug users from pushers, who are subject to different penalties, or for handling offenders who voluntarily turn themselves in to authorities (Amended Comprehensive and Dangerous Drugs Act: Republic Act No. 9165, 2002)? Insults and threats have come from the government, but no coherent, credible response to the report. After thousands of deaths, we still lack the foundation of a reliable, robust and transparent information system.

Without baseline data, we lack the benchmarks to determine the scale of the drug problem, monitor the progress we are making in addressing it, and measure the true costs and benefits of our efforts. The Department of the Interior and Local Government (DILG) recently launched an Anti-Illegal Drugs Information System that promised to provide comprehensive and updated data on the drug war by the end of 2019. The lack of funds cited as the reason for the delayed 2018 survey on drug prevalence is surprising, given the president's generous discretionary budgets. The new schedule calls for completion by the first quarter of 2020.

Forty-four percent of SWS survey respondents believed Mr. Duterte sincerely wanted Robredo's help in ICAD. The administration could have taken credit for work produced under its aegis that documented the problems of the drug war and provided a platform for further analysis and action. It could have helped mobilize the support of the bureaucracy and the public for the government's planned but woefully delayed initiatives to rationalize and strengthen the anti-drug campaign. The knee-jerk hostility to the Robredo ICAD report unfortunately wasted an opportunity to help unite people and government behind a common approach to the drug problem.

III

Constitutional Questions

A wake for a mutual close friend gave me a chance to ask Carlos "Sonny" Dominguez about the rumors that his high school classmate at the Ateneo de Davao and bosom buddy, Rodrigo Duterte, was planning to enter the 2016 presidential race. Sonny went on to college at the Ateneo de Manila University, a year behind me. We also served together in the Cory Aquino Cabinet.

At that time, he dismissed the idea. He said that Duterte was allowing, perhaps encouraging, the rumors to promote support for his long-term advocacy of moving the Philippines from a unitary to a federal system of government. A migrant from Cebu to Davao, Duterte was among those who believed that Imperial Manila's control of the national policy agenda and national resources prevented the development of the Visayas and Mindanao and this had to be dismantled through constitutional change.

Later, of course, Davao insiders acknowledged that Duterte's inner circle had concluded that a credible Mindanao candidate could capture Malacañang Palace. They believed that the presumptive 2010 candidate, former Sen. Manuel "Mar" Roxas was vulnerable to a challenge. The resurgence of Cory Aquino's popularity after her death from cancer convinced Roxas that Noynoy Aquino had a better chance to win the presidency and decided to switch places with him and run for vice president, instead. The Duterte supporters agreed with Mar's reading that Noynoy would be unbeatable in 2010 and deferred their own plans for a Duterte presidential campaign.

If Sonny Dominguez was less than forthright about Duterte's presidential ambitions—which would have run counter to the narrative that Duterte was a reluctant candidate—he was completely candid about Duterte's conviction that the Philippines needed a federal system to break the grip of the national capital on the local governments. The belief was that greater autonomy to regional and provincial governments, beyond what the Local Government Code provided, would allow them to formulate development plans more responsive to their needs.

What was less than clear were the specific features of the federal system that Duterte wanted to establish. For meaningful development to take place, local governments needed more than the autonomy to formulate plans; they also needed resources for their implementation. Economists and finance experts doubted that rearranging the boxes on the government organizational chart would by itself result in a more equitable and effective sharing of resources.

Meanwhile, the federal system agenda could not be realized without constitutional change. This requirement opened up a whole can of contentious issues: what would be the process for constitutional change; when should the process begin; what changes should be priority. The last item was particularly problematic.

Many agreed that there was a need to review and introduce changes to the 1986 Constitution. But even advocates of constitutional change worried that the people selected for the task might exploit the opportunity to remove the elements that protected the liberal and democratic rights that, in the wake of EDSA I, were enshrined in the Aquino Freedom Constitution. The authoritarian inclinations of the Duterte government demonstrated in attacks on human rights advocacy groups and independent media tended to reinforce these concerns.

1

"If Federalism Is the Answer, What's the Question?"

(*PDI*, January 06, 2018)

This was the rejoinder of a 2016 University of the Philippines School of Economics forum to the claim that federalism was the only solution to the country's problems. Responding to the question, social science professors produced the *Debate on Federal Philippines: A Citizen's Handbook* to identify the issues to consider before committing to a radical change in political structure.

Unitary states govern the majority of the 193 countries in the UN, and twenty-seven countries, comprising 40 percent of the world's population, have adopted a federal system of government. Both systems include strong and weak states. Hence, the handbook recommends that the move to change systems start by specifying the problems to be corrected and the goals to be achieved.

For much of its history, the Philippines has functioned under a unitary, presidential system of government. But it has failed to meet expectations for a government that could provide the effective and equitable delivery of public goods and services, maintain the rule of law, control corruption, and protect democratic and human rights, including the people's right to take part in policymaking and to hold public officials accountable for their actions.

The failure, according to one hypothesis, stemmed from the perpetuation of the unitary political system, inherited from colonial regimes, where authority, responsibility, resources and power flowed from the national government to subordinate territorial units. A system that allowed lower levels of administration greater autonomy in addressing local problems would arguably enable them to respond more effectively to the needs of their constituencies.

Politicians have applauded this argument and periodically tried to expand the autonomy of LGUs. In 1959–1991, the legislature passed six laws aimed at expanding LGU autonomy. Cumulatively, these laws gave LGUs greater administrative authority to manage their affairs, more taxing powers over their resources and a higher, guaranteed share of taxes collected by the national government.

But twenty-five years after the passage of the Local Government Code (LGC), complaints persist over Imperial Manila's political, bureaucratic and financial grip on the LGUs. There is reason to complain. The law enacting the LGC, for instance, called for a mandatory review after five years, or in 1996. After two decades and counting, the formula for the distribution of the internal revenue allotment—the LGUs' share of national tax revenues—remains frozen to that set in 1991.

Federalism proponents blame the LGC's failure to the fact that it was only a congressional enactment. A constitutional change to federalism, they believe, would ensure that decentralization is achieved. The handbook suggests testing this belief against the evidence available in the region.

The Philippines, Thailand and Indonesia are unitary states; Malaysia is federated. The handbook compares the forces promoting centralization (C) and decentralization (D) in the administration and the politics of these countries. In the administrative sphere, it assessed the strength of the national agency managing LGUs, usually the Ministry of the Interior (C), and prior experience with the devolution of government functions to lower administrative units (D). The political sphere considered: whether LGU officials are elected (D) or appointed (C); the strength of local political bosses (C); and the coherence and strength of political parties (C).

Among the unitary states, the Philippines was the most decentralized, followed by Indonesia and Thailand. But among the four ASEAN countries, the most centralized was Federal Malaysia. The analysis suggests three conclusions. Federalism does not guarantee decentralization. Decentralization can be achieved within a unitary state. If decentralization efforts in the Philippines are failing to yield the expected benefits, it is not because of its unitary political structure.

A problem-and-goal-driven approach must then look into the preexisting conditions that frustrate the progress toward genuine LGU autonomy and how these can be addressed—as a step toward evaluating the costs and benefits of shifting from a unitary to a federal regime.

Our congratulations and thanks to the Ateneo de Manila University Press and the handbook's authors, Eduardo Araral Jr., Paul D. Hutchcroft, Gilberto M. Llanto, Jonathan E. Malaya, Ronaldo U. Mendoza, Julio C. Teehankee, for this timely contribution to the federalism debate. The issue is too important to leave to congressmen.

2

Con-ass for Federalism?

(*PDI*, January 13, 2018)

The body politic has long been ailing. While recent years have brought some relief, its tolerance for pain has weakened, its anguish sharpened by the evidence of other polities enjoying better health and the claims of current political doctors that they have the single, surefire remedy—federalism—to end its suffering.

The shift in political structure is major surgery. What benefits will federalism bring, and by what means will they materialize? Which limbs or organs will the surgeons amputate? What foreign elements will they implant? How much will the operation cost? How long is the expected period of convalescence? The doctors prescribing the cure have not yet given a comprehensive explanation of the process to the patient.

The lack of a credible, cost-benefit analysis for the change to federalism is understandable, since its detailed framework remains undefined. The devil is in the details. While a legitimate and viable model, the benefits of its adoption is theoretical. Its success will depend on the patient's preexisting condition and the operating surgeons' expertise.

Federalism, for instance, seeks to address the disparity in regional development and prosperity. The taxes extracted by the national government from the regions and the often tardy and inequitable flowback of budgetary resources to LGUs present only one source of disparity. It also stems from the difference in God-given resource endowments among LGUs and the stewardship practiced by their respective political leaders, many of them during decades of dynastic rule. Political restructuring will not magically give poor, badly governed LGUs more natural resources or better leaders.

Research has demonstrated that even if they retained all the 2015 revenues they raised, eighty-eight of ninety-three provinces (95 percent), eighty-seven of 152 cities (57 percent), and 1,937 of 2,044 municipalities (95 percent) could not support even half of their operating costs. National government efforts to improve the fiscal position of the poor LGUs through the 1992 LGC have not succeeded. Success can come only if the richer LGUs, whose control over their resources federalism will reinforce, voluntarily agree to share their wealth. Changing systems will not necessarily displace current LGU leaders or their political priorities.

The benefits of the change are hypothetical, but the higher cost of running a federal system is inevitable. Education Secretary Leonor Briones, once the national treasurer, has expressed doubts that the government can sustain these costs.

The experience of other countries gives us more understanding also about the risks of undertaking a systems overhaul. The first risk is the constitutional change process itself, which erases anything good in the old constitution and leaves a blank slate on which anything can be inscribed. Joaquin Bernas, SJ and former Chief Justice Artemio Panganiban have both sounded this warning, which has led other analysts to prefer the piecemeal amendment of the Constitution, focusing only on provisions that have become dysfunctional.

This fear also reinforces the argument that an elected constitutional convention (con-con) should craft a new constitution rather than legislators convened as a constituent assembly (con-ass). Even if we naively assume that serving congressmen will robustly resist the temptation to promote personal interests, they would likely be more prone to focus on immediate political concerns. A con-con would allow for a more diverse, deliberative body that will have a better chance to take a longer-term, more inclusive perspective to produce a constitution to which unborn generations of Filipinos will be subject. Is this not worth the investment in a con-con?

Con-ass advocates assure us that our fears are unfounded. What is our basis for trusting this assurance? The benefits they promise are conditional and they cannot yet compute the costs and risks of their project. But these political doctors are supremely sure of three things: that they have perfectly diagnosed the disease; that the surgery they propose is the necessary treatment; that they must perform the operation themselves. This excess of confidence that the Greeks called hubris, must cause us concern.

Prudence dictates that anyone contemplating major surgery seek a second and third opinion: to review the soundness of the diagnosis; assess the aptness of the proposed cure; and evaluate the surgeons' integrity and skill. This precaution comes especially with the possibility that the doctors may profit from the surgery.

We can still hope that the Senate can offer a second opinion.

3

Charter Change? At What Cost?

(*PDI*, August 25, 2018)

Provoked by Finance Secretary Sonny Dominguez's brutally blunt critique of the Consultative Committee's (con-com) Bayanihan Charter, some members reacted in the spiteful manner described as "*pikon*" ("poor sport"—though that's a grossly inadequate translation). Fr. Ranhilio Aquino ran to Daddy Digong, challenging him to sack or silence cabinet members criticizing their output.

Others faulted the economic managers for ignoring the con-com's request for guidance on economic issues. Given only a general overview of the proposed charter, however, finance officials were understandably reluctant to provide the hard numbers the con-com probably wanted.

It would have been improper for Secretary Dominguez to require the con-com to keep the costs of their new charter's governance structure within his budget cap. The con-com was not buying a car, a process that normally begins by setting a budget, which determines the affordable brands. A million pesos would give buyers several options. But they would not bother inspecting BMW or Benz models clearly beyond their budget. A budget limit at the outset would have constrained the con-com's deliberations on reforms the country needed. Its mission was to propose remedies for specific ailments afflicting the body politic.

The con-com's first responsibility was to identify the weaknesses in the current Constitution most urgently requiring attention, and to prescribe the necessary treatment. Money should not dictate the diagnosis. It would be senseless for Finance to say that the con-com should not exceed the costs of herbal medicine and Zumba dance instructors, such as were prescribed for drug addicts; or should adopt the cheaper option of radical amputation, when less invasive robotic surgery may be the correct recourse. Efficacy, not expense, should be the con-com's first concern.

Once completed, the design should give Finance enough information to assess the likely flow of revenue and expenses and financial viability of the con-com proposal. Secretary Dominguez found the draft charter still "confusing." But with their experience managing their current budget, economic managers worry that they cannot meet all the costs of the designer drugs prescribed by the con-com without compromising other priorities.

Compared to governance, unfortunately, the effectiveness of prescriptions is easier to determine in medicine, where corrections—should projected results do not materialize—are also easier to make. Which is why business corporations prudently conduct pilot projects to test the feasibility of costly, complex innovations and to surface potential problems, before risking company-wide implementation.

This is still the argument for making sure the Bangsamoro regional autonomy succeeds, before proceeding to federalism. The Bangsamoro "pilot" would reveal, at a lower cost, what must be done to achieve federalism's professed objective of collective prosperity through regional empowerment.

While the costs of charter change are certain, the benefits are speculative. The economic managers now plead inability to give local governments their correct share of tax revenues promised under the LGC but never delivered. How can LGUs trust that federalism will give them a greater share of resources than what they are presently owed? Would they not prefer to get their proper share of resources under prevailing laws, before yielding them for the promise of more under an untested system?

Even granting the excellence of all proposed charter provisions—discounting the doubts of experts from different disciplines—their effectiveness in delivering benefits will ultimately depend on the character and the motivations of the implementors. Con-com chair Reynato Puno blames the elite for opposing charter change. But he is counting on the elite in Congress to push the charter change that surveys show the masa repeatedly rejecting. To his credit, he has declared that he would oppose charter change if it did not ban political dynasties. He admits he cannot ensure congressional approval of this ban.

Charter change will gift us with three absolutely certain results: more bureaucrats, more politicians and more taxes to support them. People want change, but they have been saying that charter change is not the change they want. This message they must deliver through their votes in the 2019 elections.

4

Development, Democracy, Dictatorship and RevGov

(*PDI*, December 02, 2017)

Enrique Razon Jr., President-CEO of International Container Terminal Services Inc., may have reason to complain. The headline of the story that covered his comments at the ASEAN Business Investment Summit ran: "Exec says infra dev't, democracy can't mix." Direct and indirect quotes in the story cannot establish that he made such a categorical and incorrect conclusion.

The print report began with an accurate statement: "[Some] countries with the best infrastructure in the world are dictatorships." This was also the basis for the online version's headline: "Countries with best infrastructure are dictatorships—Razon." But the online version also attributed to him the view that infrastructure development and democracy cannot go hand in hand, "hinting that there might be a benefit in being [run] by a dictator."

The "hint" picked came from Mr. Razon's suggestion that dictatorships did better than democracies in delivering infrastructure development. He offered, as the exception that proves the rule, the example of the US: the only country "that advocated for democracy and achieved development but only because it was 'so vast and has so much resources.'" But Canada and Australia also achieved development and democracy. Admittedly, both nations are also vast and well-endowed with natural resources. What about Japan?

Or the Netherlands? Mr. Razon conceded that Europe was "well-advanced," asserting that "its infrastructure was built over a hundred years ago and they weren't a democracy yet." But the most advanced European nations, even a hundred years ago, were already working democracies, whose World War I victory in 1917 was prematurely hailed as the triumph of democracy. Europe, however, was not then and is not now, one country.

The conceptual problem that confounds sweeping conclusions about democracy, dictatorship and development often arises from the attempt to reduce these complex terms to a single definition. The democracies of twentieth-century Europe differed in their approximation of democracy, as they do today. Democracy will always remain a work-in-progress. In an ever-changing environment, maintaining a consensus among free individuals requires continuing effort.

Ultimately dependent on coercion, a small cabal of ruthless leaders can more easily maintain, for a time, a dictatorial regime. Technology facilitated efforts by despots in Nazi Germany, Soviet Russia and Red China to aim for totalitarian control. But dictatorships also vary in their aspiration, ability and willingness to concentrate and deploy power. Critics may dismiss Cuba and Zimbabwe as infrastructure-deficient dictatorships but acknowledge that they achieved different levels of human development. China and Singapore both have excellent infrastructure but cannot be described as equally "dictatorial."

Some countries with the worst infrastructure in the world are dictatorships, something Mr. Razon might have acknowledged. That both democracies and dictatorships display good and bad infrastructure suggests that the system of government does not by itself guarantee infrastructure excellence. Not a particularly stunning insight worthy of headlines, but it would have left Mr. Razon unscathed by doubts as to his political preferences.

Having lived through the martial law years and with his international business experience, Mr. Razon knows more than most, the difference between democracies and dictatorships. Retreating from the slippery slope to which his comments on political economy had led, he declared that he was not "'endorsing' one form of political system over another."

This disclaimer only distinguished himself from most Filipinos, who continue to believe that they have better chances under a democracy, even when it has yet to deliver a better life to many of them. Unlike Mr. Razon, who has prospered even within the country's flawed democracy. He did not need a dictatorship to expand the family fortunes.

It also fed fuel to the controversy over the proposed revolutionary government. His unqualified profession of indifference to the choice between democracy and dictatorship for the Philippines at a time when the country may be compelled to choose, is disappointing and sad.

If democracy again dies in the Philippines, critics will likely blame the ignorant masses for failing either to elect leaders of proven competence and unquestioned integrity or to hold them accountable when they betray public trust. But the leadership elite—in politics and the professions, in the church and civil society, in the bureaucracy and business—will bear the heavier burden for its death.

IV

Mindanao

Shortly after the 2016 elections, I participated in a series of focus group discussions with voters, mainly from the C and D economic sectors, who were willing to talk about their presidential choices. The majority had voted for Duterte, for various reasons. But for most of them, one factor trumped everything else: Duterte was from Mindanao. Though they were not all from Mindanao, they felt that it was time for someone from Mindanao to move to Malacañang Palace.

There was merit to this line of thinking. Since the fifties, the country's second biggest island had beckoned as the "Promised Land." Rich in agricultural potential and mineral resources, its development would propel the growth of the entire country. Sadly, rather than providing the engine for development, Mindanao became the fertile breeding ground for violence arising from dynastic political competition that, complicated by the communist insurgency, religious conflict, cultivated a Muslim secessionist movement and jihadist terrorism.

The poorest, least developed communities in the country languished in the promised land. They lagged badly behind on development indicators; their scores on poverty incidence, education achievement, life expectancy, development metrics dragging down the country's numbers. Mindanao became the killing ground for the young soldiers deployed to suppress the Moro National Liberation Front (MNLF) that University of the Philippines faculty member Nur Misuari had organized and gave Marcos a justification for the declaration of martial law in 1972.

Some fifty years later, Mindanao again made an impact on the national scene. A poorly-planned and badly-botched operation to capture the Malaysian jihadist Marwan (Zulkifli Abdhir) cost the lives of forty-four Special Action Force (SAF) commandos of the National Police. Marwan was killed in this encounter in Mamasapano, but this lone terrorist accomplished more in his death than he could have hoped for. The controversy caused by the operation derailed and delayed the replacement of the Organic Act that had established the Autonomous Region of Muslim Mindanao (ARMM). The new law constituting the Bangsamoro Autonomous Region of Muslim Mindanao (BARMM) would have permitted its territorial expansion, subject to referendum, provide it with a parliamentary structure and additional features, including the Bangsamoro designation, that reinforced its cultural distinctiveness. The Mamasapano investigations effectively scuttled plans already being formulated for Manila big business to explore investments in BARMM to strengthen the economic foundations of the reorganized autonomous region.

Arguably more important than the disrupted timetable for greater autonomy and economic opportunities for Muslim Mindanao, the Mamasapano massacre reawakened religious animosities, discredited Noynoy Aquino in the tail end of his administration and depreciated his political support for Mar Roxas, his presumptive successor. Roxas, Department of Interior and Local Government (DILG) Secretary, had authority over the PNP.

Roxas himself was clearly out of the loop on the Mamasapano operation. This raised questions about why he was out of the loop, leaving him vulnerable to charges that, given his position, he should have been involved and could have done more to prevent the SAF fiasco. The controversy eroded his credibility and damaged his candidacy. On the other hand, the Senate inquiry on the Mamasapano massacre gave Sen. Bongbong Marcos a platform to boost his bid for a higher office, the vice-presidential slot as a stepping-stone to a presidential campaign in 2022.

The backlash against the Aquino administration triggered by Mamasapano was a boon for all opposition elements. Duterte claimed to have been with Noynoy Aquino in the base camp in Zamboanga during the Mamasapano incident and expressed his willingness to offer what he knew, if summoned by the Senate to testify. The massacre was a useful, easily retrievable club to use against the "*Dilawan*," the yellow color identifying Aquino supporters. As president, Duterte supported calls for its continuing investigation and benefits for the families of the SAF casualties. In April 2018, he conferred posthumously the PNP Medal of Valor to the SAF 44.

Duterte was only marginally involved in the Mamasapano incident. He had his own Mindanao moment. As in Mamasapano, an operation on May 23, 2017 to capture Isnilon Hapilon and his brothers Omar and Abdullah Maute, who had sworn allegiance to the ISIS Caliphate, misfired and triggered five months of urban warfare. On the evening of the attack, Duterte declared martial law over the entire island of Mindanao but expressed confidence that the city would be liberated within weeks. On October 16, five months to the day of the ISIS occupation of Marawi, after government troops managed to kill Hapilon, Duterte proclaimed Marawi liberated. On October 23, National Defense Sec. Delfin Lorenzana gave the assurance that the city had been cleared of all jihadist militants.

The battle for Marawi destroyed fifty-four out of ninety-eight barangays spread over 250 hectares of the city's central district, immediately displacing about 350,000 of their residents. About 95 percent had to find informal housing elsewhere. Of the 46,000 families registered as "internally displaced people." (IDP)

A briefing by the Task Force *Bangon* Marawi (Arise Marawi), or TFBM, in February 2020, reporting March 2019 data, indicated that nearly 18,000 families remained displaced from their homes and renting accommodations or staying with relatives and friends outside Marawi. Nearly 400 families only had housing in evacuation centers.

Three years after the liberation of Marawi, the city has not been fully reopened for the return of the residents.

1

Interrogating Mamasapano

(*PDI*, February 07, 2015)

Two foundational premises must inform the inquiry into the Mamasapano misencounter. First, no unjustified death by violence of any Filipino should be condoned. In one day, a Moro community, suffering what it experienced as an unprovoked attack, lost seventeen members. Did not these casualties also leave grieving parents, widows, orphans?

The Philippines is a multiethnic, multireligious community. Many statements in mainstream and social media, some quite vicious, obviously reject the principle that the national government is responsible for the welfare of all Filipinos, regardless of their religious or racial identity. But this is the fundamental premise upon which rest the peace negotiations aimed at bringing back the Bangsamoro community into the national polity.

Second, no failure of leadership or discipline or training should diminish the value of the ultimate sacrifice that the SAF 44 paid in the service of their country. Sadly, failures did occur on both the Christian and Muslim sides that resulted in the bloody clash at Mamasapano. Senior officials on both sides bear the burden of probing how and why and by whom these came about—to ensure that justice is done and to prevent similar disasters in the future.

To his credit, SAF Director Getulio Napeñas immediately accepted responsibility for his role in the misencounter. He chose not to use the mechanisms established under the provisional peace agreement to avert accidental armed confrontations, because he did not trust the Moro Islamic

Liberation Front (MILF). According to a military source, this framework for coordination has actually worked; no "misencounter" has taken place between the Army and the MILF since 2010.

Neither did Napeñas coordinate Operation Wolverine with the armed forces, which the SAF later tried to summon to its aid. Army units available to help did not have, and could not get, the information they needed to provide timely support to the beleaguered troops. Initial reports indicated that the SAF could not communicate directly with military reinforcements, because they were on different radio frequencies, and did not have the equipment to direct artillery or air assets against enemy positions.

These were serious lapses. But Napeñas maintained that he made a judgment call, command decisions that he believed followed from his mission order or within his authority to make. The PNP will need to conduct its own internal review of the incident, which will include a judgment on whether Napeñas, since suspended, deserves censure.

Whatever verdict it eventually reaches, Napeñas is already suffering the punishment and the pain of knowing that he had led forty-four men to their deaths.

The MILF must conduct its own inquiry into the conduct of the troops it controls. The public expects MILF commanders on the ground to be as forthright as Napeñas in admitting to their superiors, accountability for any action that contributed to prolonging the firefight. This information MILF leaders themselves should want to know. An earlier disengagement would probably have reduced SAF fatalities, but it might also have averted some deaths among their own troops.

However difficult for those who lost loved ones, they may yet accept death in the heat of combat as part of the occupational risks that security forces accept. But the MILF must quickly disprove reports that its troops robbed and mutilated the SAF casualties or charge and sanction those who were responsible for the crime.

An internal investigation would be mandatory for any institution confronting a crisis on the scale of Mamasapano. Since such postmortem assessments would focus mainly on institutional systems and interests, we would also need an impartial, third-party commission credible to the MILF, the government and the general public.

But the eight distinct bodies reportedly now being contemplated to conduct separate inquiries seem an excessive and potentially dysfunctional investment of the scarce human and material resources of agencies already burdened with their own responsibilities. Should these inquiries reach divergent conclusions, who will determine which one is right?

With the presidential election drawing closer, the danger that partisan political interests will drive these inquiries will become more pronounced. To prevent a protracted and inconclusive process that will not serve our national interests, the review must keep a close focus on the planning and execution of Operation Wolverine.

The misencounter at Mamasapano has already exacted a heavy toll. Placing on the balance the loss of forty-four men against the elimination of Marwan, SAF leaders believe that the expenditures of these lives was a hard but acceptable bargain—because allowing Marwan to train more terrorists to explode bombs would eventually have cost more casualties.

A similar calculation of potential costs should guide our thinking on the peace process. How many more lives will be sacrificed, like those of the SAF 44, should the Mamasapano misencounter provoke the dismantling of the peace agreement and the resumption of war?

The prospects for peace in Mindanao should not become another casualty in Mamasapano.

2

Roles Reinforced, Roles Reversed

(*PDI*, March 07, 2015)

Overlapping Mamasapano Senate hearings, the twenty-ninth anniversary of EDSA 1986 and the launch of the Almonte memoir underline continuities and discontinuities in our history.

The bravery and fidelity to duty of the SAF 44 are not in doubt. But investigative findings raise questions on how the planning, coordination and execution of Oplan Exodus contributed to the SAF casualties. Nevertheless, bishops demand that PNoy apologize and resign over the Mamasapano debacle.

Did these bishops demand that the Marcoses apologize and renounce public office for participating in, and profiting from, the crimes committed during the martial law years? PCGG Chief Andy Bautista recently reminded us that plundered wealth still remains under Marcos control.

Delayed deliberations on the Bangsamoro Basic Law (BBL), which Mamasapano made more urgent, risk breathing new life to the Muslim-Christian conflict exacerbated by Ferdinand Marcos. As Amina Bernardo recalled, it was the Marcos Jabidah massacre, exposed by Ninoy Aquino on the Senate floor, that transformed Nur Misuari from University of the Philippines academic to revolutionary. Perhaps, Sen. Bongbong Marcos has forgotten that his father provoked the Moro National Liberation Front (MNLF) secessionist insurgency.

But the EDSA commemoration might have refreshed his memory and helped him comprehend what had appeared to confound him in the hearings. Gen. Rustico Guerrero of the Armed Forces' Western Mindanao Command had explained that according to military doctrine, information was required before unleashing artillery fire to reduce the risk of harming friendly forces and non-combatants.

Doctrine notwithstanding, Sen. Bongbong asked whether Guerrero would have disobeyed a presidential order to fire artillery in support of endangered SAF units. Had Guerrero said "no," critics could have faulted PNoy for failing to give the command that might have saved SAF lives. Guerrero stood his ground; the prudential principle would preempt even a presidential order.

This response, Sen. Bongbong clearly did not expect. Neither did his father expect that soldiers would defy his command to fire on rebel soldiers and the civilians protecting them at EDSA '86.

After the post-World War II Nuremberg and Tokyo Trials, military officers charged with war crimes can no longer depend on the defense that they were merely following orders. A terrorist suicide bomber gives up his life to kill his victims. Artillery fire indiscriminately dealing death from a distance could have exposed Guerrero to criminal charges.

Mamasapano offered legislators a chance to demonstrate their grasp of conflict-resolution and peace-building processes, the complex threat of international terrorism, and the protracted Muslim-Christian conflict in Mindanao. This chance was largely wasted.

In sessions marked by badgering and bullying, confusing and incoherent questioning bordering on bigotry, the exchange between the son of the dictator and the professional descendants of the post-EDSA military offered a glimpse of hope. The trajectory has not been straight or steep, but the Armed Forces of the Philippines (AFP) appears to be keeping in step with humanity's slow evolution toward higher ethical standards.

The most instructive and edifying episodes in the Mamasapano hearings have come from those closest to the combat: the military and the MILF's Chief Negotiator Mohagher Iqbal. Both parties had kept their guns muzzled for three years. Both recognized the threat that uncoordinated police action in contested territory posed to the lives of soldiers and non-combatants and to the progress of the peace process.

The MILF did activate the ceasefire protocol when it realized that its forces and those of the government had clashed at Mamasapano. While the AFP mobilized to lend support to the SAF, its officers rightly worried also about how the escalation of the conflict would impact on the peace process.

Beyond the congressional hearings, AFP leaders also showed their sensitivity to the complex character of the Mindanao conflict. At a forum of business leaders convened by the Institute for Corporate Directors on February 24, Gen. Ariel Bernardo opened the discussions by explaining his support for the BBL process.

At the FEU Public Policy Center forum that same day, former AFP Chief of Staff Emmanuel Bautista made an impassioned argument for peace. Both men know the costs of war. General Bernardo's first assignment in Mindanao dates back to the '80s. General Bautista's father, Gen. Teodulfo Bautista, died in an MNLF ambush.

Meanwhile, our fearless politicians talk about "pulverizing" the enemy. We have seen before this role-reversal of professional soldiers preferring peace and civilians urging war. President Joseph Estrada had won many splendid battles—in the movies. President Fidel Ramos had experienced actual combat. But it was the *artista* (actor) who declared all-out war against the Muslims and the veteran soldier who pursued a peace agreement.

Police officers have justified the 44 SAF casualties as the price for eliminating Marwan. The question that should have been probed before launching Exodus: was Marwan's elimination worth the risk of derailing the BBL process and the prospects for peace in Mindanao?

If the resumption of war turns out to be the cost of Exodus, Marwan, with assistance from our politicians, would have achieved his biggest triumph.

3

Presidential Accountability

(*PDI*, March 21, 2015)

Sen. Grace Poe's conversation with CNN Philippines' Pia Hontiveros on March 19 provided a more nuanced assessment of Mamasapano than the print media coverage of the Senate report. It also offered insights into her view of the presidency and her reluctance to contest the post in 2016.

Every president stands on the shoulders of those who came before—not necessarily beneficial to an incumbent whose immediate predecessors had dug themselves deeply into a hole. Sen. Poe is keenly aware of the complex, contentious problems confronting the country. She wonders why anyone would want to be president.

Vice President Jejomar Binay's long campaign for the presidency is a different case. Election would ensure at least a six-year immunity from possible prosecution arising from the investigation of multiple crimes of corruption he allegedly committed during his term as Makati mayor and beyond. Delaying the judicial process until the hoped-for installation as president appears to be his current legal strategy.

Poe believes that only the desire to serve the country should drive the quest for the presidency because the post is both boon and bane. The president basks in the bounty, but also bears the burden of everything that happens during the term of office. Poe expressed sympathy for PNoy, whose good intentions she recognized. She clarified that PNoy's accountability discussed in the report was neither criminal nor, perhaps, even legal, but political. The buck could not go beyond PNoy's level.

Poe takes the chain-of-command concept, now threatening to tie up the public in legal knots, as it must operate in any large organization with some level of hierarchy. Any CEO takes ultimate responsibility for overall organizational results but cannot assume direct control and responsibility for operational field decisions delegated to subordinates.

Perhaps, command responsibility weighs more heavily in the Philippines, where the president is head of state and government as well as commander-in-chief, and figures as "*Ama*" (Father) or "*Ina ng Bayan*" (Mother of the Country). PNoy's first report on Mamasapano used this parental metaphor, acknowledging his failure as "Father of the Nation." Beyond the issue of presidential performance, his accounting included its deep personal cost; he confessed that he would carry Mamasapano's consequences to the end of his days.

This heartfelt and humbling admission of guilt proved inadequate. Later evidence of the criminal execution of SAF personnel provoked a fresh wave of public anger and awakened historically-embedded hostility toward the Moros. Predictably, the motley collection of Marcos partisans, Arroyo allies, disgruntled clerics, "leftist" ideologues, and "*trapos*" (traditional politicians) gearing up for the 2016 elections fueled the outrage, striving to channel it toward a demand for PNoy's resignation.

This call for resignation would benefit from a confession that PNoy: 1) planned Oplan Exodus with US operatives; 2) assumed control of the strategic and operational chain of command for the "real-time" monitoring and direction of its execution; and 3) made the decisions to decline various options for military assistance to beleaguered SAF troopers.

Such a confession would be necessary to give plausibility to the desired conclusion that the blood of the SAF 44 stain PNoy's hands. Official reports have already rendered dubious, if not refuted, these charges. But, as Sen. Antonio Trillanes noted, even an "apology" by the president at this late point, apart from the issue of whether it will do any good, may simply refresh these allegations.

During World War II, British government agents developed Enigma, a code-breaking machine that enabled them to intercept Nazi military plans. Nevertheless, they limited their use of the device and intervened sparingly, allowing the deaths resulting from their inaction. The command decision was to hold Enigma in reserve for strategic, decisive gains in the war. Winston Churchill knew about Enigma. What was his accountability for the deaths permitted to happen because the machine was not used?

Command decisions, sadly, have led and can lead to casualties. How many died from the secessionist movement that resulted from Ferdinand Marcos' Jabidah massacre? Or when Joseph Estrada decided on all-out war? Getulio Napeñas thought Exodus would cost only ten casualties; he did not expect to lose forty-four. Would a higher estimate have caused Napeñas to modify his plan? How many SAF lives would have been saved, how many SAF and other people lost if artillery had been fired? And who can really offer unimpeachable answers at this point?

The decision-maker factors in the casualty count as only one consideration. The larger context and the bigger issue would be the motivation driving the decisions that would predictably result in casualties. We can sympathize with Sen. Poe's reluctance to risk responsibility for bearing the presidential burden.

She stressed that the Senate hearings over which she presided were not the venue for addressing the issue of the BBL, on which media coverage had focused. Untangling the connections between the BBL and Mamasapano will now again call for prudence and wisdom on a life-and-death issue.

4

Seeking Silver Bullets

(*PDI*, April 25, 2015)

With distinguished academic credentials and political family connections, Francis "Chiz" G. Escudero surfaced as an electable young politician, who could, hopefully, bring competence, integrity and youthful idealism into public service. His performance at the Senate hearings on the BBL has dimmed these hopes.

Citing an International Alert (IA) study, Chiz warned government peace negotiators not to "raise false hopes that the BBL will bring peace to Mindanao," as it would "only provide peace between the government and the [Moro Islamic Liberation Front]." The IA research actually sounded a different note.

IA did say that private armies and criminal syndicates accounted for the majority of violent incidents in Mindanao. Chiz uses IA data, but rejects its conclusion: the urgency of resolving the MILF insurgency through a negotiated BBL. Assuming that the *Inquirer* quotes were accurate, Chiz either misunderstood or misrepresented the research, thus misleading the public.

Clan feuds, criminal operations and political rivalries lead to a high number of violent incidents, but these do not trigger the massive displacement of people and the level of casualties caused by clashes with the MILF. It is the insurgency that creates the conditions of lawlessness, breeds criminality and compels the community to arm itself, raising the potential for more violence.

The MILF controls the largest non-government armed force in the Bangsamoro. To dismiss the peace negotiations because it would not eliminate the other threat groups measures the peace process by an impossible yardstick. There is no silver bullet that will slay all sources of violence, whether in the Bangsamoro or in the rest of the country.

The IA conclusion was neither unclear nor guarded: "Without a doubt, ending the GPH-MILF conflict as a major source of rebellion-related violence retires a significant source of political violence with huge costs in terms of death, injury, and displacement, and will impact positively on the prospects of peace and stability across the Bangsamoro."

Misrepresenting the IA analysis was bad. Even more damaging, because exposed on television, was partnering with Bongbong Marcos to pursue the issue of aliases. Probing the crimes that Mohagher Iqbal may have committed by using an alias while engaged in rebellion, wasted government time and resources. Mercifully, TG Guingona restored a moment of sanity, explaining the obvious: revolutionaries do not submit to the laws of the state. Would we expect them to secure gun permits?

Iqbal has been using his current alias for decades because of security concerns. For this same reason, Jose Protacio Rizal Mercado used a pen name for his subversive *Noli Me Tangere*. Should Chiz and Bongbong file a bill revoking Jose Rizal's status as national hero or renaming his monuments?

"Iqbal," as alias, does not hide from the government a person it has been dealing with for decades. This is unlike the case of "William Saunders" and "Jane Ryan," the aliases behind which Ferdinand and Imelda Marcos concealed plundered wealth. For Iqbal to revert to his real name would actually confuse the public, who would not know to whom it referred. Fans probably know Mrs. Chiz Escudero better under the alias Heart Evangelista than her real name Love Marie Ongpauco.

Bongbong questioned why Iqbal should fear the government already negotiating with him. From the IA study, however, Chiz should know that Iqbal faces other threat groups, including the Bangsamoro Islamic Freedom Fighters (BIFF). Since 2012, MILF clashes with the BIFF have increased, while those with the government have "dropped dramatically," according to IA. This pattern disproves the claim of BBL critics that the MILF and BIFF acted as two hands washing each other.

Nevertheless, Chiz also pressed Iqbal for his real name, a small concession, he insisted ("*maliit na bagay lang*"), to build confidence.

Here was a senator of the republic bargaining, as in a bazaar, for Iqbal to demonstrate trust. Should it not be the senators, secure in their seat of power and backed by the resources of the state, to give Iqbal assurances that they could be trusted?

Bongbong asked Iqbal: "Who are you?" Iqbal is a rebel leader who has committed and risked his life fighting for his people and who now seeks a principled peace for his community and the country. He has earned his dues and deserves some respect. It was edifying to see this old man bearing with composure, grace and dignity, the badgering from inquisitors, many years his junior.

But who are Bongbong and Chiz? What have they risked? And for whom? Their highest achievement has been election to the Senate, and this may explain the preoccupation with names. Would they have been elected, without the names they happened to carry?

Protocol requires those invited to congressional hearings to address the legislators as "Your Honor." Sadly, those Senate hearings revealed to the public a deficit of honorable, magnanimous and even civil behavior that could serve as a model for our citizens.

5

Finger-pointing on Mamasapano

(*Rappler*, January 28, 2017)

No additional information on the incident can take away the pain of those who lost loved ones in the Mamasapano encounter. Nor can it diminish the sacrifice that the SAF 44 made in the service of the country. That they were poorly prepared and badly led in a poorly-planned and badly-executed operation was not their fault.

Reviving the Mamasapano controversy may benefit an administration battling the backlash from the build-up of high-profile cases of corruption and murder involving government officials. Media will refocus on the Mamasapano controversy, diverting attention from such cases as: the liquidation by the police of Albuera Mayor Rolando Espinosa in his jail cell; the killing of Zenaida Luz in Mindoro by two motorcycle-riding police officers; the Bureau of Immigration bribery; and the abduction/murder by the police of Jee Ick Joo.

While distracting from unanswered questions about these cases, President Rodrigo Duterte was badly advised in adding even more glare to the scrutiny of Mamasapano that will come with the charges filed against former PNP Chief Director General Alan Purisima and former SAF Director Getulio Napeñas for their handling of this mission. Hardly the most glorious operation conducted by the PNP and the SAF, Mamasapano was a reminder of their institutional weaknesses. It has also threatened to rekindle the animosity that inflamed the relations between the PNP and the AFP.

Command responsibility, which appears to be the premise for pinning responsibility for Mamasapano on former President Benigno Aquino III, is a double-edged sword. In Duterte's own words, "If it's sauce for the gander, it's also sauce for the goose." Like the directive to pursue drug lords, the pursuit of Marwan was a legitimate mission that Aquino did not even have to order; the PNP had been chasing Marwan since 2002. Marwan was the Malaysian terrorist on the US Federal Bureau of Investigation's (FBI) most wanted list.

If Aquino was ultimately responsible for Mamasapano—which he has acknowledged—should not Duterte accept ultimate accountability for the murder by PNP officers of Jee Ick Joo, and any murder subsequently discovered to have been perpetrated by the police?

That said, it is true that critical aspects of Mamasapano remain unclear, despite a year-long investigation by nine independent bodies, including those that commanded boots on the ground: the PNP, the AFP and the MILF. It is possible that Duterte can prompt answers to two contentious questions: who killed Marwan and what role did the US play in the operation?

But answers are not likely to come through another investigative body whose members will use their own lenses to look at old evidence; what is needed is not new lenses but new evidence from parties that also had boots on the ground: the BIFF that broke away from the MILF on the issue of peace negotiations with the government, and, more important, the US.

As part of the post-2001 expansion of the global war on terror, the Americans had been supporting Philippine anti-terrorist operations through Operation Enduring Freedom-Philippines. The Joint Special Operations Task Force-Philippines was organized in early 2002 and had been assisting in the hunt for Marwan since 2012.

According to the PNP, troops of the 84th SAF had shot Marwan and had cut off his right index finger, which was given to the FBI to serve as proof of his death. But a Mindanao-based, party-list group called AWAT (Anti-War, Anti-Terror) surfaced in January 2016, and claimed that the killing of Marwan and the amputation of his right index finger had been accomplished, not by the commandos of the 84th SAF, but by Marwan's own security aides. AWAT maintained that the 84th SAF found Marwan already dead and that it was Marwan's left index finger that they turned over to the FBI.

Duterte can possibly unearth new information by ordering the exhumation of Marwan's body. According to the MILF, the government had custody since March 2015, of Ali Tambako, a BIFF leader whose men had buried Marwan. But locating Marwan's grave, digging up his corpse and counting its fingers would be time-consuming and messy.

With Duterte's new friend in the White House, a simpler approach may be possible. Perhaps, he can request US President Donald Trump to ask the FBI to give him the finger or at least declare whether it belonged to Marwan's left or right hand. The FBI response would catch either AWAT or 84th SAF in a lie.

Confirmation that the FBI received Marwan's right index finger from the 84th SAF would disprove the AWAT story. Unfortunately, it would not conclusively credit the SAF 84th with the killing of Marwan. Taking Marwan's life and taking his finger could have been done by different parties.

We do not know whether the US is able and willing to shed light on this point, which could yield more information on the extent of US involvement in Mamasapano. But resolving at least the finger issue would be a good start to testing how much Mr. Duterte can count on Mr. Trump's friendship.

6

Enemy of the Good

(*PDI*, May 16, 2015)

To conclude an acceptable agreement would be a mistake, if a better deal is available. To reject a good bargain in the hope that something better will come along in the future could possibly be a bigger mistake.

Businessmen place much importance on the concept of "present value;" in simple terms, "bird in hand is better than bird in bush." One hundred pesos in your pocket now is worth more than P100 provided to you, twelve months hence. Cash in hand allows a person to address urgent, perhaps, unpostponable needs or opportunities, say, a medical emergency or a one-time investment offer.

Delay can also be more costly, especially if the rejection of the bargain involves a significant measure of risk. A Tagalog proverb, "*Aanhin pa ang damo kung patay na ang kabayo*" (What use is grass to a dead horse), implies that the timely delivery of benefits, the grass, might have kept the horse alive.

The peace council has endorsed the draft BBL, as compliant with the Constitution and responsive to the needs of the Bangsamoro region. It has recommended refinements in the bill, but believes that these, while affirming constitutional provisions, do not renege on what government negotiators have offered at the peace talks—because they are consistent with the MILF's acceptance of integration into the Republic.

The draft BBL is not a perfect law. Elements of the current BBL draft, or of any BBL law, will remain ambiguous, partly because some provisions will need implementing rules and regulations that the Bangsamoro Assembly will pass.

We do appear to demand perfection, a laudable virtue that has earned compliments for our skills in preparing comprehensive, carefully-constructed plans. We get lower marks on implementation and enforcement. Perhaps, our strength in planning relates to our weakness in execution. Plans and laws admirable for their detail may become difficult to implement when overtaken by unexpected developments, for instance, a storm surge of "Yolanda" intensity.

The drive for perfection is commendable, as long as we remember that only God (or Allah) is perfect. What mere mortals produce must remain imperfect. Legislators impose an impossible task on themselves when they ambition to craft a law that will deliver all potential benefits and avert all potential problems.

Some of the laws promulgated by the Bangsamoro Assembly may prove vulnerable to challenges on constitutional grounds. Happily, our system provides for a Supreme Court that can rule on these issues. To those who questioned the constitutionality of some provisions in the draft LGC, constitutional law expert, Joaquin Bernas, SJ, offered a standard reply: "Let the Supreme Court decide."

We do not need a perfect BBL. Peace advocates (and legislators) must avoid trying to load all of their noble ideas into the law. Better to focus on ensuring that the law is clean of any provisions that are obviously unconstitutional, demonstrably discriminatory, or clearly impractical. What is crucial is the availability of mechanisms that permit Bangsamoro and national institutions to make corrections in the law as needed.

These mechanisms exist. The BBL will not curtail the oversight powers of the president, Congress and the Supreme Court. But the Bangsamoro government needs space and time to test the relevance of their law to the realities on the ground. Following the principle of subsidiarity, the national government must give the Bangsamoro leaders the chance to exercise their mandate for autonomous rule.

What we need, therefore, is a workable BBL that can be passed as quickly as possible. The peace council takes comfort in the fact that fourteen of the eighteen living framers of the 1987 Constitution, which mandated the establishment of autonomous regions in Muslim Mindanao and the Cordillera regions have expressed support for the present BBL draft.

Autonomy for Muslim Mindanao has been on the agenda for nearly thirty years, when it emerged as an issue for the 1987 Constitutional Commission. Over seventeen years of discussions and debates with the MNLF have informed the process that led to the crafting of the framework agreement for Bangsamoro autonomy. Finally, the MILF and the government have reached a consensus on an acceptable BBL draft.

Much work has gone into this draft—and much blood spilled in the decades-long delay in its formulation. Given the country's diversity and many divisions, there will be parties that will oppose BBL for reasons both noble and ignoble. The danger is allowing their presumed passion for perfection to mask their unwillingness to accept any meaningful autonomy for the Bangsamoro.

They claim they want only the improvement of the law, but actually seek to prevent its passage through a never-ending process of fine-tuning—even at the cost of spilling more blood. This strategy makes the unreachable perfect the enemy of the attainable good.

7

Birthing the Bangsamoro Autonomous Region

(*PDI*, November 03, 2018)

As with planned caesarean procedures, we know beforehand this baby's birthday. On January 21, 2019, the people within the ARMM will determine in a plebiscite whether to welcome the birth of the Bangsamoro Autonomous Region (BAR). But, as with any delivery, we cannot predict with absolute certainty the baby's health condition at birth, or its future life prospects. It will take many years and much effort before we can proclaim the BAR a success.

The plebiscite to ratify the Bangsamoro Organic Law (BOL) is only one part of the Comprehensive Agreement on the Bangsamoro concluded between the Government and the MILF to end nearly fifty years of the separatist insurgency. The "normalization" process requires settling security issues, such as the decommissioning of MILF combatants. A ceremonial decommissioning of 145 combatants took place in June 2015. But by the time of BOL ratification, 30 percent of MILF forces or about 4,000 combatants should already have been decommissioned and absorbed into the government's security forces or provided alternative livelihood opportunities.

Some combatants may also require amnesty for actions committed during the insurgency, a process now complicated by the government handling of the Trillanes amnesty. Promoting the socioeconomic development of the BAR, especially addressing the needs of the population driven out of their homes by the fighting, constitutes another formidable normalization track. The delay in returning the refugees from the Marawi siege has added to the burden of this task, and to the even more daunting challenge that the track on Transitional Justice and Reconciliation must face—resolving the claims of victims of human rights violations.

But, first things first. A successful plebiscite to ratify the BOL is the necessary condition for completing the rest of the normalization process. Presumably, President Duterte will want to see a safe and successful delivery of the BAR. This will allow him to claim progress in delivering on his campaign promise to correct the historic injustice perpetrated against Muslim Filipinos. The MILF has also committed to the BAR. Despite its reservations, the MILF did support the BOL, whose passage in July triggered the scheduling of the plebiscite.

The BOL permits specific LGUs in Basilan, Cotabato, North Cotabato and Lanao del Norte contiguous to the ARMM territory but not subject to its jurisdiction to vote for inclusion in the new BAR. The issue will test the capacity of the government to persuade Christian and Muslim voters on the advantages of belonging to the BAR.

As a minimum, two conditions appear necessary for both the government and the MILF to judge the plebiscite a success. First, it should not result in a BAR smaller than the ARMM, a result that would deeply disappoint the Muslim constituency. Because this outcome is possible, the second condition becomes even more critical: the process must be transparent, fair and untainted by violence or irregularities, so that the public can accept the results as legitimate.

Although the plebiscite covers a smaller geographic area, the timeframe is tighter and the decision-making process more complicated than for the midterm national and local elections in May 2019. The pressure thus falls on the principal midwives to the BAR birthing: the COMELEC and the Office of the Presidential Adviser on the Peace Process (OPAPP).

The COMELEC bears the burden of ensuring that the questions for the plebiscite and the rules to guide the campaign for ratification that it issued on September 26 reach the voters and are explained to them. The OPAPP must be able to convince the voters of the merits of inclusion in the BAR, whose features it had negotiated.

Only the registered voters of the ARMM will cast a ballot in the plebiscite. But we all have a stake in its outcome and must pay it close attention.

Without a peaceful and prosperous Mindanao, the Philippines cannot realize its dream of inclusive development. And Mindanao cannot prosper if the Muslim and Christian communities in the region remain mired in identity politics and religious conflicts.

8

Balik Marawi, Bago Balik Probinsya

(*Rappler*, May 23, 2020)

Three years ago, Maute/Abu Sayyaf followers of the ISIS Caliphate drove government forces out of Marawi City, forced an estimated 350,000 people to flee their homes, and occupied the center of Lanao del Sur's provincial capital for five months between May 23 to October 17, 2017.

To root out entrenched enemy forces, the military had to use artillery fire and aerial bombardment, in effect, destroying much of the city to recapture it. The Most Affected Areas (MAA), extended over some 250 hectares, covering twenty-four barangays and their Maranao population of nearly 130,000.

The Maranaos expected much from President Duterte, who often and publicly proclaimed his Maranao descent, presuming that he would also share their urgent concerns—to tend to the injured, find and bury their dead, and meet daily subsistence needs.

Within the week of Marawi's liberation, President Duterte appointed Eduardo del Rosario, Chair of the Housing and Urban Development Coordinating Council as concurrent Head of TFBM to facilitate reconstruction and recovery efforts. TFBM promised the completion of these efforts by the end of 2019. For immediate aid to Marawi's internally displaced persons (IDPs), it had received by November 2017, nearly P37 million from Philippine and foreign donors.

Despite this promising start, the administration of Duterte, who claimed kinship with them, failed to meet Maranao expectations. For the year 2018, TFBM paid out only P10,000 to the family of one siege casualty. By end-2019, it had disbursed only 3 percent of the fund, which had increased by almost the same amount because of foreign exchange gains. The "poor utilization of donated funds" intended for the much-needed support of the Marawi siege victims earned a COA rebuke for frustrating "the good intention of the donors for human consideration."

The larger goals of compensating victims and supporting the city's rehabilitation, after three years, still await congressional action. Around 15,000 residents had filed with the Integrated Bar of the Philippines (IBP) damage claims worth over 90 billion, including more than 5,600 totally destroyed "dwelling units." The IBP transmitted the documents to the House of Representatives, whose Committee on Disaster Management was sitting on three bills filed by Muslim legislators in August 2019 to cover such claims.

At a meeting of the Senate Special Committee on Marawi Rehabilitation, held in Iligan on February 21, Ronald dela Rosa, Francis Tolentino and Bong Go, respectively committee chair and vice chairs, together with Imee Marcos, and Majority Leader Juan Miguel Zubiri, promised to file on February 24, their own version of a Marawi compensation bill. *MindaNews* reported that, as of March 4, the five senators had not delivered on the commitment. Zubiri and Marcos filed three bills between them, but none on Marawi.

Bong Go's contribution was to arrange a meeting with the president in Malacañang on March 4, where Maranao leaders aired their grievances against TFBM. The president continued to vouch for del Rosario as a good man from Davao, retaining him as TFBM Chair, but promised a monthly visit to Marawi to oversee the Bangon program personally. And then COVID-19 happened, preempting promised presidential visits to Marawi and adding to IDP problems.

Threat from Bong Go's Project

Thirty months after liberation, they remain locked out of ground zero, including some 17,000 who had assumed the costs of biometric tests that validated them as Marawi residents.

At this point, after three years of exile, they are no longer waiting for government completion of rehabilitation projects or immediate reconstruction assistance. They only want to exercise their right to return to Marawi and rebuild their homes on their own.

What has now alarmed them is the threat to their *Balik Marawi* (Return to Marawi) advocacy of competition from the *Balik Probinsiya, Bagong Pag-asa* (Return to the Province, New Hope) or the BP2 Program. When first proposed at an Inter-Agency Task Force (IATF) meeting, Bong Go acknowledged that implementation would have to wait until the country had better control of the pandemic. But the project has taken off on fast-track mode.

Two days after the May 6 signing of EO 141, making BP2 a national priority program, National Housing Authority G.M. Marcelino Escalada, Jr., appointed head of its secretariat, reported receiving 5,000 applications online. Within six months, he projected applications to increase to six figures. The projection of 1 million such settlers applying to return to their home provinces may be a conservative estimate.

For those locked down in Metro Manila's informal settlements, joining BP2 is almost a no-brainer. Programs to rebalance population distribution are most attractive to those who have the least to lose by moving, a number the pandemic has increased. But these are costly and complex programs to sustain.

White Elephants

With free transportation and assurances of homes and jobs, relocating people with few options is not the difficult part. Keeping them in the relocation sites is the problem that has turned many such programs into wasteful white elephants. Government would not have to risk this problem with a project to bring Marawi IDPs home. And it can serve as a pilot for BP2.

The government has yet to end the IDPs' now three-year exile. To give them priority over any group wishing to avail of the BP2 program would be both rational and just. If the government cannot deliver on this project, what would be our basis to believe that it can effectively implement a much larger, more complex BP2 program? Especially at the time of a pandemic and the risk of provincial travels spreading the contagion?

The Maranaos plead on priority for their return to Marawi, before a program to resettle informal settlers in the cities to their home provinces: Balik Marawi Muna, Bago Balik Probinsya!

V

International Relations

Among the colonized people of Southeast Asia, Filipinos arguably became the earliest to develop an "international" orientation. This was the result of several factors, including the early dependence of the colony on the galleon trade that carried Asian products to sell in Mexico for silver currency.

Compared to other colonial subjects, Filipinos received relatively early access to higher education; this was necessary to prepare a few of them for Holy Orders. Spain needed to supplement their missionaries with Filipino priests to fulfill the objective of keeping the colony Catholic. This required the colonial government to provide Filipinos the opportunity to learn Spanish, which later made it possible for some Filipinos to get an education in Europe. Filipinos also experienced what others might consider the dubious privilege of tutelage under two colonial masters, Spain and the US.

American colonial policy in education nipped in the bud the spread of the Spanish language, but its promotion of a public education system enabled more Filipinos to learn English in fifty years than the number who learned Spanish in 300 years of Spanish rule. While regaining its independence after the end of the Pacific War, the Philippines remained tied in trade and foreign policy to the US, which had emerged as the dominant great power in the world, and especially in Asia. Without this special connection to the US, Carlos P. Romulo's election of a Filipino as President of the UN General Assembly (UNGA) in 1949, the first Asian to hold the post, could not have happened.

I think it was probably during the martial law period when the Philippines began to turn inward, or, perhaps, when other countries began to turn away from the Philippines. But if the content of mainstream media provides any gauge, the country's concerns had become less cosmopolitan and more parochial.

The internal problems of the country and the competition for power among political and business elites tended to consume all of the space, lightened only by show business and celebrity scandals. By the turn of the century, it had become obvious that the English language newspapers of Singapore, Thailand, Malaysia and even Indonesia, gave more pages to international news and served even broader coverage of international sporting events beyond basketball.

It was ironic that this inward turn happened even as more and more Filipinos were traveling all over the world to find as OFWs the employment that they could not get at home. When the government and media took notice of massive disasters or large-scale violence overseas, often the only concern was to report on whether the casualties included Filipinos.

Certainly, there were national interests that affected bilateral relations with other countries, such as the Philippine claim to Sabah, which had become part of Malaysia, or the American military bases in the Philippines. Other issues required involvement with larger international organizations. To address the Muslim secessionist movement, for instance, the Philippines had to make representations with the UN and the Organization of Islamic Countries. Although the Philippines was founding member of the ASEAN, its activities mainly involved meetings among government officials and the executives of big business corporations. For the most part—and this was true among all the member states—ASEAN made less impact on the population than their leaders had hoped for.

With a background largely limited to local government concerns, Duterte had little experience and interest in international relations. Nevertheless, he has received credit or blame for driving a pivotal change in Philippine foreign relations: distancing himself from the US and drawing closer to the PRC. The issue that catalyzed this move was the decision of the UN Court of Arbitral Award rejecting the PRC's claims of maritime boundaries that violated Philippines EEZ in the SCS.

While expressing reservations about the wisdom of the Aquino appeal to the UN, Duterte could not categorically reject a decision favoring the Philippines during the campaign. Public opinion surveys showed overwhelming support for resisting PRC encroachment on Philippine waters and the harassment of its fishermen. Elected president, he was more forthright about his preference for deferring any action on the UN award and focusing instead on maintaining amicable relations with China. Although competing claims in the SCS involved other ASEAN countries, Duterte also preferred dealing with China on a bilateral basis.

Duterte's disenchantment with the US drew from many sources, ranging from deeply personal to broadly ideological considerations. He claimed himself a victim of sexual abuse by an American priest and expressed resentment at having been denied a visa to enter the US and, after his election, of being disrespected by President Obama. He remained resentful of American colonial exploitation of the Philippines and, especially, of human rights violations against the Moros, from whom he claimed descent, during their struggle to retain their autonomy from the Philippine state.

What rankled most intensely, however, was the attack from American institutions and officials on his record for human rights violations committed when he was Davao mayor and in the course of his war against drugs. American support for moves to elevate these violations to an international forum angered Duterte and provoked the most vigorous denunciations and threats.

The international concerns of the president were tightly tied to his domestic policies and politics. From this perspective, the friendship cultivated with both Russia and China were also strategic. Should the complaint against Duterte brought to the International Court of Justice ever prosper, he would need the support of Russia and China to veto any adverse decision.

1

Who's Afraid of Sergei Magnitsky?

(*PDI*, July 22, 2017)

He is, after all, dead. He died in 2009, according to Russia's Presidential Human Rights Council, after severe beatings while detained in a Russian prison for abetting tax evasion. But the circumstances of his death led to US legislation carrying his name. Meanwhile, current international concerns over human rights violations and the US election controversy have suddenly thrust to new prominence the laws he inspired.

An auditor in a Moscow legal firm, Magnitsky exposed a US$230-million tax fraud scheme that he discovered while engaged as legal adviser for the London-based Hermitage Capital Management (HCM), one of the largest private equity firms investing in Russia. Human rights groups and HCM blamed his arrest and death on government officials, who wanted to silence him. The government also subjected the whistle-blower to a posthumous trial to undermine his credibility. The investigators, who included parties implicated in the tax fraud case, concluded that he had been legally arrested and had not been tortured.

Undeterred, Magnitsky's supporters compiled a list of some sixty officials from the interior ministry, police and tax authorities whom he had identified as involved in the corruption. In 2012, as retribution for Magnitsky's death, the US Congress passed the Magnitsky Rule of Law Accountability Act. With rare bipartisan support, Congress expanded the scope of the law in 2016, by enacting the Global Magnitsky Human Rights Accountability Act.

The law empowers the president to deny entry into the US and to freeze the assets of any foreign person or entity found responsible for torture, EJKs and other gross violations of internationally recognized human rights, as well as anyone acting as agent in such activities. Explicitly covered also are government officials and their senior associates responsible for, or complicit in, committing these violations and other acts of significant corruption.

These laws have not been widely enforced, even against Russians; the earlier, narrower law had resulted in action against eighteen Russian individuals. But the ongoing investigation of possible collusion between Donald Trump's presidential campaign organization and Russian government agents to discredit Hillary Clinton has focused attention on these laws. The mission of the Russian group that met with Donald Trump, Jr. was apparently to lobby against the Global Magnitsky Act. Two factors may explain why this law would concern Vladimir Putin and why its repeal or weakening would become an important foreign policy priority.

First, President Trump, writing to Congress last April, said his administration was "actively identifying persons and entities to whom the Act may apply and collecting the evidence necessary to apply it." He also expressed the intent to "fulfill our commitment to hold perpetrators of human rights abuses and corruption accountable." While there is no assurance that Trump can deliver on this promise, the issue of Russian meddling in the US election will make it difficult for him to take a stance that appears to soften the law.

Second, other countries have begun the process of passing their own versions of the Global Magnitsky Act. During the third reading of the Criminal Finances Act in the Commons, UK Security Minister Ben Wallace stressed the need, in an increasingly global marketplace, to "make the UK a hostile environment for those seeking to move, hide and use the proceeds of crime and corruption." In 2015, then Canadian Justice Minister Irwin Cotler tabled a unanimously adopted parliamentary resolution for a Magnitsky Act to protect international human rights as a key foreign policy goal of Canada and the expression of its principles and core values.

In deploying the Magnitsky Act or its equivalent as a weapon against cross-border corruption and human rights violations, governments can apply punitive measures on specific individuals implicated in these crimes without imposing sanctions that indiscriminately punish an entire country. This targeted response sends a clear signal that the rejection of corrupt business practices and respect for human rights have emerged as values shared worldwide.

Those whose current control of political institutions enjoy impunity at home for gross human rights violations, such as complicity in EJK, enjoy no assurance that this control is permanent. Their world will shrink into an increasingly smaller place as more countries reject granting them impunity abroad for their crimes at home.

2

What Makes Callamard "Scary"?

(*PDI*, September 02, 2017)

On the day of Kian delos Santos' interment at La Loma Cemetery, Agnes Callamard, the UN's special rapporteur on EJKs, said in a tweet: "My heartfelt condolences to #Kian family and to all families victimized by this cruel war." The tweet carried the hashtags #Makehisdeaththelast and #Philippines.

Asked for his reaction to the Callamard tweet, President Duterte could have responded in several different ways. Perhaps he could not honestly commit to a war on drugs that did not result in casualties. But he could have reassured Callamard that his administration did not condone the EJK of Kian and would take the necessary steps to avoid adding to the list of EJK victims.

He had already arrived at the same conclusion—emerging from surveillance cameras, the testimony of witnesses, the autopsy conducted by the Public Attorney's Office (PAO)—that the Filipino public and Callamard reached: police operatives had murdered Kian. After seeing the CCTV footage, he reportedly called PNP Chief Ronald dela Rosa to order the arrest and detention of the policemen involved.

In many of his public speeches, Mr. Duterte routinely repeats his standing orders to the police: in the performance of their lawful duties, they can kill suspects who offer violent resistance and he will defend them against potential charges of human rights violations. But the Kian killing prompted an explicit warning against going beyond the bounds of their mandate: "You are not allowed to kill a person who is kneeling down, begging for his life. That is murder."

Kian was not the first EJK victim in the war on drugs. But his was the first EJK that Mr. Duterte has tacitly acknowledged. Accordingly, Mr. Duterte does not consider himself obliged to spare the killers from the legal consequences of their crime. The incident might also explain the candid confession: "I promised that I will do away with *shabu*. Now I know it won't be fulfilled, that this really will not end."

A response to Callamard, based on his public response to the Kian case, would have helped improve the government's relations with UN human rights officials. Instead, Mr. Duterte reverted to what appears to be the presidential default option when confronting perceived criticism; he cursed Callamard and warned her not to "scare" (*takutin*) him. This allowed Callamard to take the moral high ground: "Kian and others like him deserve dignity and justice . . . our respect and empathy. Not expletives."

A couple of earlier Callamard tweets perhaps explain why Mr. Duterte went ballistic. One claimed Kian was the "latest symbol of a massive, government-led, human rights crisis," and the second said "all unlawful deaths must be investigated. To stop all murderers." While the first was clearly critical, it would be difficult to disagree with the second, and it is not clear why the president should find either tweet scary or threatening.

Mr. Duterte also criticized the French legal system as based on the presumption that the accused is guilty and bears the burden of proving innocence. The French Embassy quickly responded, asserting that the presumption of innocence is "enshrined in the French Declaration of Human and Civic Rights of August 26, 1789," and adding that "France strongly believes in the importance of the rule of law, due process and respect for human rights in all countries, including the Philippines." Unfortunately, the French correction will probably fail to reach most of the people who listened to Mr. Duterte and who will remain victims of fake news.

By speaking out against the Kian killing, meeting with the parents and giving assurances that justice will be served, Mr. Duterte has managed to temper the public outrage against EJK. But the immoderate reaction to Callamard raises questions about how differently the war on drugs will be waged. Will there be greater supervision and control of anti-drug operations to prevent EJK? A faster pace to the investigation of drug war deaths, now that the Kian killing has prompted collaboration between the PNP and the CHR?

If these are genuinely new objectives in a war he insists must continue, Mr. Duterte will need the public's assistance in monitoring its conduct, to avert more Kian killings or ensure that the killers are punished.

3

Topping the Impunity Index

(*PDI*, October 07, 2017)

Ranking sixty-nine countries, the 2017 Global Impunity Index (GII) gave us first place. This suggests that if you are a criminal, you are safest practicing your profession in the Philippines. You would be less likely to be arrested; if arrested, prosecuted; if prosecuted, convicted; if convicted, punished. If you have the lofty connections of, say, a senator or a president, you can, after sentencing, hope for pardon.

To be fair, the Duterte administration cannot take sole credit for this dubious distinction. Impunity has plagued us for decades, leading many to favor tough action against suspected criminals and, up to a point, to excuse police violations of due process. The backlash against EJK shows this point may have already been reached. A law-and-order president should want the GII image of the Philippines corrected.

Addressing impunity requires interrogating two factors affecting the framework of security, justice and human rights. First, has the state invested resources to provide enough policemen and jails, judges and courtrooms, and human rights monitors to ensure the rule of law? Bureau of Jail Management and Penology (BJMP) Director Serafin Barretto said the jail congestion rate of 558 percent was the world's highest in 2015, beating Haiti's 454 percent.

Looking at the number of judges against population, GII figures showed a global average of one judge overseeing 6,250 people. In Croatia, the least afflicted by impunity, the ratio was 1:2,200 and in Mexico, 1:23,800. The ratio of Philippine lower court judges to population in 2006–2009 was over 1:60,000.

In 2017, the Philippines maintained one police officer for 650 people, against the global average of 1:315. Mexico surpassed this average number with 280 people for each police officer. But Mexico's fourth-place finish in the 2017 GII drives home the centrality of the second factor affecting impunity: the operational effectiveness of the security and justice systems. Do the people running these systems possess the requisite knowledge, skills and values? Consider Caloocan City cops convicted in killing Kian de los Santos.

Raising the number of police officers and judges to a minimum level is necessary, but not sufficient, to avert the problem of impunity. Law enforcers must also have the necessary qualifications for the job and follow the rule of law in their application. Monitoring their respect for human rights is thus a necessary measure to ensure the proper functioning of the security and justice systems.

The Duterte administration inherited deeply flawed systems—and made problems worse in three ways. It launched the war on drugs without serious planning for the issues of detention and rehabilitation. The BJMP predicts drug arrests this year to approach 200,000. In the urban areas, drug suspects make up 75–80 percent of prison inmates. Will a prison sentence in overcrowded jails, at the 2012 budget cost of P19,345 per prisoner—higher than the P15,000 conditional cash transfer family subsidy—contribute to the rehabilitation of drug addicts?

Second, opinion surveys reflect a widespread concern that a large number of crimes concealed by impunity are now committed by state agents. Consider Quezon City and the killing of Korean Jee Ick-joo in Camp Crame. Senators have recognized that EJK does happen and thousands of "under investigation" cases remain unresolved. Even more alarming, the president has encouraged, by word and deed, the belief that constitutional guarantees of human rights and due process will not deter the war on drugs. Consider the municipality of Albuera in Leyte and the downgrading of the charges against the nineteen killers of Rolando Espinosa, its mayor while in jail.

Third, resource constraints that systemically impede the delivery of justice politicize and aggravate the issue of implementation. On the corruption cases, the protest is not that those charged are innocent, but that equally guilty parties have not been prosecuted. If we cannot simultaneously prosecute all "big fish" criminals, do we abandon convicting those we can?

Mr. Duterte gallantly insists that ladies should go first; he should be investigated for hidden wealth only after the investigation of the chief justice and the ombudsman. The ladies have declared their willingness to undergo investigation. Mr. Duterte has rejected investigation by the Office of the Ombudsman. In rejecting constitutional processes to check abuse of power, he gives further substance to the GII judgment giving the Philippines the global prize for tolerating impunity.

4

The Philippines in the ICC

(*PDI*, April 07, 2018)

Since its formal establishment in 2002, the ICC has indicted thirty-four individuals from eight African countries for war crimes, crimes against humanity and genocide. Some of us may have read media references to Darfur, Uganda and the Democratic Republic of the Congo. Most Filipinos, myself included, would need a map to pinpoint their precise locations.

I am sorry and sad that the ICC has now found sufficient cause to open a "preliminary examination" of possible crimes committed since July 2016 in President Duterte's drug war. While more people voted against Mr. Duterte than for him, he won the presidency convincingly. That the ICC, after monitoring the situation for almost two years, has placed the administration of our legitimately elected president on its agenda, also reflects on the Philippines and on us.

I am even more sorry and sad that Mr. Duterte has responded to the ICC by following the leadership of Burundi in rejecting cooperation with the ICC and withdrawing from it. Burundi? It's a small, landlocked country in East Africa with a population of 10.5 million, ranked by the 2018 World Happiness Report as the "least happy people." Mr. Duterte has declared that he would campaign for other countries to leave the ICC. How many will rush to join Burundi and the Philippines? Our likely company would be those similarly under investigation by the ICC.

Lashing out against the ICC is shortsighted and self-defeating. First, because weaker, less developed countries have a greater need for the protection of an internationally accepted, rule-of-law regime. One of the ICC cases, for instance, is looking at the conduct of British military personnel in Iraq.

Second, the ICC had barely begun a process, which needs the government's assistance, through which the Duterte administration could demonstrate that an ICC investigation was unnecessary. The administration would need to present the results of a serious effort to investigate EJKs and punish the perpetrators. Compliance with the Supreme Court demand, supported by members of the Senate, that the police turn over copies of the drug war files would be a good start.

Third, Mr. Duterte had little to lose as he was still very far away from prosecution. The ICC's file of eleven cases in 2017, again, all but one from Africa, includes some which have been under investigation since 2004. The ICC does not even begin a formal investigation until it has completed a preliminary evaluation, which may, as happened in four cases last year, result in a decision not to proceed.

The cases that feed into the ICC pipeline for preliminary examination come from member states, others from the UN Security Council (UNSC). It also acts on communications that report ongoing commission of its category of crimes. Between October 2016 and October 2017, the ICC received 568 communications. Only sixty-two of them (11 percent) merited a closer look from the ICC that could lead to preliminary examination. Its process appears serious and rigorous.

Mr. Duterte has dismissed the ICC evaluation as "rude" and insulting to his position as the leader of a sovereign country. Unfortunately, he cannot wrap himself in the Philippine flag and expect the people to rally to his defense. Not when the ICC is asking for what the people and coequal branches of the government also want: an end, not to the campaign against drugs, but to the alleged impunity protecting EJK perpetrators. Two years into the Duterte term, not one EJK suspect has been convicted and given commensurate punishment. Some of the other ICC cases involve fewer deaths than have resulted from the Duterte drug war.

Given the ICC's protracted process, Mr. Duterte himself faces no threat of imminent indictment; chances are the investigations would extend beyond his lifetime. But there are also the closest subordinates and political allies implicated in the alleged crimes, which are continuing in the wake of the war. The ICC is not bound by any mandatory deadline within which to complete its investigations. Which means that the stigma of an ICC investigation would continue to hang over the Philippines for we don't know how many years.

This is one of the legacies the Duterte administration will likely bequeath to us: the dubious distinction, though no longer a member of the ICC, of a place in its "Rogues' Gallery."

5

Choosing Enemies and Friends

(*PDI*, May 05, 2018)

President Duterte's determination to prevent foreigners from offending the country's dignity and sovereignty deserves support. But we need to understand his priorities. Was the participation of a 71-year-old Australian nun in a protest rally a graver offense than Chinese infringement on Philippine rights over its exclusive economic zone?

Photographs showing Sister Patricia Fox with a political placard and a microphone drove Mr. Duterte to order her immediate investigation. He declared that, as a foreigner, she could not claim the right of free speech, accorded to citizens, to criticize him. Such criticism amounted to maligning the government, insulting the people and "trampling" on the country's sovereignty. A zealous Bureau of Immigration forthwith picked up and detained Sister Pat and subsequently ordered her deportation.

Photographs of Chinese military planes landing on Panganiban (Mischief) Reef, after two weeks, has provoked no impassioned denunciation from Mr. Duterte or Foreign Secretary Alan Cayetano. And now, China has installed missiles on three Philippine reefs, justifying the deployment as designed to protect its sovereignty over geographical features within our EEZ, the claim which the Permanent Court of Arbitration at The Hague rejected in 2016. China had dismissed this decision and continued to deny Filipino fishermen access to traditional fishing grounds in the Scarborough Shoal. It even accelerated its reclamation program, completing projects on seven reefs within Philippine EEZ that have degraded the marine environment, and now has militarized international waters.

And when Mr. Duterte raised the possibility of the Philippines prospecting for oil and gas within its EEZ, Xi Jinping threatened war. But it was Sister Pat, not Xi Jinping, who provoked the president's rage and the warning not to "mess with the sovereignty" of the country or to "treat the Philippines like a mattress there to wipe with your feet."

No one expects or wants Mr. Duterte to berate Xi Jinping, for whom he has professed love and admiration, the way he did Sister Pat. Some people crave pizza, others prefer *paksiw* (sour stew). In cuisine, as in the choice of friends and enemies, there is no arguing with taste. But his enemies are not necessarily the enemies of the entire nation. There is grave danger when differences on policies are projected as personal attacks, especially if the bully pulpit of the presidency and the coercive powers of the state are used without due process against the president's perceived enemies.

Despite Mr. Duterte's personal rapport with Xi Jinping, China remains the foreign country least trusted by Filipinos. This worries Presidential Spokesperson Harry Roque, who pleads for Filipinos to give China more time to prove its friendship. His assurance that we would later thank China when it turns over to us, lands it reclaimed within our EEZ, drew incredulous laughter from ASEAN colleagues at a gathering in Kuala Lumpur. Can a senior government official who speaks for the president be so totally naïve? Or, is it his countrymen he considers so naïve that they will swallow anything he tells them?

But Mr. Roque takes his cues from the president, who would prefer mothballing SCS issues for a century. So does, apparently, National Security Advisor Hermogenes Esperon, Jr., who declared that internal security problems should take precedence over maritime disputes with external powers. Sister Pat presumably exemplifies the internal threat that must be vigorously suppressed.

Mr. Duterte has reportedly told the prime minister of Vietnam that, "in due time," he would address the SCS issue. Playing for time is a strategy, but time is not on his side. Mr. Duterte, on his own, cannot win the SCS battle. But he can lose it by himself. Supreme Court Justice Antonio Carpio has repeatedly warned that the Philippines can forfeit the game, when leaders disdain the use of available legal and diplomatic tools to assert the righteousness of its cause in the court of international public opinion. Unfortunately, many of his colleagues in the Supreme Court are more interested in hunting for missing statements of assets, liabilities and net worth.

Mr. Duterte may be comfortable with the idea of the Philippines becoming a province of China, or may believe that bartering our EEZ for Chinese aid and loan packages is a good bargain. As president, he can argue this case. But is this a decision that any president can unilaterally and irreversibly make for the Filipino people? Where are our other leaders?

6

Return to Great Power Geopolitics

(*PDI*, June 02, 2018)

President Rodrigo Duterte sees the Chinese militarization of the WPS as an issue in geopolitics, a subject he said he took and enjoyed in college.

The musical *The King and I* is an unlikely reference in a geopolitics course, but one Mr. Duterte might have appreciated. Like him, Siam's King Mongkut worried about the usefulness of allies perceived as weak in military capacity or political resolve.

Despite our mutual defense treaty, Mr. Duterte doubts that the US would invest treasure and blood to defend the Philippines. The constraint to follow constitutional processes before it can take up arms to protect the Philippines, in his view, makes America an unreliable ally. He also distrusts the US because American leaders have openly criticized his drug war and, presumably, supported its review by the ICC.

China, in contrast, has more powerful forces closer to the Philippines and appears more aggressive in their use. It has also defended the drug war. Mr. Duterte has celebrated China's pledge to protect the Philippines, a commitment he said he was counting on "in case of an outbreak of violence in Mindanao."

But the Islamic State and the NPA, which pose the biggest security threats in Mindanao, remain, thus far, internal insurgencies, notwithstanding evidence of foreign support to local jihadists. Will we ask China to send troops to Mindanao, as it once did to North Korea? From which enemies is China going to defend us?

Choosing allies is problematic. As King Mongkut recognized: "If allies are weak, am I not best alone?/If allies are strong, with power to protect me/Might they not protect me out of all I own?"

Now we know that Chinese missiles protect our reefs in our EEZ, precisely the kind of "protection" that King Mongkut feared. In an age of Great Power rivalry over colonies, King Mongkut faced a more difficult situation. He knew that Thailand could not win a war against the Western colonial powers. But he learned to use the rules of international engagement that the Western powers themselves had established and, therefore, could not completely ignore.

Since World War II, a more robust framework of international law and collective security has tempered, though not fully ended, the gunboat diplomacy practiced by the Great Powers. Enough progress has been made to expand the options for weaker countries beyond unwinnable wars and abject appeasement (rendered more palatable as "accepting the reality on the ground").

Inexplicably, however, these are the choices that Mr. Duterte has aggressively promoted. He has continuously harped on the theme that we cannot win a war against China, which no one disputes.

Thus, China does not even have to engage in saber-rattling to threaten us, which would be bad for its international PR. Mr. Duterte does it himself. Because we are weak, he has said, we should remain meek and humble so that China will have pity on us. And, maybe then, China will allow us a bigger share of the WPS resources that rightly belong to us.

Does this posture reflect the "*puso*" (heart) that Secretary of Foreign Affairs Alan Peter Cayetano said will help us compensate for the material superiority enjoyed by China?

We understand the benefit of the warm personal rapport that Mr. Duterte has established with Xi Jinping. But it seems short-sighted to rely on our "newfound friendship" with China to protect us from the dangers of a militarized WPS. A mid-nineteenth century geopolitical insight remains pertinent: a country has no permanent friends or enemies, only permanent interests.

What happens when Mr. Duterte, as he says he wants to do, exits the stage? And what happens now that he has drawn lines on the sand that, if crossed, will lead him to war? "*Bahala na*" (Leave to Fate) is not a strategy, especially since he has brought us back to the game of great power geopolitics, where military force is the principal currency.

Over thousands of years, humanity has struggled to escape from the law of the jungle to the rule of law. Ironically, despite their training in the craft and ethics of the legal profession, the president, the presidential spokesman and the foreign secretary seem more inclined to believe that might makes right and laws do not matter.

Even sadder, no one in the top ranks of the administration seems to disagree.

7

A Beijing World Order

(*PDI*, June 01, 2019)

The Trump trade war is apparently inflicting damage on China. But it is hurting other countries as well, not least the US itself, thus weakening the Washington world order. It bolsters the belief that the birthing of a Beijing world order is inevitable. Whether such development is desirable is another matter.

In his latest "Tomgram" essay, Alfred McCoy presents a compelling picture of what that world order might portend. Filipinos may still remember McCoy as the historian who unearthed the archival documents demolishing the Marcos claims to medals of valor, allegedly awarded to him by the American government for heroic exploits against Japanese occupation forces. These medals were as fake as the claims for compensation submitted by Marcos for his Maharlika guerrilla unit, which makes mystifying why President Duterte would revive the Marcos idea of renaming the country after his scam to defraud the US government and genuine Filipino guerrillas.

McCoy's outline of the potential Beijing framework for a new global system will be credible to Filipinos who are witnessing its contours emerging in their backyard. The contrast between the Washington world order could not be sharper, particularly in how they define the limits of state sovereignty and the nature of human rights.

The Iberian world order (1494–1805), established by the Treaty of Tordesillas (1494), gave Catholic Spain and Portugal papal authority to subjugate "barbarous" (i.e., non-Catholic) peoples and to exercise dominion over open seas. The Dutch and the British happily accepted the right to establish colonial rule over barbarian infidels, but enshrined the principle of freedom of the seas, which the succeeding British world order (1815–1914) sustained. At the Berlin Conference on Africa (1885), Britain modified the basis of colonial rule from religion to race, denying "native tribes" both sovereignty and human rights.

The current Washington world order, arising in 1944 from the ashes of the world wars, retained the freedom of the seas doctrine but rejected the religious and racial divisions previous world orders had imposed. Instead, it promoted the universal declaration of human rights, proclaiming the "equal and inalienable rights of all members of the human family" under the protection of the rule of law. Affirming the right of self-determination for all nations, the Washington global system also established the infrastructure for international collaboration: the UN, World Bank, North Atlantic Treaty Organization and World Trade Organization.

The 2017 Beijing Belt and Road Forum, attended by 130 nations, marked for McCoy, the "formal start of the Chinese era." Already, China has paved the path it wants the world to pursue. In rejecting the UN ruling that denied its unilateral claims over the SCS, China was returning to the fifteenth century Iberian principle of the "closed sea," subject to the control of one country. It was also demonstrating its dismissal of the framework of international law supporting the Washington world order.

A Beijing system is unlikely to defend the exercise of individual political rights, freedom of expression and freedom of religion—values cherished by Filipinos. A million Uighurs in Xinjiang are reportedly captives in "reeducation camps" for living their Muslim faith. China has taken steps to cleanse historical records of content that reflected badly on the Communist Party and the regime. It controls the flow of information within its borders, blocking online sources deemed dangerous by the state. Reporters Without Borders has warned that China is exporting its methods of censorship and control of information to other countries, promoting a Chinese "new world media order" that threatens press freedom globally.

Without mutual commitment to international covenants based on the rule of law, state transactions will require scrupulous attention to economic costs and benefits, crafty diplomacy anchored on balance of power calculations, and a sharp focus always on national interest. With a political system driven by factional, partisan interests and a leadership so shamelessly complacent and submissive in its dealings with China, a Beijing world order promises formidable challenges for the Philippines.

Demanding fortitude in defending our rights in the WPS, and transparency and prudence in negotiating Chinese deals, will help guard against the premature imposition upon us of a new world order.

8

Authoritarian Kleptocracy (AK)

(*PDI*, October 05, 2019)

AK defines a country ruled by a narrow elite that seeks self-enrichment as its primary goal. Business tycoons have always benefited from their ability to influence the government to favor their interests. The center of gravity under AK shifts to political leaders. With the centralization of government powers, they can bend even "Big Business" to their whims. The consolidation of political and economic resources results in the most powerful politicians becoming the country's wealthiest. Or the reverse.

The emergence of new entrepreneurs riding on the coattails of the top political leader is a second AK marker, facilitated by the dismantling of the system of divided powers that protects democratic governance. As the executive acquires dominance over the legislature and the courts, the government gains control over tax funds and revenue flows from franchises and rents. These provide the executive with wealth to dispense to family and friends, and to assemble a new set of loyal cronies.

We have long and extensive experience with one way of diverting public funds into private pockets: the common complex of illegal corrupt practices that every presidential candidate condemns. Actual implementation of anti-corruption rhetoric generally fails to realize the promise. Still, the standard anti-corruption measures sometimes manage to trap "big fish" in their nets. The safer strategy is to take funds right off the top.

Control of the legal and political system permits the appropriation of funds to support new offices—for instance, for additional deputy ministers and vice chairs; or to transfer them into discretionary expenditure items not subject to normal reporting and accounting requirements, such as "intelligence funds." Legislated budgetary measures to raise compensation or allowance levels of officials on a selective basis can also mask potential corruption. These schemes provide a legal cover for appropriating public funds for the private enrichment of those with political clout. But they essentially support a corrupt environment.

AK's third characteristic follows from the other two: government powers centralized in the executive and the consolidation of political and economic resources in the same set of self-interested elites. Together, they weaken the check-and-balance framework of government. The oversight responsibility to hold the executive branch accountable for its actions rests on the legislature and the courts. Their abdication of this duty permits kleptocracy to flourish. AK applies Robert Klitgaard's formula: Corruption = Monopoly + Discretion – Accountability.

The 47th anniversary of martial law last month reminded us that "kleptocracy" and "crony capitalism" entered our political vocabulary during the Marcos regime. Chris Miller's review of Anders Aslund's *Russia's Crony Capitalism: The Path from Market Economy to Kleptocracy* (Yale University Press, 2019) supplied another prompt for this piece. Aslund updates the concept and practices of kleptocracy in Russia under President Vladimir Putin.

Filipinos do not know much about Russia. President Duterte's second visit to Russia in three years should alert us to learn more. Aslund's book offers useful information on the most influential cronies today and insights on how the government transacts business with them. Aslund identifies Gennady Timchenko, Arkady Rotenberg and Yuri Kovalchuk among those entrepreneurs who were neither notably prominent nor wealthy, until Putin became the dominant power. Like many of the old, established business elite, they have fallen in line to pledge loyalty to Putin. They have now amassed billions, according to Aslund, from "preferential state orders" from state-owned firms to "unique access" to licenses. Such relationships assure mutual advantages.

With his long service in government and his proclaimed concern over corruption, Mr. Duterte himself may not need any assistance from Aslund's book. He would have learned already, from his familiarity with the Marcos regime and his own experience as long-serving Davao mayor, how corruption works in our local context and how to control it. He does not need any lessons from Russia and what Putin does or does not do.

For government officials expected to implement agreements resulting from the visit, Aslund's research should provide relevant reading. It is they who must ensure that whatever promised benefits come from Russia with love, genuinely contribute to the country's welfare.

9

Consensus on the South China Sea

(*PDI*, October 03, 2020)

Department of Foreign Affairs (DFA) technocrats must have experienced some unease when President Duterte decided that he would address the 75th UN General Assembly. He would join this annual ritual, even if only in virtual mode, for the first time since his election in 2016. During his term, he has not found many kind words to say about the UN. He has publicly cursed and threatened UN officials and dismissed the institution itself as worthless.

But the president surprised critics with a speech that praised and proclaimed the UN as "humanity's essential organization." He delivered the prepared text without indulging in the ad-libbing familiar to a Philippine audience. He was composed and circumspect, omitting the profanities. He could have played it safe by staying on the COVID-19 pandemic and other broad international concerns. Unexpectedly, he diverted, in a more direct fashion than he had done before, to the sensitive SCS issue that he could have easily avoided.

His statement deserves memorializing in full: "We must remain mindful of our obligations and commitment to the Charter of the United Nations and as amplified by the 1982 Manila Declaration on the Peaceful Settlement of International Disputes. The Philippines affirms that commitment in the SCS in accordance with United Nations Convention for the Law of the Sea (UNCLOS) and the 2016 Arbitral Award. The award is now part of international law, beyond compromise and beyond the reach of passing governments to dilute, diminish or abandon.

"We firmly reject attempts to undermine it. We welcome the increasing number of states that have come in support of the award and what it stands for—the triumph of reason over rashness, of law over disorder, of amity over ambition. This, as it should be, is the majesty of the law."

Unwilling to admit a presidential change of mind, Spokesperson Harry Roque discounted the message as nothing new. But UN delegates familiar with the issue would appreciate, as Filipinos did, that the statement was the president's strongest affirmation of the Arbitral Award and his most categorical rejection of China's claim to boundaries that would violate the Philippine EEZ and maritime rights in the SCS.

The president has changed his mind before—on peace talks with communist insurgents, the timing of constitutional change, cabinet appointments—without damage to his popularity. Only the foolish and the dead never change their minds. New facts may justify new views. On the SCS issue, even a change in presidential tone should improve his approval rating. SWS surveys have consistently shown overwhelming popular support for resistance to Chinese encroachment into Philippine waters and the bullying of Filipino fishermen.

The president's speech also offers the hope that, going beyond political colors, leaders in the administration and in the opposition can come together to craft a common strategy to promote national goals. Consensus on the principles the president enunciated in his statement will, hopefully, herald broader collaboration among DFA technical experts and those of independent policy think tanks on how best to protect the country's interests in the SCS.

Already suffering from the challenge of the pandemic, the country would welcome a united effort to promote the common good. There seems to be a growing frustration with the tendency of some government officials to cast every policy debate as a battle between good and evil, where only one side has the right answers and no constructive criticism is possible. In recent weeks, the strongest critical comments on administration performance—on COVID-19, PhilHealth, the budget process—have come not from "*Dilawan*" (yellow) opposition leaders but from politicians and columnists supportive of the president, and from the president himself.

Addressing the "Great Powers" locked in geopolitical competition, Mr. Duterte pointed out that "escalating tensions benefit no one." Surely, his admonition to them applies also to the partisans in national politics: "if we cannot be friends as yet, then in God's name, let us not hate each other too much." The president can do much to set the tone of political discourse, starting with the rejection of troll-driven fake news and the promotion of dialogue, to—in his words—"pursue a common purpose."

10

The Conflict-Collaboration Game

(*Rappler*, March 13, 2021)

Bilahari Kausikan had served as Singapore ambassador to Israel, Russia, and the UN, and as Permanent Secretary, Singapore Foreign Affairs. In a recent Foreign Affairs essay, he recalled a Vietnamese counterpart's response to his question on what leadership changes in Vietnam meant for relations with the PRC: "Every Vietnamese leader must get along with China, every Vietnamese leader must stand up to China, and if you can't do both at the same time, you don't deserve to be leader."

This tension in the relationship between China and Vietnam has endured over many centuries, beginning long before their common engagement in the anti-colonial struggle and embracement of the Marxist/communist ideology. China supported Vietnam's resistance to French colonial rule, which led to the country's division into North and South Vietnam. In contrast, Thailand and the Philippines, two founding members of ASEAN, sent soldiers to serve with the UN forces to fight against the PRC in the Korean War. The PRC again supported North Vietnam in its war to reunify the country under its rule.

While still under British rule, Singapore and Malaysia had faced their own struggle with communist insurgency. Both also feared the "domino effect"—that the fall of the South Vietnam piece would topple other governments in the region, beginning with Laos, Cambodia and Thailand. Unlike Thailand and the Philippines, they did not send troops to South Vietnam, but they cooperated in training South Vietnamese soldiers in jungle warfare and providing rest-and-recreation facilities for American troops.

For most of the twentieth century, China's relations with Vietnam were warmer and stronger than with ASEAN's founding members. In the preceding period, however, the Vietnamese had sustained a protracted, 1,500-year struggle against Chinese colonial rule. China invaded and occupied Vietnam for the first time in 111 BC. Intermitted rebellion forced the Chinese to invade Vietnam on three separate occasions, until the Vietnamese regained their independence in 1428.

If China wanted to turn back the clock, it has more historically-founded claims to control over Vietnam than the SCS and the nebulous nine-dash line (originally eleven-dash line) generated by the Kuomintang Government in 1947. This would be analogous to the UK asserting rights over Canada or Spain over the Philippines, but still perhaps contributes to Vietnam's sensitivity to China's "Great Power" politics.

Like other ASEAN countries, Vietnam also contests Chinese claims over land and maritime boundaries. Since the Korean War, only Vietnam among ASEAN members has engaged China in a shooting war. In 1978, Vietnam invaded Cambodia to overthrow Pol Pot's Khmer Rouge government, whose troops had been raiding Vietnamese border settlements and whose harsh regime eventually led to the death of an estimated 2 million Cambodians. Vietnamese troops captured the capital in less than two weeks but failed to catch Pol Pot, who continued to wage guerrilla war. Initially welcomed as liberators, the Vietnamese overstayed their welcome and became regarded as invaders. Vietnam ended its occupation of the country after a decade and some 30,000 casualties.

China, which had offered refuge to King Sihanouk, had been Cambodia's patron and protector. Concerned over Vietnam's ascendance in the region and its close ties with the Soviet Union, China mobilized 300,000 troops and launched a punitive invasion to "teach Vietnam a lesson" in February and March 1979. Vietnam and China have also clashed in the SCS, most seriously in 1988, when Vietnam lost three ships and seventy-four sailors.

Much weaker than Vietnam and more beholden to the PRC, Laos and Cambodia, as Kausikan noted, also found it necessary to stand up to China. In January 2018, Cambodia complained about a surge in crime and insecurity accompanying Chinese investment in the province of Preah Sihanouk. In 2016, the president and general secretary of the Lao People's

Revolutionary Party lost their posts for being "too pro-China." Both countries now worry about China's valve-like control from its upstream position to regulate the flow of water to the Mekong River, on which their agriculture depends.

Although wary of communist China from the start, Singapore and Malaysia have benefitted from the economic expansion in the region promoted by its pivot to capitalism. These economic benefits have not diminished their wariness nor discouraged the pursuit of common goals with the US. Aggrieved at the Chinese ambassador's support for the rival party in the Malaysian elections, Mahathir warned during his visit to Beijing in 2018, that Chinese actions in the region might suggest a form of colonialism.

Lee Kuan Yew had grave reservations about American prosecution of the Vietnam War. But anyone who wanted the US to leave the region, in his view, was either a communist or a fool. With the termination of the US occupation of military bases in the Philippines in 1990, Singapore promptly offered use of its facilities to American forces, an agreement renewed in 2019.

Kausikan acknowledged that ASEAN avoided publicly opposing China but pointed out that it did not publicly criticize the US or any other major power either, "because public criticism forecloses options and reduces the room for diplomacy." Philippine officials seem less observant of this norm. While careful about offending China, they have been less concerned about offending the US and other Western powers. But Kausikan's main point bears noting: "The diplomacy of ASEAN and its members is naturally promiscuous, not monogamous."

All the ASEAN members together cannot match China's military power. It would be insulting, however, to assume they were all "so irredeemably corrupt, terminally naïve or simple-minded that they would sell their national interests for a mess of pottage." Each member has the burden of proving to the others that this assumption is false.

VI

Pandemic Challenge

No country was really prepared to cope with the sudden challenge of COVID-19. But the pandemic was not really a totally unexpected Black Swan event, impossible to anticipate. Just since the turn of the century, even beyond the earlier HIV-AIDS (Human Immunodeficiency Virus-Acquired Immunodeficiency Syndrome), epidemiologists have served in the last couple of decades a rich alphabet soup of acronyms designating various viruses: SARS (Severe Acute Respiratory Syndrome), MERS (Middle East Respiratory Syndrome), the H1N1 varieties of Asian and Swine Flu.

Rather than a Black Swan, the pandemic was more like a Gray Rhino, a menace looming in the horizon whose attack was inevitable but the timing, uncertain. A rich super power like the US, which reputedly had a prepared playbook for the next pandemic, obviously failed to put in place the precautions prescribed by the plan. But countries like Taiwan, South Korea and Singapore, which had suffered the SARS virus, learned from the experience and responded more effectively to COVID-19.

The Philippines had also coped with the SARS attack in 2003 reasonably well. But it lacked the resource base already established by its more developed neighbors to counter COVID-19. Other countries had the financial resources and the industrial capacity to acquire or produce the protective equipment and the medical supplies and facilities to deal with the disease. They had a more advanced communications and information system to implement contact tracing of infectious cases to contain the spread of the virus.

COVID-19 also exposed the fragility of the country's public health system. The pandemic assault found the Philippines with only one institution, the Research Institute for Tropical Medicine in Alabang, Metro Manila, equipped to diagnose the virus; its capacity 200 to 250 tests a day. The Philippines was thus poorly positioned to implement the World Health Organization's (WHO) main strategy against the pandemic: test, trace and treat. With private sector support, the government ramped up testing capacity to the level of 30,000 tests a day by August 2020.

More difficult to address was the institutional weakness of the system that made it vulnerable to the danger that political interests and partisan politics would muddle issues of medicine and science. In 2017, the Aquino administration had launched a program for the mass inoculation of school children with the Dengvaxia vaccine to deal with the dengue epidemic. The Senate conducted hearings to investigate claims that Dengvaxia had caused the deaths of some schoolchildren and allegations of corruption in the purchase and use of the vaccine.

Although the charges have not been proven, these inevitably damaged not just the credibility of health officials, but even public confidence in vaccines. It has not helped either that corruption charges also assailed the Department of Health (DOH) and PhilHealth—the agency providing a social safety net for the health needs of the population—in the handling of their response to COVID-19.

The China provenance of COVID-19 also proved problematic for public health authorities. The first case recorded in the Philippines was a 38-year-old Chinese national travelling from Wuhan, the epicenter of the contagion, via Hong Kong. But early public calls for a temporary ban of visitors from mainland China met resistance from the secretary of health, who echoed the president's concern that the move may be deemed an unfriendly act by the Chinese government.

The pandemic was clearly the most formidable challenge that President Duterte has faced in his term, and it came on the tail end of his administration at a time when he has not been at the peak of health himself. Apart from the delays in closing down the country's borders, the initial decisions were sound. Given the state of the public health system, the imposition of community quarantine or lockdown was necessary to buy time to mobilize medical resources against the pandemic. The decision to organize the IATF with cabinet-level representation was also well-received. Defeating the virus would need a comprehensive, coordinated national response. That the IATF and its weekly presidential briefings did not live up to its promise, was part of the problems government failed to deal with.

The Philippines has endured one of the longest, continuous lockdown restrictions in the world. The issue that will continue to divide public opinion, perhaps to be resolved only later by historians, raises cost-benefit calculations: how effective was the IATF in realizing the gains expected from comprehensive, serial lockdowns?

Duterte's immediate, intuitive response to the pandemic reflected his long experience as a local government executive. He wanted the lowest level of government, the barangay and its heads, to take the lead in the fight against the virus. This approach would also have been consistent with his advocacy for a federal, decentralized structure of government. When local government officials began to exercise initiative, however, the president reverted to type, asking them to subordinate themselves to the decisions of the IATF or face charges.

In the end, Duterte fell back on the strategy with which he was most comfortable: appoint military and police officials he implicitly trusted and wage war on COVID-19, as he would against insurgents, terrorists and drug addicts—even as he realized himself that this was not a winning strategy against the pandemic. His frustration was palpable in nationally televised briefings where he repeatedly complained that things would be so simple if he could just deploy his soldiers to shoot down the virus.

The president depended on another plank in his policy platform to buttress the anti-COVID-19 campaign: his personal friendship with Xi Jinping and the PRC for its support in providing medical assistance, equipment support and finally, the supply of the COVID-19 vaccine.

The president talked about plans for financing the purchase of the vaccine, the use of the military to deliver the drugs and priority access for the poor. Despite weekly reports on encouraging results of vaccine development work by the Chinese, however, the public really had no solid evidence as 2020 drew to a close that it would be available any time soon. The doubts raised by the Dengvaxia controversy about vaccines in general was reinforced, as expected, in the case of the Chinese COVID-19 vaccine—when finally delivered—by the low public trust in China.

All countries stumbled at some point in their management of the pandemic. But some countries did better than others. As important in the success of these countries as the depth of their resources and the coherence of their institutions, has been the fund of social capital built up in the community—the trust of the people in their government. Opinion surveys in October 2020 reported that only a third of the population regarded the government data on COVID-19 prevalence and mortality rates as reliable. Halfway through 2021, problems with the vaccine roll-out, recurring surges in coronavirus cases, uneven enforcement of lockdown restrictions, and opposition to government policies beyond public health, like those on internal and external security issues, continued to deplete the administration's resources of social capital. Low levels of trust in the competence and trustworthiness of public officials undermine even honest efforts at improvement and reform.

1

Filipinos Becoming "Scientifically Illiterate"

(*PDI*, January 05, 2019)

Prompting this lament from Lulu Bravo of the Philippine Foundation for Vaccination was the rise in measles cases by November 2018 to 17,000, five times the count from the previous year. In 69 percent of the cases, parents had declined vaccination for their children. Equally alarming, confidence in vaccines reportedly declined from 93 to 32 percent between 2015 and 2018, a drop unseen in the other thirty-seven states of the WHO's West Pacific Region.

Blame for this descent to scientific illiteracy has focused on the investigations conducted by Sen. Richard Gordon and the PAO Chief Persida Acosta on the use of the dengue vaccine Dengvaxia in a 2017 vaccination program that covered some 830,000 children. While prompted by the warning that the use of the vaccine on those who had not been previously infected by the virus may aggravate the symptoms of the disease, medical practitioners criticized the investigations for promoting sensationalistic media reporting that appeared more focused on political than public health objectives.

Delays in the DOJ decision on the first batch of Dengvaxia cases, expected in November 2020, prolong public anxieties about vaccines. The group Doctors for Truth and Public Welfare has called for a halt to "fear-mongering" by spreading unproven claims against Dengvaxia that erode public trust in all vaccines.

Gordon has not addressed the problem to which he had contributed. Acosta and PAO officials remain unrepentant. Director Erwin Erfe of the PAO forensic laboratory claimed that "increasing number of deaths of Dengvaxia vaccinees, now numbering hundreds, are real—the result of a criminal act perpetrated by doctors of DOH."

But PAO has brought to court only nine cases. Erfe has claimed that autopsies conducted on 105 vaccinees showed a "Dengvaxia death pattern" of hemorrhages, edema and internal organ bleeding, without explaining how this pattern differs from that of dengue deaths, which claimed 730 casualties in 2017. His statement slides from "deaths of Dengvaxia vaccinees" to "Dengvaxia deaths," suggesting that vaccinees died because of Dengvaxia—precisely what he has to prove.

In a parallel effort, a University of the Philippines medical team investigated 14 dengue-related deaths. Only three were attributed directly to dengue. Dengvaxia could not be conclusively determined as the cause of these deaths. If the PAO cases involved dengue-related deaths, we cannot conclude that Dengvaxia killed the vaccinees, only that Dengvaxia failed to save them.

Rarely does any vaccine guarantee 100-percent effectiveness. A *New England Journal of Medicine* (NEJM) study reported that Dengvaxia reduced rates of severe disease and hospitalization for previously exposed children aged nine and older, by 80 percent. Given to those not previously exposed to dengue, Dengvaxia could result in more severe infection and increased risk of hospitalization. Unfortunately, no quick, safe and inexpensive way to test prior exposure is currently available. The required blood test itself poses some risks to children. Hence, individual testing is dispensed with in dengue-endemic areas where 50 percent or more of the population is likely affected.

The NEJM study quantified the tradeoff in using Dengvaxia without prior testing: hospitalization cases prevented for the group previously exposed to dengue would be eleven times higher than the number that may be required for the group without previous exposure. The reduction in number of severe cases for the first group would be five times higher than might occur with the second group. The Dengvaxia risk of severe infection for those without prior exposure would be one in 2000.

Meanwhile, PAO will be striving to prove that nine of the 830,000 vaccinees died because of Dengvaxia. In 2015, the Philippines registered over 140,000 dengue cases, resulting in over 400 deaths.

Deaths averted provide little comfort to those families who lose members to dengue. But bureaucrats and politicians involved in managing public health issues must calculate the tradeoffs and consider the lives risked and lost, when vaccination programs for dengue and other diseases are undermined by reckless fear-mongering. The ethical principle guiding the medical profession must apply equally to them: "First do no harm."

2

Dissonance in the Acosta–Gordon Duet

(*PDI*, March 09, 2019)

PAO Chief Persida Acosta and Sen. Dick Gordon have shared the blame for the sudden drop in public acceptance of vaccination. Health practitioners have alleged that their unsupported denunciation of the anti-dengue Dengvaxia as a dangerous, deadly vaccine drove people away from vaccination in general, contributing to the spike in measles cases and deaths. In the first two months of 2019, the DOH reported over 16,000 measles cases and over 260 deaths. Most of the dead had no anti-measles inoculation.

Most of the people following this complex issue, like me, have no medical training. Which is why Acosta and Gordon, also without medical training, needed to exercise prudence in their public statements. Both have been unrestrained and unrepentant. Acosta now claims the suit against those who decided on the mass Dengvaxia immunization program constituted "proof PAO didn't start vaccine scare." Huh? The DOJ issued the indictment on March 1, 2019; the vaccine scare started in 2017.

Still careless with dates, she accused the DOH of proceeding with mass inoculation, disregarding the danger of administering Dengvaxia without prior blood test and screening. Sanofi, the Dengvaxia producer, learned of the risk only after the mass vaccination had started. Receiving the information, the DOH stopped the program on December 1, 2017, after 830,000 pupils had undergone inoculation.

Independent health experts have been unable to confirm that any of the dengue deaths they have examined resulted from taking Dengvaxia, the PAO's allegation in the thirty-five complaints, covering thirty-three deaths, that it has filed. But the PAO has yet to present a single case proving that Dengvaxia caused death. It declared discovery of a "medical link" between deaths of dengue-infected children and the Dengvaxia vaccine, without explaining the nature of that link.

Surprisingly, Gordon, in an *Inquirer* article changed his tune, effectively sabotaging his partner's case. He reportedly "expressed doubt that the [PAO] charges . . . would prosper in court." In a quote from a radio interview, Gordon reportedly said: "They only focused on the complaint about the deaths [of those inoculated with Dengvaxia]. But there's no problem with those deaths . . . Because it has yet to be proven that [Dengvaxia] is the principal cause of the deaths. We really don't have any evidence to support [that allegation]." Nor did he have evidence at the time of his Senate hearings last year, when these allegations about Dengvaxia triggered fears about vaccination.

Gordon's admission that his hearings had not discovered any evidence against Dengvaxia documented the flaw in the approach he and Acosta had followed. They failed to distinguish between two aspects of the Dengvaxia case: the effectiveness of the vaccine as a measure against dengue; and the compliance, in its purchase, with pertinent rules and regulations. Both elements are important but must be separately evaluated.

The report quoting Gordon alluded to the "failed immunization program." In what way was the program a failure? How many of the 830,000 pupils who received the vaccine did Dengvaxia fail to protect? But neither Gordon nor Acosta seemed interested in the dengue victims and the public health issue confronting the DOH. They appeared oblivious to the 2015 surge in dengue cases, when the number of deaths reached 2,000, provoking alarm among doctors and hospitals. Their priority concern was the possible corruption in the Dengvaxia procurement, which they have yet to establish.

Could Dengvaxia have been an effective vaccine, but its procurement tainted by corruption? Certainly. Also possible is a transaction immaculate in the observance of procurement rules, but providing a vaccine ineffective in moderating the impact of the disease. Or, sadly, we could get a useless vaccine corruptly procured. People are rightly enraged by the number and scale of corruption cases that have lately assailed them. But people, especially those with loved ones at risk, also fear the dengue danger. We deserve both good governance and timely protection against epidemics.

But, bottom line: Acosta and Gordon have arguably aggravated the public health problem, without advancing the anti-corruption agenda. They did get good media coverage.

3

Health Is Wealth

(*PDI*, September 07, 2019)

So goes the saying preached in earlier times to schoolchildren. The adage applies both to individuals and communities. Even more than education, the population's health sets limits on the pace of its progress. The demographic dividend yielded by a young population to fill up the labor force becomes a demographic drag if the youth lack the physical or mental capacity to benefit from education and produce value for the country.

Promoting public health, however, requires balancing a complex mix of issues relating to household economics, medical and technology research, business interests and government policies. Where regulatory authorities must interpret and rule on the views of differing domain experts, complexity opens opportunities for corruption. A steady stream of media reports alleging corruption against pharma companies and high officials of the DOH, FDA, PAO and PhilHealth, has given the "health is wealth" prescription a cynical meaning.

Sen. Richard Gordon and PAO Chief Persida Acosta are not medical doctors. Their approach to the Dengvaxia vaccine focused on corruption, a concern that excites the electorate and can be conveniently directed against political enemies. But prosecuting criminals does not eliminate the danger from infectious diseases already punishing the public. National and international health experts have attributed to the high drama of the Dengvaxia investigation, the drastic drop in vaccination rates, not just against dengue but also against other diseases, from 93 percent in 2015 to the current 40 percent. We are now farther away from the 95 percent coverage necessary for effective disease containment.

Over 830,000 children received Dengvaxia shots. PAO has yet to establish conclusively one death caused by the vaccine. The DOJ ruling on the PAO cases was expected nine months ago. The delay in resolving the issue prolongs the anxiety among vaccine-takers. Meanwhile, the number of dengue cases now approaches 230,000 with over 950 deaths. Measles cases have tripled from last year's 11,800 to over 39,000, with deaths rising five times from 100 to 500.

The Philippine Foundation for Vaccination wants a law to punish scaremongers complicit in producing and spreading fake news that undermines vaccine confidence in the country. While admitting the backlash against vaccination, Gordon and Acosta absolve themselves from accountability for it. But they continue to project Dengvaxia as an untested, defective drug, damaging and even deadly to the health of children. Politicians rarely admit mistakes.

The government stopped mass Dengvaxia immunization in 2017, trusting the WHO warning against the use of Dengvaxia on children not previously exposed to dengue. But what was the basis for its February 2019 decision to prohibit its sale to everyone?

In July 2019, WHO added Dengvaxia to its List of Essential Medicines that should be available to the public. This time, DOH did not accept the WHO advisory, calling for further studies before possibly bringing the vaccine back to the market. Two months later, the FDA reaffirmed the ban, without clarifying the basis for rejecting the WHO recommendation on Dengvaxia that most of the world accepted. Meanwhile, wealthy families get the vaccine abroad.

The statement of Health Secretary Francisco Duque that the FDA decision had nothing to do with the efficacy of the vaccine raised further questions about how health authorities made decisions on issues critical to people's health. Health Undersecretary Enrique Domingo reported that international WHO experts could not comprehend the Philippine response to Dengvaxia: "Nobody understands why we're acting this way . . . On a global level, it seems only the Philippines is reacting this way to the Dengvaxia issue."

Perhaps, these foreign public health experts were "stumped," because they approach issues narrowly, according to the methods and norms of their discipline. They may not appreciate how health problems can become political issues, or the burden placed on professionals in government service to massage their messages to avoid contradicting politicians who reject expert judgment.

When they publicly and stubbornly cling to conclusions unsupported by evidence, politicians put pressure on the bureaucrats to bend professional judgment to political interests, at the risk of violating professional ethics—a situation that invites a kind of corruption in the bureaucracy.

4

Crisis Response

(*PDI*, February 15, 2020)

On December 31, 2019, the WHO noted in China, a new, SARS-like virus, later labeled COVID-19. By the week of January 20, 2020, Philippine media began covering the contagion that had already spread from Hubei beyond China's borders. Netizens called for quick action, including a ban on tourists from China, arriving since January 2020 at around 4,800 a day and promising to exceed the 1.6 million visitors in 2019. The WHO warning on January 26 of a high-risk global epidemic reinforced public alarm.

On January 29, President Duterte delivered mixed messages. He declared that he would delegate to the proper authorities what precautionary measures to take—after first flagging his concern about the difficulty and unfairness of unilaterally refusing entry to travelers from China. Health Secretary Francisco Duque III readily agreed that even a temporary ban on mainland China tourists would be "very tricky" and "unfair," as COVID-19 had already appeared in other countries. Responsible for public health, his concern was not medical but diplomatic—"possible repercussions" on relations with China. Sen. Bong Go, chairing the Senate Committee on Health, echoed this perspective on January 30, asserting that a ban applied only against China would be "improper" and "unfair".

China's Consul General Jia Li had weighed in on the issue, dismissing the need for a ban, since China had already imposed a travel lockdown on Hubei since January 24. Meanwhile, the DFA, charged with managing foreign relations, was waiting for advice from health authorities. But the highest health officials had kicked the ball back to the president, whose goal remained fixed on China. Only after the WHO declaration on January 31 of a global COVID-19 emergency, did Mr. Duterte ban the entry of travelers from Hubei, extending the ban on February 2 to all of China.

Sen. Vicente Sotto III reinforced the diplomatic dimension of the health issue on February 4, contributing his "interesting, if not revealing" video suggesting that COVID-19 had been deployed as a bioweapon against China. Foreign Secretary Teodoro Locsin Jr. ridiculed the claim as "an example of the craziest video I have ever seen," prompting Go's warning against people spreading fake news and Justice Secretary Menardo Guevarra's instruction for the National Bureau of Investigation to probe "alleged deliberate spread of misinformation and news" about COVID-19. Any suspect can invoke in defense, the introduction in a Senate hearing, of an unvetted YouTube video peddling conspiracy theories.

Continuing his discourse on international relations, Locsin debunked any Western hopes that COVID-19 would weaken China. China's response to the epidemic, he predicted, would project it as "a power that just cannot be defeated even by nature." He also defended China against allegations that it had suppressed information about COVID-19, recalling the January 7 advisory that the Hong Kong government had sent to the Philippine consulate. Netizens wondered why Philippine officials seemed more concerned with the rights and reputation of China than the "health and safety" of Filipinos, later invoked for the travel ban against Taiwan.

Locsin correctly noted that Beijing was sharing COVID-19 information with the world in early January. In December 2019, however, a 34-year-old doctor had already posted for his medical alumni chat group an alert on the new virus that went viral. Chinese authorities were not prepared to circulate such information among its own citizens. Police investigated Li for rumor-mongering and forced him to withdraw his warning. Catching the virus himself, Li Wenliang died on February 7, 2020. Hailed as a whistle-blower hero, his death triggered a massive online movement that defied Beijing's censorship apparatus. In a last interview, Li regretted the delay in defending against the virus: "I think a healthy society should not only have one kind of voice."

Though more muted in the executive branch, many voices can still be heard in the Philippines, in media, academe, civil society, even in the legislature. Diverse voices make more difficult the crafting of a concerted response to crises. But when the threat is deadly, its origins still uncertain and its trajectory unpredictable—as with COVID-19—a single voice dictating possibly mistaken diagnoses and treatments, risks unmitigated disasters.

5

Calamities and Democracies

(*PDI*, March 07, 2020)

"No famine has ever taken place in the history of the world in a functioning democracy." Amartya Sen's comment and the criticism it received from some academics apparently made little impact on the panel that awarded him the Nobel Prize in Economic Science in 1998 for his work on poverty, gender inequality and the UN's Human Development Index (HDI). But it was this observation that caught the attention and assent of public intellectuals and the general public.

Famines do not suddenly strike without warning, and experience has established measures to address their occurrence. In democracies, access to opposition leaders and a free press make it difficult to conceal emerging problems. Free and regular elections hold ruling governments accountable and pressure leaders to respond or risk rejection by angry voters at the polls. Unencumbered by such restraints, Mao Zedong's Great Leap Forward, the grand project to place agriculture under a collective system, left an estimated 30 million peasants dead from famine.

A democratic system obviously does not provide a country the same kind of protection against other calamities, like epidemics. A new virus can suddenly appear and spread at a speed that challenges the scientific, bureaucratic and financial resources of even highly developed, wealthy democracies, as demonstrated by the quick migration of COVID-19 from Wuhan in China to Japan, South Korea and Italy. Unlike famines, the cure for stricken patients needing immediate care is not clear and preventive vaccines must undergo time-consuming tests.

An authoritarian, centralized system can mobilize with impressive speed. China built two hospitals in ten days, set up 500 quarantine hotels, and sealed off 50 million residents in their cities, if not in their homes. Such draconian measures democracies would find difficult to implement quickly.

But the authoritarian system that enabled the efficient deployment of the state's coercive powers also permitted the punishment of Wuhan doctors who had sounded the alert about the new virus without government authorization. As had happened with SARS in 2003, censorship delayed countermeasures against the spread of COVID-19. Knowing the aversion of authoritarian leaders to public exposure of government failings, equally authoritarian local officials instinctively protect themselves by suppressing bad news, and thus blindsided Beijing on the scale of the problem.

Tight, top-down management also restrains remedial action at lower levels. In the Philippines, greater autonomy from the center arguably helped contain COVID-19. The presidential ban on travelers from Hubei, the province of Wuhan, came on January 31, 2020. On January 23, Presidential Spokesperson Salvador Panelo had dismissed any need to ban travelers from Wuhan.

Notwithstanding this opinion, Carmelo Arcilla, Executive Director of the Civil Aeronautics Board (CAB), ordered on the same day, the immediate suspension of the six weekly direct flights between Wuhan and Kalibo provided by Pan Pacific Air and Royal Air Charter Services. The CAB initiative, supported by Tourism Secretary Bernadette Romulo Puyat, was implemented even before the WHO announced on January 26 that COVID-19 posed a high global risk. On January 28, the Bureau of Immigration officially stopped issuing visa-on-arrival to Chinese nationals (although the policy was unfortunately undermined by corrupt officials through the "*pastillas* (milk candy)," the code word for bribery arrangements).

LGUs also exercised their authority to avoid the risk of infection in the case of the cruise ship *World Dream*. Cleared by the Board of Quarantine as "safe and clear" from COVID-19, *World Dream*, sailing from Hong Kong with 778 passengers "authorized to travel," docked at the Port of Manila on January 28. Its itinerary called for a tour of Subic Bay, the following day. Protests from their constituencies enabled Olongapo Mayor Rolen

Paulino Jr. and Subic Mayor John Khonghun to press successfully for the cancellation of this tour and *World Dream*'s return to Hong Kong. In Cebu, Gov. Gwendolyn Garcia on January 31 ordered a 14-day quarantine for arrivals from China.

Epidemics may require drastic control measures at which authoritarian governments are adept. But the public backlash provoked by China's action to discipline COVID-19 whistle-blowers recalls Sen's insight that public health experts applaud: democracies recognize their accountability to their citizens, whose access to information and ability to act on their own, enhance the acceptance and effectiveness of coercive precautions.

6

Conflicting Instincts

(*Rappler*, March 21, 2020)

Crafty and cruel, the coronavirus attacks people by exploiting intuitive human responses. How natural it is to visit loved ones who are sick and to greet them with a kiss, a hug, a touch. But contact spreads contamination; people must suppress this instinct to show love and concern through expected physical signs.

Lockdown to control contagion is also the intuitive response. Countries from Argentina to New Zealand are closing their international borders and increasingly imposing domestic quarantine. Protecting healthy people by barring their entry into infected areas and the exit of potential virus carriers into still secure spaces appear logical.

But experts disagree. Roy Anderson, professor of infectious disease epidemiology at Imperial College, dismissed travel bans as "a complete and utter waste of time." Bruce Aylward, formerly WHO emergencies chief and last month's team leader in China, declared, as a "pretty robust principle," that restricting movement does not help, possibly justified only at the outbreak's earliest stage. With virus carriers asymptomatic for as many as fourteen days, and with the delays in the response of most governments, the horses have typically bolted before the barn doors were bolted.

Still, Dr. Clare Wenham, London School of Economics scholar on health regulations, explains the strategy's popularity: "It is good political placebo." It allows an impressive show of government activity, even when implementation can cause economic, social, public and public health harm. Photos of massed travelers at Chicago's O'Hare Airport and crowds milling about Manila checkpoints and supermarkets mock warnings to maintain social distance. Might the mandatory lockdown have fostered rather than weakened conditions for breeding coronavirus infections?

The human impulse to touch to show love and to impose lockdowns to counter threats is instinctive, but against the coronavirus may be counterproductive. Banning travel to and from Manila denies outsiders access to the resources and the expertise in many sectors, including health, that are more abundant in the capital.

People have also become used to operating within the sprawl of Metro Manila. Wage workers from Cainta did not expect encountering barriers into Quezon City. Exceptions are allowed but delays are inevitable. It also devolves decision-making at the discretion of border guards.

Expanding the lockdown from Manila to Luzon was not as perversely problematic as simultaneously permitting its progressive constriction to smaller areas, from the capital region to the barangay. The ultimate logic of lockdowns left individuals to deal with the pandemic on their own: quarantine for the patient, the family, the household—only mediated and enforced by the weakest agency of government and the police while prevented from seeking help outside. This will punish the poorest, weakest sectors of society. What is the government doing now about the coronavirus cases in the informal settlements of Baseco and Payatas?

South Korea and Singapore practiced selective quarantine, but used public information infrastructure and aggressively adopted the WHO focus on locating virus cases and tracing their contacts—by building testing capacity for 10,000 and while administering 2,000 tests a day. Targeted lockdowns also permitted more direct assistance and more rigorous enforcement. Singapore isolated almost 5,000 cases and imposed criminal charges on violators. It did not confine millions of untested households in their communities.

Meanwhile, lacking comparable institutions and resources, the DOH will not test those with only "mild" symptoms outside the "at-risk" population. And we must now accept the community lockdown as a done deed and strive to convert government compulsion to personal compliance. Hopefully, this would allow the redeployment of resources for law enforcement to other concerns.

Such concerns include providing transport for the sick to get to doctors, personnel to essential occupations, and buyers and sellers of necessary goods to market; or ensuring continued collection of garbage. Surely, government could have introduced these measures to mitigate the burden on the public of the decision to suspend public transport.

Pandemics do not respect social, gender, economic, ethnic or national divisions. They require a concerted response from all countries and all communities, because the weakness of one endangers all.

The threat, as historian Yuval Harari observes, is not the violation of man-made distinctions among peoples or of boundaries between political or administrative units, but the breaching of the border between the virus and the human species.

7

Launching the ARK

(*PDI*, May 9, 2020)

Business leaders have stepped up in their individual and corporate capacity in the campaign against COVID-19. They responded quickly to cushion the Enhanced Community Quarantine (ECQ) impact on their employees, including contractuals compensated on a no-work-no-pay basis, suppliers and customers. Acutely sensitive to business and economic signals, they recognized the resumption of "normal" life as urgent and began dealing more directly with the pandemic.

As RFM president and CEO, founder of Go Negosyo, and Presidential Adviser for Entrepreneurship, Secretary Joey Concepcion, wearing both corporate and government hats, has emerged as the leading advocate for the relaxation of lockdown restrictions. He represented sixty other business leaders in recommending the selective reopening of malls, restaurants and other commercial establishments, as well as the provision of some public transport services, provided that every enterprise practiced social distance and health security precautions.

The recommendation came on April 2, when the country had registered over 2,600 COVID-19 cases and over 100 deaths. Two weeks later, the COVID-19 count had more than doubled to over 5,400 cases, while deaths had more than tripled at nearly 350. Although probably relieved that the business recommendations had not been immediately accepted, Concepcion continued to push for them. But Concepcion has maintained that epidemiology must guide public health decision-making and that life must take precedence over livelihood.

Whatever the preferred descriptor—gradual, phased, selective, calibrated—everyone accepts the need for careful deliberation on lockdown lifting. But the focus on dates for ECQ modification has distracted from the more difficult issue: determining the bases for relaxing lockdown. Concepcion has fixed on location as a critical element: "Determine where the virus is."

The country's archipelagic setting does provide an advantage; some areas have natural features that help isolate them from cross-border infection. If it is true that thirty provinces have not encountered COVID-19 cases, as the Union of Local Authorities of the Philippines or ULAP claims (twenty-six, according to the DOH), why should they suffer quarantine? The problem is verifying the ULAP assertion. The WHO has been preaching the answer—by testing; the first step in the test-trace-treat strategy. Project ARK (antibody rapid test kits), which Mr. Concepcion unveiled on April 23, aligned his advocacy for gradual lockdown lifting to the WHO mantra on testing.

The lack of test kits has stalled the testing program. Given supply constraints, it makes sense to test the people who need it most, such as frontliners in the health centers. But this rationing raises the number of positive test results. Since the people subjected to the test are those most exposed to the infection, the high test-positivity rate is unsurprising. The US and the UK have registered rates at 20 percent (55 percent in New York!) and over 30 percent, respectively, compared to 2 percent in South Korea, Australia and New Zealand, which have undertaken more widespread testing.

Information on how many new cases on a daily basis are being tested, where these are conducted, and their results, would enable more reliable estimates of the virus prevalence rate, the proportion of the general population infected by COVID-19, and the number of infected people likely to die. With these data, experts can better trace the trajectory of the disease and map the areas for selective lockdown relief. Declining daily infection rates, while maintaining the pace of general testing, would prove progress against the pandemic.

New York established seven requirements for relaxing quarantine restrictions, including a fourteen-day decline in hospitalization and death rates, and thirty tests per 1,000 residents each month. For Manila's 13 million residents, the requirement would come to about 13,000 tests a day. The *Rappler* count of tests conducted between mid-March and May 4 averages at less than 3,000 a day. The DOH is targeting capacity for 30,000 tests per day by end-May. If achieved, Manila can meet the New York benchmark, although leaving less for the rest of the country.

Private sector projects like ARK are thus important initiatives. Working to ensure they have virus-free personnel for their operations, business can help close the testing gap and improve the bases for deciding where and when to restart the economy.

8

Public Well-being for Public Security

(*PDI*, March 14, 2020)

On March 11, 2020, the WHO declared the coronavirus a global pandemic, as it was sweeping across 100 countries in six continents, infecting more than 120,000 and killing over 4,300 people. With commendable speed, President Duterte, surrounded by cabinet, civilian and police/military officials, announced over television on March 12, the intent of an executive order to deal with COVID-19.

Although unnecessarily detouring to praise Xi Jinping, implicitly shading other world leaders, Mr. Duterte pitched some important messages. He stressed the seriousness of the pandemic but cautioned against panic and urged the public to look at the government and the military as dedicated to its safety. He appeared more in command, compared to an earlier press conference and the alarming incoherence of a rambling discourse on the bubonic plague, the Spanish flu and the Spanish Inquisition's attack on witches.

Mr. Duterte established IATF headed by the health secretary, to craft the details of the executive order and monitor its implementation on a "day-to-day basis." He warned that dealing with COVID-19 would require compliance with regulations restricting personal rights normally taken for granted, such as freedom of movement. From March 15 to April 14, domestic air, land and sea travel to and from Manila would be suspended.

Hopefully, the IATF will carefully explain the planned restrictions. Will the Manila quarantine also control the movement of goods as well as people? Banning both will substantially impact supply chains and business activities. How will this ban be enforced? Easy enough to close air traffic. Possible to restrict vehicular entry and exit through the tollways. But control sea traffic in an archipelago?

Mr. Duterte admits that he does not have enough soldiers to enforce anti-COVID-19 regulations. Thus, his reliance on the DILG and the barangay heads to disperse mass gatherings, catch school truants taking advantage of suspended classes to patronize bars and night-clubs, and enforce community quarantine in coronavirus-infected areas. He ordered local officials and the military to execute IATF decrees, or face dereliction of duty charges. He repeatedly called for obedience to government orders, warning those who forcibly resist "persons in authority" that they can be subject to criminal penalties.

The focus on law enforcement appears to spring from his fear that COVID-19 precautions might provoke resistance, resulting in public disturbance and the breakdown of peace and order. This is not an entirely unreasonable apprehension, especially if the pandemic, ignoring the one-month plan for its containment, decides to extend its Philippine tour. At one point, the president cursed the SOB virus, as he had earlier demanded to know where it lived—which Presidential Spokesperson Salvador Panelo will assure us was just Mr. Duterte being humorous. But COVID-19, a public health and well-being concern, does present a problem to a president who tends to look at governance through a mailed fist, law-and-order prism. The virus is immune to insults, bribes and threats; impervious even to a president willing to kill.

Transparency and clarity must provide the first line of defense against public unrest. People must appreciate the scale of the problem, the design, and reasonableness of regulatory measures to protect public well-being and provide the help that people need and expect from government. Having acknowledged lacking medical expertise, Mr. Duterte might have permitted Health Secretary Francisco Duque III to explain the public health aspects of the anti-coronavirus strategy.

Testing on a broader basis is necessary to ascertain the extent of the contagion and the commensurate response required; does the DOH have enough test kits to do this? Where can people get tested and, if infected, get treatment? At what and whose cost? Most crucial for the IATF, how will government help wage-earners and employers cope with the income losses imposed by COVID-19 precautions? Without assurance on these medical and livelihood issues, coercion will encounter evasion and disobedience. Despite the risks, people will do what they must to support their families.

As emphasized in other countries, the effective implementation of community quarantine heavily depends on the people's regard for the credibility and competence of the government, and their trust in its capacity to enforce reasonable coercive measures in a humane and compassionate manner.

9

A Matter of Mutual Trust

(*Rappler*, March 28, 2020)

Pressure for quick action against COVID-19 should not prevent authorities from pausing to align strategies along the best practices discovered by frontline experts.

Cluster Containment

Lockdown effectiveness increases with the isolation of infected individuals, not in their homes but in dedicated facilities where they can be treated without endangering kin and neighbors. In China, 75 to 80 percent of all transmissions took place within households. A harsh measure to separate the sick from their families, but stories of households losing three to four members paint a grim picture of the alternative.

Contact Tracing

The identification of symptomatic COVID-19 cases up to their contacts' contacts is crucial for quarantine, monitoring and, hopefully, cure. The Taiwan government had the infrastructure to trace and transmit to the population, the contacts and the places visited by tourists on the port call of a cruise ship. Singapore tapped military personnel to expand its contract tracing teams, as needed.

Widespread Testing

Patients under investigation or monitoring and their contacts, as well as medical frontliners, for whom infection is an occupational hazard, are obvious priorities. If we followed the testing rate of South Korea or Singapore, we would need to be conducting at this time, at least 100,000 to 680,000 tests.

The three elements buy more bang for the buck when bundled together as an integrated response package and also allow for more targeted and productive lockdown. They were also more effective the earlier in the pandemic cycle it was implemented, as South Korea, Singapore, Taiwan and Germany did.

Like many other countries, we may have missed, for various reasons, such as not displeasing China, the early window for action; no reason for not implementing them now.

Controlling the Contagion

It has been over two weeks since the activation of a cabinet-level IATF on March 11. It is prudently developing plans to stabilize the economy, protect jobs, provide safety nets for self-employed gig workers and support those at the bottom of the pyramid. But controlling the contagion is the urgent priority and calls for IATF attention to best practices.

Experts predict that we will get more coronavirus cases. PhilHealth reports 70,000 beds in the health system, but not supported by the equipment and staff needed against COVID-19. Already, the health system is under stress, with personal protective equipment (PPE) lacking even for frontliners, and hospitals already turning down patients.

Who is responsible and what is the plan for implementing cluster containment? This may require acquiring, by purchase or lease, and building quarantine facilities. What progress has been made in ramping up PPE supply and the more expensive respirators and ventilators?

The WHO mantra has been testing, testing, testing. Widespread testing will give us more reliable information on the scale and worst locations of the pandemic and more reliable models of its behavior. More systematic testing would permit the gradual loosening of quarantine restrictions. It would also bolster the confidence of the public, which wants it.

We hear assurances that symptomatic cases can get tested for free, but not the specific information on how people at risk can access these tests. Now that the president has emergency powers, we should no longer see the absurdity of critically needed supplies held up in Customs.

Judgment Calls

Government has focused on the pandemic as a law-and-order problem, threatening enforcement agents with dire penalties for dereliction of duty. Judgment in the interpretation of rules ultimately becomes the burden of border guards trained to follow orders, unprepared and likely afraid to exercise discretion.

It is unsurprising that literal compliance with directives would serve as their default demand. A doctor is detained at a checkpoint, because his document does not identify him as "doctor." Fortunately, the guard was persuaded to accept that "physician" also means "doctor." Provincial mayors still complain that their cargo trucks are prevented from entering their home base after making their NCR deliveries.

Two weeks after the freeze on public transport, coping mechanisms apparently still await implementation. Frontliners without private cars still face problems getting to and from their stations. Clear and uniform rules need wide dissemination. The limit of one travel pass per household imposed by some barangays is a burdensome and short-sighted restriction, when many urban households typically consist not only of nuclear, but extended families; it requires review.

It imposes the burden of external housekeeping on one person, expected to be able to drive, or walk distances loaded with provisions, empowered to sign checks and credit cards, and familiar with household management. The same person, who can better stay healthy with the assistance of a companion, may be the only one who can do hospital care with a sick family member.

The emphasis on enforcement suggests that government places little trust on its citizens or wants even more power over them. At a time when the public needs information, for instance, why should media, exempted by the president from lockdown, now have to get a permit from the Presidential Communications Operations Office (PCOO)? It must be admitted that violations of lockdown protocol occur—although, apparently, many who violate social distance and quarantine norms with impunity, are high government officials.

10

The Midnight Show

(*Rappler*, April 18, 2020)

I watch the televised broadcast of President Duterte. Because COVID-19 terrifies me. Under lockdown, I follow the global coverage of the pandemic's seemingly inevitable spread. Horrifying stories of rich nations staggering under the weight of the sick and the dead make me wonder how we will cope with COVID-19. We have lost good friends to the plague. We fear for the frontliners and pray for them every night; we have family members among them. Also, family members with health conditions requiring regular confinement in hospitals. They must now face the risk of COVID-19 infection assaulting weakened immunity systems.

I listened to the foreign secretaries of South Korea and Spain and epidemiology experts like Dr. Anthony Fauci, as they explained their evolving responses to the health crisis. I cannot help the sad and forlorn wish that our president had such advisers to help him. After many messages urging me to watch Singapore Prime Minister Lee Hsien Loong addressing his country, I eventually and reluctantly did. I watched him speak to the nation, using in turn its three official languages. In one briefing, he spent under ten minutes to explain a new surge of infection among migrant workers, the response of government and what the public had to do. He also thanked the workers and their families for their contribution to Singapore's development and reassured them of government assistance.

Idle waste of time to compare the personal credentials and communication styles of the two leaders. It is what it is, Mr. Duterte is what we have.

Enough Filipinos voted him president and we must respect that choice. I listen to him because he is president. I want authoritative information on the state of the pandemic, what government has accomplished from one week to another to address identified problems, and what the public should prepare for. In this context, it is permissible and useful to compare how leaders use the resources of their offices to communicate to their people.

After so many appearances, I have to ask: what is the purpose of *The Midnight Show*? What is it achieving? It is not a press conference, as the first one was originally billed; no independent media were present. Some analysts suggest that the program enables executive compliance with the Bayanihan Act requirement for a weekly report on the exercise of emergency powers and its results. I wonder if the show meets the accountability requirements of the law.

The Midnight Show offers valuable bully pulpit that can ideally project Mr. Duterte's leadership. It can serve to inspire and rally the people behind a common cause. But some changes can make it more effective, starting with scheduling the program on prime time to reach a bigger, hopefully, more awake audience. Keeping the program short would also help.

Brevity would require that the presidential briefings focus on disseminating decisions, on which we assume IATF, after vigorous debate as a collegial body, had reached consensus. We do not need a reality show exposing the conduct of IATF discussions; we are not grading class participation.

But the April 13 episode featured recommendations from Sec. Joey Concepcion on the reopening of the economy that Mr. Duterte was apparently hearing for the first time. He did promise a response within two days.

In a time of crisis, we do not need a public catfight among IATF members. Who cares if Sec. Locsin's foul-mouthed tirade in media against the ban on the return of health workers to their overseas jobs impressed anyone?

Whether gaining him more or less PR points, the big loser was the IATF and the president. Was not the IATF constituted precisely to discuss and settle contentious issues before they become media fodder?

Government can and should provide another forum where independent media and the public can question, critique and clarify IATF decisions.

For both brevity and impact, the president needs a simpler, shorter script and bigger fonts. The image of authority is diminished when Sen. Bong Go has to put his finger on the text to indicate points that the president had overlooked. Admittedly, Mr. Duterte is clearest when venting his anger and attacking critics, or alternatively, complimenting Sen. Go and other friends. But the adlibs distract and drag him off-message and make it more difficult to follow his thinking on policy issues. The April 9 episode began auspiciously with upbeat reports from Sec. Bautista and Sec. Dominguez. Purporting to recap the discussion, Mr. Duterte proceeded to undermine what his action officers had reported.

Mr. Duterte does not seem to need, and certainly not the public, the profusion of praise that Donald Trump appears to require from his followers. Enough already about the comments from his subordinates about his decisive, proactive measures against COVID-19. It would be sad and worrisome to believe that respected professionals may now find themselves compelled to proclaim in public what many, and they better than most, already know stretches the truth. They damage their own credibility.

The Midnight Show can do much to help reach and reassure the public. But government must first evaluate its current costs and benefits and what must change for it to do better. Not too difficult, if abiding by Obama's plain and modest advice: "Speak the truth. Speak it clearly. Speak it with compassion. Speak it with empathy for what folks are going through. The biggest mistake any us can make in these situations is to misinform."

11

War against COVID-19

(*PDI*, April 04, 2020)

The Duterte administration could use some creative writer or literary scholar to supply it with a fresh stock of metaphors. To date, "war" has provided the dominant image to brand the government's priority programs: war against drugs, terrorism, poverty, corruption; wars without definitive endings. War does evoke images of courage and commitment, self-sacrifice and patriotism in the nation's service.

Ironically, President Duterte will vigorously avoid invoking the war imagery on the problem proper to the military, the defense of the WPS; that might involve a real, not a metaphorical war. Heaven forbid that his army and his people should take any risk to oppose a stronger foe, when war, as he has learned from history, can cause painful consequences. That is why Filipinos did not fight the Spaniards, the Americans and the Japanese, or defy the forces of the Marcos martial law regime.

With the pandemic threat, the government smoothly slides into the familiar, figurative language: war against COVID-19. But the literal interpretation of the war metaphor is problematic. Primary responsibility for waging the pandemic war then logically falls on the armed forces and their ranking officers. But we have to recognize that this has been Mr. Duterte's personal default button for his other wars, from which no one in his inner circle apparently dares to deviate. Hence, against corruption, generals in DILG and Bureau of Customs; against poverty, a general in Department of Social Welfare and Development (DSWD); against ignorance, a PNP deputy chief in Technical Education and Skills Development Authority.

Against COVID-19, Presidential Spokesperson Salvador Panelo proclaims the need for military leaders who have developed a "culture of discipline, obedience to superiors, training in organization, tactical strategies in fighting the enemies of the state and thorough preparedness in organization." One might inquire what training they had received to defeat a largely unknown and invisible enemy that hides among the people they are supposed to defend.

Still, as the British mathematicians who cracked the German World War II Enigma code, and the scientists of the US moonshot that helped launch the internet have demonstrated, the management and technical expertise available in security agencies has gone far beyond combat skills. The armed forces also command their own equipment and personnel. In the US, the military can deploy hospital ships to decongest civilian hospitals and medical personnel to reinforce the public health system in the most infected areas. In our case, the role of the military appears focused on enforcing lockdown controls, arresting violators and maintaining public order.

But clearly, for Panelo, the most highly-prized virtue that the military brings to the government's different wars is their obedience to the chain of command. He commended the leaders of the armed forces because: "They are not embroiled in bureaucratic rigmaroles. They abhor useless debates. They are silent workers, not voracious talkers. They act without fanfare. They get things done." This was an extraordinarily contemptuous putdown of the civilian bureaucracy that might have embarrassed even the military officers themselves.

Evolving in close proximity with human beings since prehistoric times, dogs supposedly developed the habit of subordination to their masters. But some dogs, still influenced by ancient instincts, display more independence and must be disciplined and trained into quick and unquestioning obedience.

Panelo and the administration seem stuck in a World War I mental frame, when the enemy was visible only several hundred meters away in their fortified trenches. It took iron discipline and unquestioning faith for soldiers to leap, on command, from their own protected positions and charge across open ground covered by enemy fire, to find safety only by occupying enemy trenches.

Modern warfare has become too complex for the military's absolute obedience to serve as the key to victory. More so with metaphorical wars for socioeconomic goals like public health. Granting that military personnel are good at following orders, how good are the orders they must follow, when the Commander-in-Chief has already disclaimed any expertise on pandemics?

The military does have much to contribute to the campaign against COVID-19. It may lack now someone like Dr. Anthony Fauci, director of the US National Institute of Allergy and Infectious Diseases, who has the credentials, the credibility, and the courage to speak truth to power. But to believe that military men merely implement top-down orders depreciates their value, reducing them to puppets on strings. This reflects a low regard for the military, so low that its proponents cannot even conceive that the military might consider this assessment insulting.

12

Heel as One

(*Rappler*, August 08, 2020)

Evolving in close proximity with human beings since prehistoric times, dogs supposedly developed the habit of subordination to their masters. But some dogs, still influenced by ancient instincts, display more independence and must be disciplined and trained into quick and unquestioning obedience. They must learn to follow the master at the command to heel.

The sound of the two words is the same, so maybe the legislators just misspelled their bill. The prescription, perhaps, was not really to "Heal as One." Placing at the top of the campaign against the pandemic the best trained and the most experienced people in the sciences and medicine, as South Korea did, would have delivered this message. Like the master of a pack of dogs, perhaps, what they really wanted was for the people to "Heel as One."

Those who had more training in the killing than the healing arts have their contribution to make, but presumably less on a public health crisis. Unfortunately, what leads the president to favor police and military leadership, even against a pandemic, is precisely the training in the killing arts, as well as his presumption that they themselves had already fully internalized the habit to heel on demand in quick and unquestioning obedience.

The coronavirus cannot be paid off, or shamed, or threatened. Mr. Duterte has repeatedly expressed his frustration that the virus could not be shot dead by his soldiers. This has not deterred the government from deploying Special Action Forces (SAF) and armored units against the pandemic. But the response to public health as a security problem, to be addressed by legal threats, arrests and sanctions enforced by police and military personnel, was also completely consistent with the way this administration has approached other issues, including drug dependency, allegedly anomalous business contracts and political/policy dissent.

Of dubious effectiveness in containing disease transmission, the approach leads to perverse results that undermine the mission objectives. Violations of mandatory health protection measures, such as the use of masks and social distancing guidelines, have led to over 200,000 arrests in mid-July, and counting. What this achieves is the relocation of the site of contagion, from the streets where the arrests are made, to the offices where the violators are processed and to the prisons where they are detained. Not surprisingly, the prisons have become hotspots of contagion.

The objective should be to disperse crowds, not to create them or reassemble them in even more dangerous places. What if, instead of sending armor, Debold Sinas equipped his troops with masks to distribute to the crowd? They would at least be doing something useful to reduce the risk of infection that people would appreciate, tamping down as well the potential for violence when security forces confront crowds. Providing masks should be less costly than the arrest and confinement of quarantine violators.

Security frontliners at the checkpoints have little latitude to question their marching orders, however counterproductive they may appear to the public. Do the checkpoints help to contain infection, or do they contribute to its spread? They do become chokepoints that keep people for a longer time in close proximity to each other, increasing the risk of infection. The process also exposes enforcement agents to the danger of the disease.

Authorities appear to enjoy some discretion in the sanctions they can impose on minor violations of lockdown rules—unfortunately, sometimes exercised to demonstrate the power they hold. Why place violators in animal cages or keep them baking in the sun or forcing them to eat six pieces of *sili* (hot pepper)? Are not people suffering enough from the pandemic without these gratuitous acts of official violence?

It is this environment that has raised the level of public concern at the thrust of government policies and action even in the period of the pandemic. Priority has not focused on sustained attention on improving the government response to manage the public health crisis and mitigate its consequences and the impact of lockdown on the economy and society.

Instead, the move has been to push controversial measures, such as the Terror and the Death Penalty bills, that reinforce state power over citizens and undermine their right to express dissent. Threats from military elements to use the Terror Bill to police social media show why there is reason for public alarm. Even the head of a Quezon City civilian task force, like a certain Rannie Ludovica, can believe himself justified to threaten on Facebook, the issuance of shoot-to-kill orders against violators of quarantine rules.

13

Lockdown Costs and Benefits

(*PDI*, July 04, 2020)

Addressing ASEAN heads of state in June 2020, President Duterte called for a "reboot of the anti-virus plan" in the context of the need for a concerted regional approach against COVID-19. A review of the national COVID-19 strategy might also be timely to consider perspectives from the six-month struggle with the pandemic.

COVID-19 remains a critical public health problem. Netizens deserve credit for raising the alarm in mid-January about the mysterious virus surging in China and urging a travel ban; January arrivals from China were averaging at almost 5,000 a day. Some executive agencies and LGUs responded quickly.

On January 23, the CAB ordered the immediate suspension of direct charter flights to Boracay from Wuhan, the contagion's epicenter. The Bureau of Quarantine, the province of Cebu, and the city of Olongapo also acted decisively to protect their communities from possibly contagious sea and air travelers.

Diplomatic concerns about appearing "unfair" to China prevailed at the national level and delayed action. President Duterte, supported by Foreign Secretary Teodoro Locsin, Jr., as well as Health Secretary Francisco Duque III and Senate Health Committee Chair Bong Go, did not order the travel ban until January 31.

Second, the Philippines, like many other countries, chose to copy China's lockdown strategy against the pandemic. An estimated 4 billion people, half the planet's population, became subject to some level of government-imposed quarantine. Especially when applied to large, densely-populated areas, lockdown was a crude instrument, the tool of feudal states in the Middle Ages to deal with unknown plagues, like the fourteenth century bubonic plague, Black Death. "Quarantine" itself came from *quaranta*, the forty-day waiting period before ships arriving in Venice could unload passengers and crew.

Since the ECQ imposed on March 15, Metro Manila has moved well past forty days into a fourth month of lockdown, already a world record. Extended lockdown made COVID-19 both an economic and a health crisis. Graduating Metro Manila to general community quarantine did little to revive the economy, because the lack of public transport services kept people from workplaces, a problem detected from the first day of lockdown when frontliners had to beg motorists for rides to the frontlines.

Third, the quarantine did reduce the speed of infection, giving time to build up the capacity for testing against the virus. Starting in March with less than ten government laboratories and a testing capacity of 300/day, nearly seventy laboratories, about two-thirds private, can now do 30,000/day and targeting 50,000 by July. This is an impressive feat, achieved by government and private sector investments in the purchase of testing equipment. Now, we face the problem of underutilized capacity. The Philippine Red Cross, charging the lowest rate for the gold-standard RT-PCR (Reverse Transcription Polymerase Chain Reaction) test, is using less than 10 percent of capacity, comparable to the utilization of public laboratories.

Much work remains to reap the benefits of higher testing capacity, starting with more intensive use of the facilities. Reduction of transmission, the key to economic revival, also requires getting test results quickly and, as the WHO noted, effective tracing procedures. Presidential Spokesperson Harry Roque denied that the Philippines had the highest number of COVID-19 cases among the twenty-two countries of the West Pacific region, which no one had claimed. But the WHO data indicated an issue of concern: despite stringent quarantine measures, the Philippines registered the region's fastest rise in COVID-19 cases in the period between June 16–27.

Fourth, lockdown is not a cost-free strategy. Its enforcement alone, dependent on military and police personnel, taxes government resources and strains relations with the civilian population. It also seemed to make little sense to arrest people (now running reportedly at 200,000) for breaching social distance rules and then risking more infection by confining them in congested jails.

SWS surveys in May reported 90 percent of respondents feeling stressed by COVID-19 and its impact on their access to transport (77 percent) and goods (80 percent). But fear of the disease encouraged the majority (87 percent) to observe health precautions (masks, social distancing, etc.) as best they could.

Despite the government narrative of Filipinos as "*pasaway*," or incorrigible scofflaws, 84 percent of respondents accepted lockdown restrictions. Effective communication of rules, their sensible and uniform implementation, and credible progress in controlling transmission will be necessary for these restrictions to remain acceptable.

14

Social Capital against COVID-19

(*PDI*, August 01, 2020)

This time, at least the rhetoric was right: "Heal as One," instead of "War against COVID-19." The Bayanihan Act itself fixed its provisions on constitutional anchors. And the initial response of a former-mayor-turned-president looked to the level of government closest to the community, the barangay heads, to take the initiative in mobilizing the people against the pandemic.

The reality quickly proved different from the rhetoric. Faced with an unfamiliar problem, President Duterte immediately reverted to the default mode: mobilize police and military elements against the enemy. To direct the cabinet-level National Task Force Against COVID-19, he appointed, as on earlier occasions, a retired general, who already had a critical job as head of the OPAPP.

In the first few publicly-aired IATF for the Management of Emerging Infectious Diseases meetings, however, Mr. Duterte repeatedly expressed frustration that his soldiers could not just shoot down the virus.

This did not stop the deployment of SAF and armored vehicles against the pandemic. Malacañang's public relations avoided branding the government response as a war; it might as well have done so. In a war, victory means imposing one's will on the vanquished. Security forces could not bend the virus to their bidding. But they could dominate the civilian population and declare victory.

The pandemic has disrupted the operations of hospitals and schoolrooms, courthouses and factories, theaters, markets and churches.

With all sectors affected, healing as one called for a unified strategy that only a central government could plan and implement. As governance experts have concluded, it will take a state to contain the coronavirus. But "healing as one" does not demand, as it seems to be interpreted, the centralization of power in only one institution or one decision-maker depending on gut-feel.

In many countries, however, the pandemic has resulted in expanding the already extensive powers of the executive, because this was claimed necessary to overcome the pandemic crisis. The literature on crisis management, particularly in the case of public health disasters, as against terrorist attacks like 9/11, questions the assumption that authoritarian governments were necessarily more effective than democracies in coping with crises.

The game is far from over, but both authoritarian governments and liberal democracies have recorded successes and failures against COVID-19.

Even democratic governments allow for temporary grants of extraordinary executive authority during periods of national emergencies. Authoritarian governments tend to be more fearful of even temporarily relaxing their powers. Denying the freedom to dissent, once permitted, may prove as difficult as returning spilled toothpaste back inside the tube.

Three factors have appeared more crucial than governance structure: the capacity of the bureaucracy, the people's confidence in government and the quality of the leadership. Public intellectuals have attributed the dismal performance of the US against the pandemic not to its liberal, democratic character, but to the weakened condition of the bureaucracy, the erosion of people's confidence in government and the character of the leadership.

The American public health bureaucracy has been blamed for failing to prepare against pandemics that epidemiologists had long warned against. The health crisis came at a time when the public was sharply polarized between those supporting and those opposing Donald Trump. Both elements fundamentally rested on the third factor—trust in the leadership that contributed to what political philosopher Francis Fukuyama described as "social capital."

Competent, compassionate leaders committed to the public good can deal with bureaucratic problems. A leader's power to retrain, fire and hire personnel can address weaknesses and corruption in the bureaucracy, actions that themselves strengthen public trust in the leadership. In Fukuyama's view, and to his regret, the pandemic struck the country when government was under the "most incompetent and divisive leader in its modern history."

The Duterte administration has had the benefit of three years to build social capital against crises like COVID-19. Any assessment of the Philippines' performance must inquire into what it has done before and at the onset of the pandemic, to earn the trust of the public in its policies, the capacity of its bureaucracy and the motivations of its leaders.

15

Starting School

(*PDI*, June 06, 2020)

Despite COVID-19, private schools had hoped for the normal June start to the 2020–21 school year. Not before August 24, the DepEd declared in April. Only after a vaccine is available, President Duterte decreed on May 25. He reconsidered on May 28, after a DepEd appeal for support of its "blended learning" plan; an August start may be possible. Playing safe, the Senate approved a bill on June 1 permitting the president to start school beyond the August deadline prescribed by law.

For many schools, this discussion on whether to start the school year in August or later was an exercise akin to rearranging deck chairs on the *Titanic*. In April, the Philippine Association of Colleges and Universities (PACU) conducted a survey on the impact of the pandemic on its members. Only 20 percent of the respondents reported budgets strong enough to meet full payroll expenses through mid-May. Why should 80 percent of schools, projected to slip under the water before the end of May, care about the advantages of an August reopening, let alone of an indefinite start dependent on vaccine availability?

The Coordinating Council of Private Educational Associations (COCOPEA), which included PACU, echoed its concern. It estimated the cost of the delayed school year to the 2,500 institutions its members represented, at P55.2 billion, rising to P142.1 billion if the 2021 schoolyear is effectively erased.

Bayanihan Act 1 provided no support to the sector. Even the handlers of Sen. Bong Go, who daily find space in multiple newspapers for articles and photographs trumpeting his advocacy for every cause voters might support, somehow missed the private education constituency. Why?

Because the ranking of values ordained by the pandemic pushed learning down to third place behind life and livelihood. Parents of K10 children instinctively supported such an ordering. "Maslow before Bloom," a UNESCO study's delightfully nerdy, catchy, capsule prescription, reinforced the paternalistic instinct: focus on survival issues in the hierarchy of needs described by psychologist Abraham Maslow, before debating goals among the taxonomy of educational objectives classified by Benjamin Bloom.

Even private schools followed this approach in the early days of the pandemic. Protection of students and staff from the disease was their immediate concern. With community quarantine, they tried to protect the income of their personnel. With lockdown extensions, livelihood became a concern, not just for individuals but also for their institutions. For this sector, however, livelihood and life depended on the continuation of the learning process in schools.

Education was not just a social service; it was an economic and business operation that directly engaged and supported over a million people. The point that learning meant livelihood for the private schools was lost, even among government officials. The president and assorted legislators were more concerned that these schools make their fees more affordable to their students by postponing tuition increases and accepting partial payments.

Why? Because the private sector accounts for only 15 percent of the basic education enrollment of about 28 million. It still held 54 percent of the higher education market, which covered, however, a much smaller number of around 3 million students. Down from its peak of 80 percent, the private school share, even before COVID-19, had been projected to decrease next schoolyear, because of free tuition in state universities and colleges (SUCs). Learning can thus continue outside the private school sector.

For personnel in state-supported schools, livelihood did not require the resumption of classes. They lose no income waiting for a January 2021 school reopening and gain more time, as the Teachers' Dignity Coalition pointed out, to address issues critical to the implementation of the new blended learning strategy, including connectivity, curricular content, and teacher training.

But the pay of their colleagues in private schools depended on tuition income from students returning to classes. Education delivered a critical social service; it was also an economic and business operation that must earn revenue to support the salaries of over a million people. Without government assistance, many such schools would collapse, with long-term repercussions on education access and quality.

Bayanihan Act 2 allocates P3 billion for SUCs and P1 billion for the Technical Education and Skills Development Authority, as well as P50 billion for relending to micro, small and medium enterprises. Private schools with proven performance records deserve comparable institutional support.

16

Going Back to School – and the Challenges Ahead

(*Rappler*, May 1, 2020)

After the premature end of school year 2019-20, schools wanted a June start for the incoming school year. The University of the Philippines Institute of Resilience recommended December 2020. The CHED decided it would be September for face-to-face classes and August for those with "flexible" systems.[3]

The decision, focused on health risks, has serious financial consequences. The COCOPEA, representing about 2,500 institutions, estimates revenue losses at P55 billion by August and P142 billion by December. These are staggering figures, considering that a survey of the PACU reporting that only about 20 percent of its members can meet their payroll costs beyond mid-May, probably reflects the state of the sector.

The proposed dates do not even assume "normal" schooling. Pandemic health security precautions must be maintained: protective masks; temperature checks at school entrances and exits; soap and sanitizers and tissues or hand-dryers in bathrooms and social distancing. Most of these measures, although involving additional costs for the schools, would be preferable to longer closure. But most schools are not structured for social distancing. Remodeling, even if possible, would entail time and heavy construction costs.

Resuming normal classes exposes commuting students to risks schools cannot control, such as the non-enforcement of social distance in public transport facilities or in the streets.

Other risk-reducing mechanisms—restricting class capacity, organizing students in blocks for staggered school attendance, or reducing class time would require complex scheduling and administrative arrangements for students and staff. They would also run into mandated rules regarding number of class sessions over the academic term.

Introducing these constraints would raise questions about how to ensure equitable access to quality education for all students. Such measures, as lower teacher-student ratios would also translate to lower revenues and/or higher costs and frustrate the goal of giving schools financial relief.

If "normal" means the pre-COVID-19 delivery of instruction in campus classrooms, where students and teachers are physically present, the honest answer is never—until a vaccine is successfully tested and becomes universally available. How long the respite will last will also remain uncertain, as the possibility of COVID-19 mutation or the emergence of other viruses will remain a threat.

It will include old reliables. Unable to hold classes, teachers have reverted to the quick, default device—requiring students to read and submit written reports on assigned texts. Moving forward, faculty may be able to prepare course packs for each subject that the students can purchase at the beginning of the term. It would contain course objectives, schedules, requirements and all the materials for the entire term. Basic education schools can effectively use made-for-television educational programs.

At the tertiary level, education on digital platforms will certainly assume a greater role, as it has done with impressive speed in other sectors.

Since the lockdown, 90 percent of the Bank of Philippine Islands' (BPI) total transactions have gone through offsite, electronic channels. Its online banking platform recorded more online users in one month than in the past year. At this rate, it will add 20 percent additional capacity to its existing BPI and BPI Family Bank branch network, roughly comparable to opening 170 new branches at a fraction of the cost.

Physical to Digital

Leading universities in developed countries quickly pivoted from physical to digital classrooms for asynchronous or even real-time class sessions on the internet. Their foreign students who had to leave their colleges with months to go in the Spring term, completed their course requirements at home, though having to settle for Pass-Fail grades.

Even in the Philippines, online learning innovations started at least two decades ago, with projects to give faculty and students access to online learning materials by providing computer labs and subscribing to content providers.

Schools began to experiment with "blended" learning strategies, putting lectures and other materials on the web to replace or supplement those provided in the classroom. Some institutions have invested in learning management systems (LMS), like Blackboard and Canvas, that allowed closer interface between faculty and students.

To move into even blended, asynchronous digital learning, schools will have to make the investments in hardware, bandwidth and LMS. About a dozen higher education institutions, several with multiple campuses, have already formed a Canvas Consortium.

From the experience of the Far Eastern University, among the earliest institutions to subscribe to Canvas, the more expensive investment would be in the training of faculty and students and in the development of robust assessment systems.

Students' Limitations

The impediment to a broader use of digital learning lies on the student side. Students manage to access online materials through the schools' computer labs and through internet cafes. With restricted access to these facilities and heavier reliance on digital sources, most students lack the funds for the phone or computer devices/peripherals and adequate internet and bandwidth services to meet online learning requirements on a sustainable basis.

And the services are not always available where the students reside. These elements are beyond the schools' control and require the support of government and the private sector.

But many private schools will not survive the extended lockdown period without immediate and substantial government assistance. A less restrictive general community quarantine will permit essential sectors to operate after May 15. Schools are not among them. They have fallen into the group that includes amusement centers, leisure facilities, gaming and tourism services.

COCOPEA can only hope that the class of non-essential sectors to which it has been consigned does not reflect the government's regard for the value of education and its willingness to give it support.

17

Victory over COVID-19?

(*PDI*, November 07, 2020)

Let us first acknowledge that the pandemic confronted the DepEd with the most formidable problems any post-war administration had to face. To its credit, DepEd managed to open on October 5 the 2020–21 academic year that COVID-19 had delayed. Secretary Leonor Briones then declared "victory is assured for education." Whoever prepared the draft of her remarks did her a disservice.

The achievement was critical and commendable, but the claim is premature, like celebrating the D-Day landing in Normandy as the triumph over Nazi Germany. It also risks the loss of focus on the critical goal: not just meeting the schedule for school opening, but also ensuring that the students achieve the prescribed learning objectives.

DepEd thus deserves commendation also for undertaking the strategic step of reviewing and revising the competencies students should master and against which they would be evaluated. Briones noted that this process had started even before the pandemic because of persistent complaints about the congested basic education curriculum. COVID-19 accelerated and expanded the scope of the decongestion process. The curriculum of senior high school (SHS), the new and more complex program, bore the main brunt of the criticism. But it was elementary education that suffered the biggest reduction in the Most Essential Learning Competencies (MELC).

Filipino (70 percent) and English (93 percent) took the biggest cuts in MELC. Math and Science, where the Philippines placed second to last in the 2018 Programme for International Student Assessment tests, lost

27 percent and 34 percent of their original MELC. Educators are now wondering whether the reduction might have been too severe and whether the graduates of the "streamlined" system will learn the competencies needed for SHS and college. We will not have enough evidence to reassure these educators, or to confirm their fears, until we see how the students are learning the new MELC.

After streamlining the MELC, DepEd had to provide students the appropriate learning materials. It had two choices. It could instruct teachers to continue using their textbooks and simply omit coverage of the MELC that had been discarded. This was the easier, safer and less costly option. The materials, perhaps, were not ideal but they were immediately available to students and already familiar to teachers. With less content to cover, teachers would have more time to review the texts for errors and, perhaps, prepare their own supplemental notes, since the ban on face-to-face classroom sessions would limit their ability to help students directly.

DepEd chose instead to require teachers to prepare new learning modules matching the new sets of MELC for their subjects, a more costly option that has apparently raised questions about the adequacy of the budget appropriated for the purpose. It also required more work for the production of the materials, and their review to ensure their quality. Media reports of errors in the materials delivered to the students underlined some quality control failures.

Given the rush to meet the deadline for the start of classes, errors were understandable and almost inevitable. DepEd teachers and staff were also coping with their own COVID-19 concerns. There was also the potential waste of committing resources to support a streamlined set of MELC that should undergo continuing evaluation. Math, Science and Language (Filipino and English) were foundation disciplines essential for building the students' capacity for lifelong learning. How do we know that the drastic DepEd reduction of their MELC trimmed away only the less essential fat but spared muscle and bone? Would the streamlining leave a foundation strong enough to support the progress of the students from elementary and junior high school, to SHS and college?

The question cannot be answered without further research, as a first step. Even with expert confirmation that mastering the 7 percent of the pre-pandemic DepEd MELC for English would adequately prepare students for higher education, educators would still have to worry about the effectiveness of the system for enabling students to gain this mastery.

But research to assure us that we have identified the necessary and sufficient MELC would allow us to move with greater confidence on the task of producing the appropriate learning modules and planning for their effective delivery.

18

Ang Vaccine Ay Sumapit!

(*Rappler*, December 23, 2020)

(The Vaccine has come!) Unlike Christmas, it will not arrive everywhere on the same date. Some concerns still remain. The vaccines will protect those who get them. For how long is not certain. Nor is the level of risk that the vaccinated may infect the unvaccinated. There is light at the end, but it is still a long and dangerous pandemic tunnel that lies ahead of us.

Logistics Management

The IATF must now face intensified pressure to accelerate the process of vaccine delivery. Securing the supply of vaccine in a global market where demand has soared for internationally vetted vaccines already in use, presents the first problem. The market, following the default response, will deliver the product to those able and willing to pay the going price. Rich countries have closed contracts for their supplies, some for more doses than their population required.

Enough Filipinos will have the connections to get the vaccine for themselves. A black market has reportedly opened in unvetted Russian and Chinese vaccines. But protecting public health is a national mandate covering all 110 million+ Filipinos. What criteria should IATF establish to determine how much of the vaccine it should buy from which suppliers? Effectiveness? Safety? Availability? Price? IATF would need to balance competing cost-and-benefit considerations to craft a plan yielding the greatest gain to the biggest number. This classic, utilitarian approach is congenial to economists because the quantitative analysis can appear conclusive and uncontroversial.

More contentious is the problem of who gets the vaccine and when. IATF follows many countries in giving priority to health frontliners. With the virus still rampaging, those engaged in suppressing its spread, need protection. They are also fairly easy to locate; they will be in the health facilities.

Beyond this segment, IATF hews to the presidential promise to put the poor at the head of the queue, starting with indigent senior citizens more vulnerable to the virus and, thus, potential sources of infection themselves.

Economic Concerns

This ranking does raise some issues. In developed countries, many senior citizens find accommodation in homes for the aged. Our seniors live widely dispersed with their families. Less mobile and exposed, recommended health practices may protect them adequately, even without vaccine.

Finally, senior citizens are mainly retired, while the poor are poor because they are jobless. How does giving them priority access to the vaccine help revive the economy?

The IATF priorities suggest that the government bureaucracy, civilian and military, constitutes the productive elements of society. And assumes that the private sector must protect their own people. The conglomerates can do this. But lockdown triggered a multi-pronged crisis because even “essential” workers could not get to their stations. How will the economy rebound without vaccine protection for the private transportation sector, the gig/services economy, the small and medium enterprises?

Political Considerations

The rationale for the pro-poor vaccine policy is political, not economic, supporting the administration’s populist governance rhetoric. Populist leaders claiming to champion the marginalized have tended to define this constituency as those who support them. With the delivery of the vaccine coming during an election season, fears that partisan politics will determine its distribution are not easily dismissed.

As it has done in every election, corruption complicates governance problems. Sen. Panfilo Lacson observed that the virus does not stop greed. The perceived administration preference for Chinese and Russian vaccines and whatever personal interests or "*kickvac*" this serves, require timely and thorough investigation to preserve public trust. But, setting this aside, the normal gamesmanship to gain control of vaccine procurement to grab political credit becomes problematic when it precludes more effective measures against a deadly pandemic.

Equity and Ethics

Vaccine delivery cannot avoid politics, because it requires tax-funded material and personnel resources and their deployment down to the barangay level. For the same reasons, neither can it ignore the issue of equity and justice involved in determining which areas get the limited vaccine supply.

We might accept in principle that every city, based on population, should have an equitable share of the vaccine. While all are vulnerable to COVID-19, they will not equally need immediate access. IATF might develop a platform for trading vaccine rights, with the cities not availing of their supply receiving alternative but commensurate government credit/benefits. The last mile issue is more difficult. Among the population of the poor selected for priority assistance, which poor person gets the vaccine first? It is at this retail level that partisan politics becomes more difficult to control.

Vaccine distribution is similar, though less fraught than the immediate life-and-death ethical dilemma that pandemic-stricken American and European cities have confronted: which of two dying patients gets the single life-saving ventilator available? In the absence of national guidelines, which have been debated in the US, frontline medical personnel must deal with desperate, on-the-spot decisions that sometimes leave them exposed to legal sanctions—such as for omitting mandatory manual resuscitation methods deemed already futile for patients but seriously life-threatening for caregivers.

We must acknowledge the heroic challenges confronting IATF. It has enough technocrats among the decision makers, though fewer recognized and respected medical experts many would have wanted. Who takes the lead in exploring equity and ethics issues? These may not even surface explicitly in the agenda. But it is important to recognize that IATF decisions, beyond affirming what is efficient and what is effective, also imply judgments on what is right and what is just.

This is not an easy mandate, but the vaccination program requires public trust. IATF can help itself: by ensuring transparency in its decision processes; by enabling the participation of the private sector and civil society in the supply chain; and by encouraging and developing mechanisms to enlist their collaboration in the program oversight.

19

SNAFU

(*Rappler*, January 4, 2021)

The term, defined as a "state of complete confusion," might describe what followed from the president's revelation on December 26, 2020 that Presidential Security Group (PSG) personnel had received Chinese Sinopharm vaccine against COVID-19. Spelled out, the acronym, attributed to World War II US Marines, implies something more serious: "Situation Normal, All F*****D Up." PSG did not violate the vaccine queue established by IATF, which had not yet been determined when they took the shots in September and October. But they could only have used unregistered, smuggled vaccines, since FDA has yet to approve any of them.

Officials thus found themselves scrambling to deny knowledge or offer confusing explanations of the president's statements. President Duterte did authorize the FDA to reduce the review period for drugs from six months to one month and, assuming positive results, to issue Emergency Use Authorization (EUA) permits. But the order only came on December 2. As Director General Eric Domingo stressed, FDA was accountable for ensuring that "only vaccines that pass standards will be made available to the public." These standards included compliance with all the requirements necessary for the proper handling, storage and preparation of the drugs before they are given to people.

Domingo disclaimed any knowledge of vaccines entering the country, as did Bureau of Customs Spokesperson Vincent Maronilla. Both acknowledged the possibility of private or government agencies bringing them in without the clearance of their respective agencies. Maronilla noted that misdeclaration of vaccine shipments as other goods would constitute "technical smuggling." Reports of a black-market trade in vaccines in the NCR indicated that this had happened.

Although aware of these reports, FDA, Customs and the PNP efforts to detect this market have so far failed. They might consult with the PSG. In taking command responsibility for the vaccination of his troops, Brig. Gen. Jesus Durante declared: "We vaccinated ourselves. It's so easy."

Durante's declaration effectively cleared the president of any blame for the use of unregistered vaccines, which FDA and Customs also did. But the agencies did not address questions already publicly raised. Had the president himself availed of unregistered vaccines? Which other government officials might have undergone vaccination? What vaccines were used and when? The SNAFU needlessly provoked questions about the competence, judgement or trustworthiness of government officials.

A situation often reaches SNAFU proportions when triggered by actions causing drastic damage to achieve benefits attainable by easier means. Heads of state and high officials in other countries got priority access to vaccines without provoking public protests. People would have understood and accepted the logic of protecting from infection the people guarding the president. A more competent and confident leadership could have managed early vaccination in a way that did not leave selected recipients seemingly guilty and reluctant to identify themselves. Nor those who knew compelled to justify withholding information by invoking privacy rights that appear more protective of high-level administration personnel.

Spokesperson Roque mistook or, as a good lawyer, misdirected the public reaction as mainly motivated by unjustified and unworthy resentment against soldiers performing their duty to protect the president. Or grave alarm at violations of the Anti-Graft and Corrupt Practices Act that banned government personnel from receiving gifts from private parties; small potatoes, the public would agree, compared to the far bigger cases of corruption it had seen this year.

The corruption issue was something of a straw man or a red herring thrown into the water to absolve from legal liability the individual PSG soldiers who accepted vaccination. Roque wanted to underline the argument that taking a non-FDA registered vaccine was not a crime. Buying the unregistered drug that is illegal, but an act the recipients did not commit, because the vaccine was given to them. Since the monetary value of the "gift" was modest, Roque could also employ two other favorite rhetorical arguments in his repertory: 1) "Trust me, I am a lawyer; nothing seriously wrong here." 2) "It happened; let's just accept this," or its alternative formulation, "Please just let the president have this."

The ultimate justification would cover a multitude of sins: "the act may have been wrong, but the intention was good." Not an original or uncommon excuse, but unexpected from an administration that projected itself as the uncompromising guardian of law and order. It was a rationalization that Prosecutor Duterte would have ridiculed out of court. Clearly, something wrong did happen that the government must explain and that the public should try to understand and not blindly accept. With his forthright admission of the need for the PSG to explain something it should not have done, Department of National Defense (DND) Sec. Lorenzana emerged relatively unscathed by the controversy.

PSG vaccination was troubling because of the possible pressure imposed upon soldiers to place themselves at risk with unvetted vaccines, and the precedent it could set for the civilian population. The issue at least established that government did not have a blanket right to force even those subject to military discipline to take unregistered, potentially dangerous medicine. The broader, fundamental concern relates to the problem that has long plagued the country—the issue of impunity and the rule of law. Do our laws apply only to some and not to others? To what extent can bureaucrats and politicians manipulate, bend or weaponize the laws to serve particular interests? And what is the citizen's recourse to those who may be tempted to exercise this power? Chain of command and military discipline notwithstanding, the PSG is still ultimately subject to higher civilian authorities; presumably, the DND secretary and the president. Sec. Lorenzana has already called for the PSG to explain how the vaccine decision was made.

Clarifying and resolving this unfortunate, avoidable controversy will help repair the breach of trust it has caused and help the country prepare for the massive task of delivering the vaccine to the people and reviving the economy. Or face the risk of extending and replicating the SNAFU.

PERFORMANCE

Coupled with the goodwill gained from an uncontested electoral mandate, Duterte, at the start of his administration, commanded the robust political platform and resources denied any of his predecessors to launch a transformative presidency. The opportunity was largely wasted in the futile effort to win a war to eradicate the drug trade. The victory promised within a year was deemed impossible to achieve even in the six years of a presidential term.

Perhaps, the goal was achievable within the confines of a city. On a national scale, as other countries, including the US, have realized, this was an impossible dream. Duterte's pursuit of this objective mainly as a police-military, rather than a public health concern, wasted the chance to move forward on other national goals. Recourse to the same top-down, police-driven approach on other goals, including that of containing COVID-19, proved as ineffective as its application in the drug war. But more than anything else, the pandemic exposed the mismatch between the capabilities of the president and many of his appointees and the challenges confronting the country.

Rodrigo Duterte's political team had conducted a tactically brilliant, populist election campaign that tapped into, revved up and converted into votes, the frustrations, fears and the simmering fury felt by the majority of the population struggling to improve their lives. The projection of candidate Duterte played on elements that have characterized this populist approach.

He was portrayed as the man from the masses, emerging from the common people and committed to their service. Actually, his father, Vicente, served as governor of Davao, then the country's largest province in terms of land area. The Duterte family, also well-connected in the province of Cebu, from which it started, belonged at least to the regional elite. Vicente also held national office as secretary of general services in the Cabinet of Ferdinand Marcos during his first presidential term.

The campaign promoted Duterte as the underdog outsider, a reluctant presidential candidate, who would have much preferred to continue serving the people's needs as mayor. His electoral platform bannered his achievements as Davao City mayor against drug criminality, which he projected as the pressing concern of poor communities. Only later did people learn that his political supporters had been exploring a presidential run as early as 2009.

In speech, behavior and manners, he was closer to the *masa* than other national politicians. To reinforce the identification, he did not need to bring himself down to the lowest common denominator. Locker room sexual banter can get pretty raw. But to describe molesting a sleeping domestic servant in graphic detail on mass media or joke about the mayor's preemptive rights in the serial rape of an Australian missionary?

Gutter language and sexual titillation, initially shocking, became quickly tedious, when repeated ad nauseam. People might take comfort in the thought of a president who shared weaknesses they might harbor but have never acted on and would be ashamed to admit in public. But did Filipinos really want a leader who pandered to the basest instincts and a common indulgence in bottom-feeding?

Mothers worried that their children might pick up the coarse language the president publicly used and had been emulated by some of his officials. Die-hard supporters dismissed this concern as a hypocritical ploy of politicians to observe "political correctness." But government guidelines continue to prescribe what movies and television shows are appropriate for different audiences. Educators call for more emphasis on civic education to reinforce the Filipino values that school children recite in the *Panatang Makabayan* (Patriotic Pledge). A nine-year-old school boy made the dailies with his letter asking the president to be a better "role model for good manners and right conduct."*

Platforms for Change

Marcos in 1972, Aquino in 1985, Arroyo in 2001 began their respective terms of office in a time of crisis. A transition to a new order with a new mandate helped defuse the danger. Estrada, the candidate of the *masa*, started on a hopeful note in 1998. EDSA II, triggered by an attempt to abort an impeachment trial for illegal gambling links, prematurely ended his term. The controversy over Estrada's exit from office burdened Arroyo's promotion to the presidency and even her election in 2004.

Unlike his predecessors, Duterte enjoyed an enviable launching pad for his administration. Victors often get to shape the eventual verdict of history. The quality of the victory can make an immediate difference. Gloria Macapagal-Arroyo won the 2004 elections but the controversy over her illegal contacts during the campaign period with officials of the COMELEC cast a shadow over the outcome, which she was never able to escape. A convincing electoral victory, quickly acknowledged by rival candidates and welcomed by the electorate, even in the short-term, generated energy to power policies.

Duterte's winning campaign thus laid the justification for the "shock-and-awe" strategy pursued in the violent war against drugs, launched even before his formal elevation to the presidency. Duterte dismissed the protests against the mounting toll of people killed in police drug operations with a reminder of his campaign warning that the drug war would result in casualties; he was simply carrying out what the voters had elected him for and expected him to do.

Duterte's party grew to control Congress. The fortuitous schedule of retirements and the judicious exercise of appointment powers gave the president unprecedented influence over the Supreme Court. During the twenty-four years he was in power, Marcos appointed six Supreme

* Joseph Peter Calleja. "Filipino Child Admonishes Duterte for Foul Language". *UCA News*. April 14, 2021. Accessed on May 11, 2021. https://www.ucanews.com/news/filipino-child-admonishes-duterte-for-foul-language/92101#

Court chief justices, five of them in twelve years (1973–1985), when the Philippines was under martial law. In five years, Duterte appointed three Supreme Court chief justices. Diosdado Peralta held the post for less than sixteen months, Lucas Bersamin for less than a year. After voting with her colleagues to oust the incumbent, Maria Lourdes Sereno, Teresita de Castro accepted the benefit of an appointment to serve as chief justice for forty-four days.

In the three years and five months between August 2017 and January 2021, Duterte appointed sixteen associate justices. Two appointees, Andres B. Reyes, Jr., and Jose Reyes, Jr., served for over two years. Samuel R. Martires and Noel G. Tijam served for less than two years and Priscilla Baltazar Padilla for less than four months. The retirement of five of his original appointees during his term gave Duterte the opportunity to appoint their replacements as well.

His historic leap from provincial city mayor to Malacañang as the first president to emerge from Mindanao gave him a large reservoir of political capital. Clergymen from Mindanao, though also repelled by the rising casualty count of the drug war, suppressed their concerns and withheld critical judgment to give their candidate the benefit of the doubt and time to achieve his objectives.

Duterte also inherited an economy that had stabilized and was averaging a respectable 6.1 percent GDP growth rate in a global market still struggling with the consequences of the US sub-prime real estate crisis. Economist Karl Kendrick Chua's positive evaluation of the Aquino Administration's economic record should carry both professional and political weight.* Starting as a World Bank research analyst in 2005, Chua rose by 2012 to head the team on the Philippines. He knew the country's problems and potential, when he accepted the appointment as finance undersecretary in 2016 and subsequently, the post of director general of the National Economic and Development Authority and secretary for Socioeconomic Planning.

* World Bank. *Philippine Economic Update: Pursuing Inclusive Growth Through Sustainable Reconstruction And Job Creation.*March 2014. Available at: https://openknowledge.worldbank.org/bitstream/handle/10986/20066/833150WP0Box380ic0Update0March02014.pdf?sequence=1&isAllowed=y.

Chua credited Aquino with getting the macroeconomic fundamentals and the national budget in order. This included improving systems to boost revenue collection by about 1.6 percent of GDP, keeping inflation in check, improving business registration processes and its standing in competitiveness surveys. Among sixteen countries, the Philippines scored the best improvement in curbing corruption. Interest rates had gone down in a decade from 12 to 4 percent. These measures helped boost its credit rating to investment grade by 2013 and reduced from 30 to 20 percent its budget for interest payments.

As Chua acknowledged, the growth had been substantial, but uneven; not strong enough to make a significant impact on reducing poverty. The income gap had not narrowed, because the poor could not readily find employment in the formal sector. Hence, the importance he attached to social reform initiatives, such as K12, that would enhance people's entry into the job market.

Litanies of promises to end corruption and promote economic development for the poor, repeated with religious fervor by politicians, no longer carried much resonance. But the kin connections Duterte claimed with the *lumad* (indigenous) and Muslim communities, provided a platform for inclusive policies that would address the plight of the most marginalized segments of the national society.

His "populist" and alleged leftist sympathies, supposedly sown during his time with his professor at Lyceum University, Joma Sison, founder of the Communist Party of the Philippines.[*] With the benefit of the "Honeymoon Period," usually granted to newly-elected presidents, Duterte could confidently risk the radical initiative to invite Sison to the Philippines and offer cabinet positions to personalities associated with the NDF, a move disconcerting to the military establishment and to business groups victimized by NPA "taxes."

Policy Setbacks

With nearly a year to go until elections, it might seem premature to render a verdict on the performance of the Duterte administration, especially as the

[*] Kristine Angeli Sabillo. "Joma Sison talks about former student Duterte, other candidates". *Inquirer*. February 14, 2016. Accessed on May 3, 2021. https://newsinfo.inquirer.net/764641/joma-sison-talks-about-former-student-duterte-other-candidates#ixzz6tmFUxQ00k.

conduct of the elections itself should constitute a key assessment measure. The incumbent government is accountable for the conduct of a free and fair electoral process, recognized by the public as relatively untainted by violence or irregularities and delivering a credible outcome. Such was the process from which President-elect Duterte benefitted in 2016.

But with the temperature of the body politic showing the beginnings of election fever, a performance review of the administration becomes inevitable. Candidate Duterte's campaign materials in 2016 provide a convenient starting point, especially the leaflet that proclaimed a 15-point Legacy Agenda:

i. Ending criminalities in 2016
ii. Ending corruption in 2016
iii. Ending illegal drugs and human trafficking in 2016
iv. Ending social injustice in 2017
v. Judicial reforms in 2017
vi. Global connectivity in 2017
vii. Adapting to climate change by 2017
viii. Ending political turncoat-ism in 2018
ix. Ending insurgency in 2018
x. Ending political dynasties in 2018
xi. National reconciliation in 2018
xii. Ending poverty in 2018
xiii. Ending traffic congestion in the metropolitan areas in 2019
xiv. Shift to new form of government in 2019
xv. Economic power in Asia in 2019

Granted these were exuberantly optimistic campaign pledges; candidates will want to produce as many as can be peddled, to as many groups from which a sizeable number of votes might be harvested. But it was extraordinary to assure substantial fulfillment of promises within the first half of the term. What would Duterte do between 2019 and 2022?

Some of the items the president-elect could not contemplate as immediately feasible or desirable. Prudently, he would reject "turncoat-ism" only in 2018; in 2016, he would need turncoats to gain a majority in Congress. He declared his personal opposition to political dynasties but subordinated this to the principle of respecting the will of the voters choosing to elect dynastic politicians.

His surprise appointment as DENR secretary, of Gina Lopez, an environmental activist but also from a family he had criticized as belonging to the anti-Duterte business oligarchy, suggested that he might transcend political interests to meet the challenge of climate change. But Lopez could not get confirmation for her cabinet seat from the Congress Duterte supposedly controlled.

The campaign promises also included millenarian goals that reflected the historic aspirations of the Filipino people: a more responsive government; freedom from corruption, crime and violence; an end to poverty, social injustice and insurgency. But national reconciliation was an agenda difficult for the administration to pursue. Its populist strategy required a polarized constituency divided into the *masa*, the president represented and its declared enemies, which were the criminals, insurgents and the elite.

Sison never came home for peace talks, although Duterte actually appointed nominees of the National Democratic Front (NDF) as Secretaries of Agrarian Reform, Social Welfare and Development, Undersecretary for Labor and Employment, and as head of the National Anti-Poverty Commission. By 2018, they had resigned or had been replaced or, like Lopez, rejected by the Commission on Appointments. Either Duterte did not command as firm a control over his turncoats as believed, or he was not completely committed to his leftist appointees. After short ceasefire intervals, government went back to waging war against the communist insurgents.

The campaign for federalism floundered, becalmed in the waters by 2018. The government never succeeded in formulating a coherent and convincing plan that could unify advocates on its objectives and architecture and on its political and economic viability, let alone allay the suspicions of its critics.

By 2021, proponents of constitutional change were only pushing for amending restrictive economic provisions in the Constitution. But even Charter-Change-Light was meeting resistance from the public, who thought the plan untimely and distracting from more urgent issues—the opposition of still suspicious senators, the congressional bureaucracy and politicians concerned about scheduling constraints as the 2022 elections beckoned.

Missed Opportunities in Mindanao

Mindanao could have offered an instructive opportunity to gain experience in the management of a federal structure, with the organization of the BARMM, and to promote the development of the poorest communities in the country. But BARMM needed sustained national government support to fulfill its two critical tasks: 1) completing the Normalization Track of the Peace Agreement with secessionist insurgents; 2) governing through a new structure a region long troubled by sectarian divisions, ethnic and clan rivalries and lawless armed groups running an extensive shadow economy.

Factors foreseen and unforeseen made the mandate even more challenging. Despite the delays in the organization of BARMM, Congress fixed the term of the Bangsamoro Transitional Authority (BTA) to the 2022 presidential and local elections. By design, the control of the BTA and the BARMM parliament went to the MILF, which had concluded the peace agreement with government. Unexpected external events hardly provided auspicious conditions for meeting BARMM goals within the three-year transition period to the elections.

The 2019 pandemic disrupted normal activities in BARMM, the country's least developed region and most vulnerable to its onslaught. Even before COVID-19, the BTA had to deal with the surprise of an ISIS-inspired insurrection that captured and occupied between May and October 2017, the center of the Islamic City of Marawi, BARMM's cultural and religious capital.

To dislodge the rebels, the government resorted to the use of airpower, which devastated much of the area and left unexploded ordnance that in 2021, had not been completely cleared. Estimates of the damage and dislocation caused by the siege, which displaced over 300,000 people, ranged from P50–70 billion. Through 2020, government fund releases have totaled only about 15 billion. While the national government was responsible for the city's rehabilitation and reconstruction, BARMM's ability to address the plight of internal refugees would affect its credibility and standing among its constituency and the country.

By January 2021, if not even earlier, regional politicians had begun to mobilize for the BARMM elections. MILF leaders, experienced in guerrilla warfare but not in governance, struggled with administrative tasks. Also inexperienced in electoral competitions, they faced the prospect of possibly losing in the elections the government positions to which they had been appointed. The election results would affect the peace process, an issue critical not just to Mindanao but to the entire republic and central to how the legacy of the first Mindanao president will be measured.

Treading Water in the South China Sea

Even in Marawi, Chinese influence was manifest. A photo-op of a visit to the battleground showed Duterte testing a Chinese-manufactured gun, advertising it as the weapon that took out Hapilon, although no soldier had been credited with the kill.[*] A one-year delay in starting the rehabilitation of the city was the attempt to implement it through a single, private–public joint venture contract, estimated at P17.2–20 billion. The National Housing Authority under Eduardo del Rosario would sign the state signatory with a private consortium of three local and five Chinese firms led by China State Construction Engineering Corp, Ltd. (CSCEC).

The Marawi community opposed the plans. So did the Office of the Government Corporate Counsel (OGCC), which questioned the legality of the joint venture agreement as the mode of procurement. The involvement of international donor agencies supporting Marawi's reconstruction presented a third problem; the World Bank in 2009 had blacklisted CSCEC and another participating firm, the Power Construction Corporation of China for corruption. Malacañang argued that those firms "deserve another chance." Not until 2019 did it concede that the OGCC was correct in judging the plan illegal.[†]

[*] "Doubts about smoking gun as Duterte lauds China role in rebel killing". *Reuters*. October 20, 2017. Accessed on May 3, 2021. https://www.reuters.com/article/usphilippines-militants-killing-idUSKBN1CP19W.

[†] Ica Fernandez. *TatlongTaongBakwit (Three Years Displaced): Towards a Review of Post-Marawi Crisis Rehabilitation and Reconstruction, 2017-2020*. A Report Prepared for the International Center for Innovation, Transformation and Excellence in Governance (INCITEGOV). pp. 24–26. January, 2021.

The partiality for the Chinese was most clearly evident on the SCS issue. It was not included in the 15-point Legacy Agenda promoted during his presidential campaign, though the population was celebrating the UN Arbitral Award that rejected the arbitrary boundaries of China's nine-dash line. China's claims over the SCS commons that belong to the international community and even to the EEZs of other countries, was an election concern discussed in one of the presidential debates in 2016.

Duterte knew that the population deeply distrusted China and supported the defense of Philippine SCS rights. But he was averse to acclaiming the arbitral award that was an Aquino achievement. He also wanted to avoid offending China and possibly, placing his soldiers at risk. It was understandable that he would try to dodge the issue during the campaign, He was more openly conciliatory towards China after his election. In August 2017, the government's Philippine News Agency even posted an editorial of China's state-run Xinhua News Agency criticizing the UN 2016 arbitral ruling.*

With his speech at the 75th UN General Assembly in 2020, Duterte appeared finally to recognize the value of the UN recognition of Philippine EEZ and maritime rights in the SCS. Was Duterte also anticipating that a new president in the White House might make it useful to hedge his position on China?

A US administration that placed greater value on multilateral diplomacy might also enlarge the space for transactional bargaining. Duterte made clear after Biden's election that he was open to reconsidering his opposition to the renewal of the Visiting Forces Agreement, which gave American military forces access to Philippine bases, if the US could offer the right price.†

Opportunities for bargaining with the US did not mean, however, that China had fallen out of favor. Though unlikely to return to the liberal

---

* Xave Gregorio. "PTV to discipline social media team over 'erroneous' #DutertePalpak tweet". *Philstar.* March 17, 2021. Accessed on May 3, 2021. https://www.philstar.com/headlines/2021/03/17/2084956/ptv-discipline-social-media-team-over-erroneousdutertepalpak-tweet.

† Mara Cepeda. "Duterte to US: 'You want VFA done? You have to pay'". *Rappler.* February 12, 2021. Accessed on March 22, 2021. https://www.rappler.com/nation/duterte-message-united-states-visiting-forces-agreement-february-12-2021.

agenda of aggressively exporting democratic values and systems around the world, the Biden administration was expected to revive traditional American advocacy for the protection of human rights, which was unwelcome to the Duterte administration. EJK remained a major issue in the Philippines.

Drug War Risks

The UN also provided the platform for reviving concerns about the drug war. Addressing the UN Human Rights Center (UNHRC) in February 2021, DOJ Sec. Menardo Guevarra acknowledged police failure to follow legal protocols and "standards of regularity" in anti-drug operations. The DOJ report had been delayed because of the incomplete documentation, described as "rubbish," initially submitted by Sol. Gen. Calida in 2018. *Rappler*'s analysis of the documents showed, for instance, that Bulacan province recorded over 500 killings between 2016 and 2017. Nearly half of the victims had appeared on police drug watch lists but were not identified as casualties in police operations.[*] Also needing explanation was the police failure to stop successive killings in the same area.[†]

These reports heightened public concern about EJK and the revival of a PNP plan, proposed in 2016, to adopt the drug war's Tokhang strategy against suspected communist sympathizers. Tokhang or the "knock and plead" strategy involved police visits to suspects on their lists to urge them to abandon their radical affiliations. Critics condemned these visits as the "red-tagging" of leftist activists, local government officials and their lawyers to identify them as targets for vigilante killing.[‡]

In a speech at a meeting of the National Task Force to End Local Communist Armed Conflict in Cagayan de Oro on March 5, 2020,

[*] Human Rights Watch. "Philippines Admits Police Role in 'Drug War' Killings". February 25, 2021. Accessed on March 22, 2021. https://www.hrw.org/news/2021/02/25/philippines-admits-police-role-drug-war-killings.

[†] Lian Buan. "DOJ Dents Drug War: PNP Did Not Follow Rules in Nanlaban Cases". *Rappler*. February 24, 2021. Accessed on May 3, 2021. https://www.rappler.com/nation/doj-drug-war-review-pnp-did-not-follow-rules-nanlaban-cases.

[‡] Christian V. Esguerra. "Leftists cry foul over police 'Oplan Tokhang'". *ABS–CBN*. December 2, 2016. Accessed on May 1, 2021. https://news.abs-cbn.com/news/12/02/16/leftists-cry-foul-over-police-oplan-tokhang.

Duterte ordered police and military forces to kill all armed insurgents, never mind human rights. This would be the way to eliminate communist insurgency by the end of his term in 2022. Two days later, police and military soldiers, reported as serving search warrants, killed nine and arrested six individuals in four Central Luzon provinces.*

The following day, Ronald Aquino, Calbayog City Mayor, was killed, along with five others, in an incident first described as an ambush and then as a "shoot-out."† The killings, linked by critics to the Duterte shoot-to-kill order, prompted calls for an investigation from both the Philippine and UN Commission on Human Rights, from the European Union and from church leaders.‡

Were soldiers implementing the shoot-to-kill order of the president? DND Sec. Lorenzana replied, "in a way, yes," adding that it applied to those rebels fighting the government.§ The prejudicial question, however, was whether the rebels were killed in a firefight or, as suspected by the DOJ, in incidents of drug-crime killings; the deaths involved the unnecessary exercise of lethal force.

In the case of Mayor Aquino's killing, irregularities in police operations led to the relief of both Lt. Col. Neil Montaño, Calbayog City police chief, and his intelligence officer, Lt. Fernando Calabria, Jr. Calabria had gone to the court to get the names of lawyers representing "Communist Terrorist Group personalities," reinforcing suspicions of red-tagging for elimination.

The rash of killings in March prompted legislators to call for a congressional inquiry. It also led to research showing, according to the

---

* Rambo Talabong. "Bloody Sunday: 9 Dead, 6 Arrested in Calabarzon Crackdown on Activists". *Rappler*. March 7, 2021. Accessed on May 3, 2021. https://www.rappler.com/nation/dead-arrested-calabarzon-crackdown-progressives-march-7-2021.

† Nick Aspinwall. "Philippine Mayor Among 6 Killed in Police Shootout". *The Diplomat*. March 12, 2021. Accessed on May 2, 2021. https://thediplomat.com/2021/03/philippine-mayor-among-6-killed-in-police-shootout/.

‡ Jezreel Ines. "Bishop Hits Duterte War on Communists: Lying, Killing Will Never Work". *Rappler*. March 15, 2021. Accessed on March 22, 2021. https://www.rappler.com/nation/bishop-pabillo-hits-duterte-war-on-communists.

§ Daphne Galvez. "Soldiers Follow Duterte's 'Shoot-To-Kill' Order vs. Reds 'In A Way'—Lorenzana". *Inquirer*. March 11, 2021. Accessed on May 2, 2021. https://newsinfo.inquirer.net/1405615/soldiers-dutertes-shoot-to-kill-order-vs-reds-in-a-way-lorenzana.

National Union of People's Lawyers, that sixty-one lawyers had been killed during the five years of the Duterte administration compared to forty-nine victims in the forty-four years from Ferdinand Marcos to Noynoy Aquino.*

Appeals for investigation and redress addressed to the Supreme Court, which was already hearing objections to the Anti-Terror Law, provoked from it a rare, if implicit, rebuke and a warning directed at its co-equal partners in government:

"The Supreme Court has always operated within institutional restraints, but it is far from resigned to spectate as clear breaches of constitutional rights are carried out beyond its halls. We remain conscious of our role to ensure that the rule of law is resilient and effective in a just, fair, and timely manner . . . At no more fitting time than now should the judiciary remain undaunted, with a clear vision of taking courage, enforcing the law and upholding the supremacy of the Constitution."†

The rising body count of EJK victims also provoked fresh international protests. Earlier appeals had already resulted in a preliminary report, issued by the ICC in December 2020 of a "reasonable basis to believe that the crimes against humanity of murder, torture and the infliction of serious physical injury and mental harm" had taken place.‡ The PRC influence over any possible ICC investigation provided another reason for cultivating a friendship with China.

Even Duterte had to recognize that reality had overtaken the vaunted drug war. He admitted, in August 2018, that "drugs will not end at the end of my term. It might just be worsened."§ In March 2019, he expressed

* Lian Buan. "Lawyers Killed: 61 under Duterte, 49 from Marcos to Aquino". *Rappler*. March 15, 2021. Accessed on March 22, 2021. https://www.rappler.com/nation/lawyers-killed-duterte-marcos-aquino-administrations-data-studies.

† "FULL TEXT: Supreme Court Addresses Calls for Action on Attacks on Lawyers, Judges". *Philstar*. March 23, 2021. Accessed on May 3, 2021. https://www.philstar.com/headlines/2021/03/23/2086434/full-text-supreme-court-addresses-calls-action-attacks-lawyers-judges.

‡ Jason Gutierrez. "Court Finds Evidence of Crimes Against Humanity in the Philippines". *The New York Times*. December 15, 2020. Accessed on May 2, 2021. https://www.nytimes.com/2020/12/15/world/asia/philippines-duterte-drugs-icc.html.

§ Julius N. Leonen. "Duterte Admits Drug Problem Won't End Under His Watch". *Inquirer*. August 14, 2018. Accessed on February 8, 2021. https://newsinfo.inquirer.net/1021310/duterte-admits-drug-problem-wont-end-under-hiswatch#ixzz6tmRadasa.

his fears that "my policemen are at the brink of surrendering."* In February 2020, Reuters ran a story quoting Col. Romeo Caramat, PNP head of the Drug Enforcement Group (DEG), that "shock and awe definitely did not work."† A US$50-million drug bust in November captured over 370 kg of crystal meth, but, according to Caramat, the trafficker's phone showed photographs of tons of meth stored elsewhere.

Caramat later claimed that the Reuters' story was inaccurate and had misquoted him.‡ But data from the UN Office on Drugs and Crime (UNODC) appeared to confirm the view attributed to Caramat on the easy availability of illegal drugs and the need to target big drug bosses rather than the street pushers, on which the campaign had focused. UNODC estimated that the drug oversupply on the street dropped the average, per gram retail cost of meth from US$164, when the drug war began in 2016, to US$136 in 2020.

The Reuters article attracted attention because of Caramat's previous assignments. Before the DEG, he had headed the PNP Counter-Intelligence Task Force that acted on cases against police officers. This was a promotion from his earlier posting as Bulacan Provincial Director in 2017.§ In this assignment, he received presidential praise for a record thirty-two drug deaths in one day, prompting Duterte's exhortation "Let's kill another thirty-two every day." Caramat acknowledged that "hundreds" died in Bulacan during his watch.¶

---

* "Duterte Admits PHL Drug Situation Had Worsened". *GMA News Online.* March 26, 2019. Accessed on February 8, 2021. https://www.gmanetwork.com/news/news/nation/689192/duterte-admits-drug-situation-has-worsened-in-phl/story/.

† Tom Allard, Karen Lema. "Exclusive: 'Shock and awe' has failed in Philippines drug war, enforcement chief says". *Reuters.* February 7, 2020. Accessed on February 8, 2021. https://www.reuters.com/article/philippines-drugs-performance-idINKBN2010IT.

‡ Rene Acosta. "Police Drug Enforcement Chief Says He's 'Misquoted' In Reuters Report". *Business Mirror.* February 11, 2020. Accessed on February 8, 2021. https://businessmirror.com.ph/2020/02/11/police-drug-enforcement-chief-says-hesmisquoted-in-reuters-report/.

§ Rambo Talabong. "Bulacan Police Chief Now Heads PNP Counter-Intelligence Task Force". *Rappler.* May 17, 2018. Accessed on February 8, 2021. https://www.rappler.com/nation/romeo-caramat-pnp-counter-intelligence-task-force-head.

¶ Prashanth Parameswaran. "Philippine Drug Enforcement Chief Admits Problems with Duterte's Drug War". *The Diplomat.* February 11, 2020. Accessed on February 8, 2021. https://thediplomat.com/2020/02/philippine-drug-enforcement-chief-admitsproblems-with-dutertes-drug-war/.

Back-sliding on Corruption

The doubts Duterte expressed about the effectiveness of his drug war strategy also extended to his war against corruption. Although recognized as a front-burner issue, the Duterte government could not sustain the momentum achieved earlier. Some of its difficulties were self-inflicted, arising from the failure to address areas of presidential weakness.

Extended service as a city mayor had not helped Duterte build up a rich rolodex of people he knew and trusted enough to place in positions of power. Hence, his key appointees tended to come from the KKK circle of "*Kaibigan, Kaklase, Kaprobinsya*" (Friends, Classmates, Provincemates). Yet, he was spared the attacks suffered by his predecessors for the disposition to depend on cronies and the danger that this would lead to corruption. Indeed, barely a year after his election, Duterte had to dismiss in short order, five of his high KKK appointees, the DILG secretary, the deputy cabinet secretary, the head of the National Irrigation Authority, and two deputy commissioners of the Bureau of Immigration.*

Compelled to venture beyond this limited circle, his inclination was to look for personnel from the security forces. First, this was consistent with the image he wished to project as a law-and-order president and his declared priority objective of fighting insurgency and criminality. Second, it followed from his assumption that he could rely on those with military training to implement orders without question. Finally, it could preemptively defuse the most dangerous threat to his rule, a potential alliance between the state's own armed forces and the opposition. Such had been the fate of Ferdinand Marcos and Joseph Estrada.

From the beginning of his term, he courted the support of the military and police, visiting and delivering speeches in their camps, promising them protection from potential charges of human rights violations, placing them at the head of the queue for benefits. Surrounding himself with appointees from their ranks was another way of courting their loyalty and support. Even when appointees proved unequal to the task or prone to

* Pia Ranada. "When President Duterte Goes on aFiring Spree". *Rappler*. April 7, 2017. Accessed on May 3, 2021. https://www.rappler.com/newsbreak/in-depth/duterteleadership-decision-making-firing-spree.

corruption, Duterte continued to retain their services, relieving them from their original assignments but parachuting them to other offices.*

Customs Commissioner Nicanor Faeldon had to step down from his post in August 2017 over Chinese smuggled drugs worth P6.4 billion that had avoided detection in May and the charge that he had accepted bribes. In December, he was appointed administrator of the Defense Department's Office of Civil Defense. His successor at Customs, Isidro Lapeña, who headed the PDEA in 2016, but was also tainted by the Chinese drug haul, whose value had been raised to P11 billion, was among the casualties, when Duterte reorganized the office by sacking everyone in October 2018. But Lapeña landed in a sub-cabinet position as Director General of the Technical Education and Skills Development Authority.

Spokesperson Roque met head-on, the charge of presidential recycling of corrupt officials. Not true, he declared; the president had appointed over twenty officials "very close to him" (*napakalapit sa kanya*) and, by his count, had reappointed only three of them. Associated Press reported that one-fourth of some twenty sacked officials had been recycled. Though his count was disputed, Roque argued, in any case, that "executive prerogative" permitted these appointments.† His defense implicitly affirmed the KKK basis of selection.

Prescinding from the logic of recycling appointees saddled with competence or integrity issues, many governance problems were not readily resolved through the shock-and-awe use of armed force, as even professional soldiers like Caramat recognized. But Duterte would not deviate from the established template. Even as he accepted the limited success of the drug war, he doubled down on the strategy, warning that the last three years of his term would be "the most dangerous times . . . *patayin ko talaga kayo* (I will really kill you)."

* Lara Tan. "Is Duterte 'recycling' fired officials? Only 3 out of 20, says Roque". *CNN Philippines*. June 7, 2018. Accessed on May 2, 2021. https://cnnphilippines.com/news/2018/06/07/Duterte-corruption-fired-officials-Faeldon-Pompee-La-Vina.html.

† Associated Press. "Is Philippines' Rodrigo Duterte Tough on Corruption? Not for the Slew of Fired Officials that He Rehired". *South China Morning Post*. July 5, 2018. Accessed on May 2, 2021. https://www.scmp.com/news/asia/southeast-asia/article/2153821/rodrigo-duterte-wavers-fight-against-corruption-philippines.

Two assumptions undermined his campaign against corruption. The first, apparently shared by congressmen, assumed that responsibility resided only on those directly appointed to the task. Thus, the House panel convened to investigate the delay in DSWD distribution of cash aid for the pandemic Social Amelioration Program (SAP) did not bother to invite DSWD Sec. Rolando Bautista to the hearing. According to Rep. Jonathan Sy-Alvarado, it would be unfair to include Bautista, a former general, who, in his experience, quickly acted on issues at his level.[*]

The president used the same premise to absolve DOH Sec. Duque from any guilt in the PhilHealth plunder case; Duque was not the PhilHealth CEO but only the chair of the board. This was an unexpected position to take, for someone so enamored of the military as an institution, where command responsibility remained a sacrosanct principle. Second, and even more surprising, was the presumption, also used in Duque's defense—he could not be guilty of corruption, because he was already rich.[†] For one thing, the contention was both conceptually unsupported and empirically untenable. Even worse, it denigrated the poor people with whom a populist leader claims to identify, implying that only the poor are corrupt.

Duterte's appointment of Samuel Martires as Ombudsman also weakened the mechanism that had proven effective in detecting and deterring corruption, public and media access to the SALNs that public officials had to submit every year. With half a year left in his term as Supreme Court associate justice, Martires took early retirement to accept the appointment in July 2018.[‡] Upon taking office, he stopped giving media access to 2018 SALNs. New rules issued in September 2020 made SALN requests for "life-style checks" subject to the approval of an Ombudsman lawyer-evaluator. The Duterte SALN for 2018 and

---

[*] "Solons Seek DSWD Secretary's Presence in Probe on Delayed SAP Distribution". *Manila Bulletin*. June 25, 2020. Accessed on March 27, 2021. https://mb.com.ph/2020/06/25/solons-seek-dswd-secretarys-presence-in-probe-on-delayed-sap-distribution/.

[†] Leila B. Salaverria. "Duterte: No Corruption on Duque's Watch". *Inquirer*. June 24, 2020. Accessed on March 27, 2021. https://newsinfo.inquirer.net/1296421/duterte-nocorruption-on-duqucs-watch

[‡] Lian Buan. "In New Official Rules, Ombudsman Restricts Public Access to SALN" *Rappler*. September 15, 2020. Accessed on March 27, 2021. https://www.rappler.com/nation/martires-restricts-public-access-saln-starting-september-2020.

subsequent years have not been disclosed, despite Freedom of Information requests for their release.

With the ombudsman appointment, Martires gained jurisdiction over the ill-gotten wealth cases against Paolo Duterte during his term as Davao mayor and on the reopening of the uncompleted investigation into the Duterte family's bank accounts.[*] Like Duterte, Martires was a San Beda Law School alumnus, but denied that he was close to the president, to whom he owed his appointment to the Supreme Court. In 2011, Martires, then with the Sandiganbayan, the court overseeing government officials, delivered the decision acquitting Duterte on a corruption charge involving a Davao project.

And yet, Duterte seemed surprised and disappointed that corruption continued unabated. In November 2019, he admitted, "*Talagang wala ng katapusan itong* corruption. *Mahirap talaga pigilin* (There is really no end to corruption. Really difficult to stop.); I offered to resign as president." And he advised officials who could not perform their tasks to resign as well. Spokesperson Roque later explained that the president would not resign but would spend the last two years of his term continuing the fight against corruption.[†] In February 2021, Duterte again conceded that he could not defeat corruption. Roque no longer registered dissent.[‡]

Viral Shock

Perhaps, the benign environment of a clear electoral mandate, a growing economy, and almost unfettered political control contributed to unrealistic promises to end on his watch the country's chronic problems: drug addiction, insurgency and corruption. These were goals that Duterte

[*] Lian Buan. "Duterte Appoints Samuel Martires as Ombudsman". *Rappler*. July 26, 2018. Accessed on March 21, 2021. https://www.rappler.com/nation/duterte-appointssamuel-martires-new-ombudsman.

[†] Arianne Merez. "#PaalamDuterte? Palace Says Unlikely for Philippine Leader to Resign". *ABS–CBN News*. September 29, 2020. Accessed on February 8, 2021. https://news.abscbn.com/news/09/29/20/malacanang-says-rodrigo-duterte-not-resigning-despitethreat-corruption-trending-twitter.

[‡] Krissy Aguilar. "Duterte Admits Eradicating Corruption 'Impossible'". *Inquirer*. February 25, 2021. Accessed on May 3, 2021. https://newsinfo.inquirer.net/1399856/duterte-admits-eradicating-corruption-impossible.

decided would be his priorities. The coronavirus pandemic was a problem forced upon him at a bad time for an administration already bothered by the downward trend lines of its flagship programs.

The crisis that threatened the health of the population came at a time when the president's own health also appeared precarious. Duterte seemed sick and tired, fleeing Manila to shelter in Davao. The 77-year-old Duterte had his own share of health problems, including Myasthenia Gravis, Buerger's Disease, Gastroesophageal Reflux Disease, Barrett's Esophagus, aside from "spinal issues" and "daily migraines," which required him to take the drug Fentanyl. Lawyer Dino de Leon counted twenty-one occasions of last-minute cancellation of appointments and public statements marked by "incoherent, unresponsive and . . . unintelligible rumblings." Concerned over the president's health, the lawyer filed a petition in April 2020 asking the Supreme Court to compel disclosure of the president's medical and psychological exam results.*

The challenge of COVID-19 distracted the public even from the hot-button topics of EJK and corruption, and bought the government some time. But the pandemic also made these problems more resistant to the usual recourse to intimidation tactics. When people fearful for the survival of their families were only a breath away from infection and possible death, the "I will kill you" threat somehow did not seem as frightening. Senior citizens and frontline workers, perhaps more fatalistic about their greater risk from the pandemic, appeared more emboldened in speaking out and pushing back.

Even as he bemoaned his misfortune at having to battle a virus impervious to bullets, Duterte formed for COVID-19, a cabinet-level IATF that still included more executives with military than medical training. Rather than prompting a rethink of strategy, the health crisis reinforced reflex reliance on law-and-order personnel and police enforcement of ad hoc rules. Broad and extended community quarantine became the government's main approach against the virus. While endorsed by WHO as a necessary tool, the timing and implementation of lockdown needed careful planning.

* "Lawyer to SC: Reveal Duterte Health Records". *Manila Standard.* April 13, 2020. Accessed on February 8, 2021. https://www.manilastandard.net/index.php/news/national/321485/lawyer-to-sc-reveal-duterte-health-records.html.

The pandemic exacerbated the problem of corruption. The urgency of releasing funds to support people who had lost their jobs enlarged the area where corruption could operate—as confirmed most clearly by the charges against officials of the PhilHealth, the government's health insurance institution. Enhanced powers to enforce compliance with lockdown restrictions inevitably opened up opportunities for petty corruption at ground level.

Although he had already declared defeat, Duterte tried to show he was still fighting corruption. The weekly, televised IATF briefings began to include a recitation of the names of officials, mostly middle-level bureaucrats, sanctioned for incompetence, immorality, fraud. He would ask to review some of these cases to see whether heavier penalties could be imposed than three months of suspension. He would also ask staff to bring some of these officials to him, so he could talk to them as he did when he was a city mayor. Or so that, he said, he could beat them up himself.

But the IATF sessions were intended to focus on the government's pandemic response, to report to Congress on the use of the pandemic funds and to advise the people on the precautions to take against infection. The proforma reading of minor officials subjected to disciplinary measures were not relevant to any of goals of the meeting and only reminded people of corruption plunder cases that remained unresolved.

The coronavirus pandemic imposed a stress test on governance systems around the world. No country anticipated the quick spread of the virus. But the narrative that people must show resilience, follow orders and just bear the pain of the pandemic without complaint—because it is no one's fault and everyone is suffering—was too glib and self-extenuating an appeal.

Some countries clearly did better than others in containing the contagion and moderating its consequences. Leadership mattered. The first confirmed COVID-19 fatality outside China, reported on February 2, 2020, was a 44-year-old male Chinese from Wuhan, who died in the Philippines. The report prompted Australia, the US and other countries to bar the entry of foreigners arriving from China and to quarantine returning residents.* The Philippines did not impose these restrictions until the end of February.

* "Coronavirus: First Death Outside China Reported in Philippines". *BBC*. February 2, 2020. Accessed on February 8, 2021. https://www.bbc.com/news/world-asia-51345855.

Government public relations experts recognized that the COVID-19 crisis called for a united national response. In a time of calamity, the country needed not just financial resources but also social capital. The president's populist strategy and the adversarial approach it required did not help to build up the social capital account.

The populist pledge to give preferential vaccine access to the poor was expected but not persuasive. High profile cases of government officials receiving favored treatment in their access to COVID-19 tests and exemption from lockdown rules cast doubt on the populist pledge to give the poor priority in the distribution of the vaccine. It did not help that the president was pushing a vaccine from China, given people's distrust of the country.

Add to this the resistance to vaccines triggered by the 2017 unproven charges by the PAO of deaths against the anti-dengue vaccine Dengvaxia. SWS reported in 2020 that only about 66 percent of survey respondents were ready to take the anti-coronavirus vaccine.

The reaction of the president to a controversy ignited by his own disclosure on December 26, 2002, that PSG personnel had taken in September and October a Chinese vaccine did not help to build trust. Since the FDA at year-end still had not approved and registered any vaccine, the PSG could only have used smuggled drugs and thus, violated laws.

Calls for a congressional investigation of the incident provoked an angry presidential response. He declared that the PSG acted on their own to protect themselves, that the law of self-preservation justified their action, and that he would instruct whomever were summoned to invoke their right against self-incrimination and refuse to answer questions. He admitted that he needed military protection and would, in turn, protect his soldiers. He concluded with a thinly-veiled warning to the Congress not to test his resolve to protect his soldiers.

The PSG case illustrated how the handling of the pandemic connected to public concerns about corruption, impunity and the tendency to take a security approach to a public health issue. It was not, however, an isolated incident. In his newspaper column, Ramon Tulfo, Duterte's Special Envoy to China, revealed that he had received in October 2020, the required two doses of the Sinopharm vaccine "along with other government officials."

FDA head Eric Domingo denied issuing any EUA for Sinopharm and added this to the PSG case that needed investigation.[*]

Tulfo explained at a Senate hearing that he had obtained the vaccine from a friend, who was negotiating to get the exclusive distributorship of the Sinopharm vaccine for the Philippines. He also wanted to acquire a Sinopharm distributorship, which raised the issue of conflict-of-interest with his diplomatic appointment. But he said he was willing to trade his post for the distributorship. He did not "entertain guilt feelings" from jumping the queue for the vaccine: "*kasi* (because) I was not doing so as a government official but as a private citizen." It was allegedly the president who asked the Philippine Sinopharm representative, through Tulfo's cellphone, to provide the vaccine for him and his family.[†] He did not identify the other government officials who took the vaccine with him.

It was Dr. Rabindra Abeyashinghe, WHO's representative in Manila, who flagged the need to "respect the prioritization" schedule established by DOH and National Immunization Technical Advisory Group for vaccine distribution. This was a condition for Philippine participation in the COVAX global vaccine sharing program designed to help secure vaccine supplies for low- and middle-income countries. Otherwise, according to Abeyasinghe, COVAX may have to consider other options where the impact of the vaccine rollout will be more useful and practical and will contribute to saving more lives." At risk from the behavior of Tulfo and other government officials, was the COVAX allocation for the Philippines of over 50 million doses for 25 million Filipinos.[‡] WHO does seek clarification from subscribed members to ensure that their vaccine

---

[*] Krissy Aguilar. "FDA to Probe Mon Tulfo's Vaccination Using Smuggled Sinopharm Brand". *Inquirer*. February 24, 2021. Accessed on March 21, 2021. https://newsinfo.inquirer.net/1399533/fda-to-probe-mon-tulfos-vaccination-using-smuggledsinopharm-brand.

[†] Cathrine Gonzales. "Tulfo 'willing to give up' special envoy post for Sinopharm distributorship". *Inquirer*. February 24, 2021. Accessed onMarch 21, 2021. https://newsinfo.inquirer.net/1399526/tulfo-says-willing-to-give-up-special-envoy-postforsinopharmdistributorship#ixzz6poGBk1Bw.

[‡] Cathrine Gonzales. "WHO Urges PH to Follow Priority List for Continued Rollout of COVAX Vaccines". *Inquirer*. March 4, 2021. Accessed on May 3, 2021. https://newsinfo.inquirer.net/1402928/who-urges-ph-to-follow-priority-list-for-continued-rollout-of-covax-vaccines#ixzz6pnakhyHn.

distribution policies align with the COVAX priorities. But it was the practice of some government personnel violating government policies that caused concern.

The Philippines marked a year of pandemic lockdown on March 16, 2021, recording over 620,000 cases and a count of nearly 13,000 deaths. Roque pronounced the government's response "excellent," although the daily incidence had risen to over 5,000 cases and was trending up.* By the third week of March, daily cases had soared up to record highs of over 8,000.† The rebound in cases was attributed to various causes: new virus variants, the relaxation of pandemic precautions to which the hopes of access to vaccines and the government's own push for the reopening the economy would have contributed. The world's longest lockdown had failed to flatten the curve of infection. The administration thus received a fair dose of criticism for the wasted year of lockdown.

Into the second year of the pandemic, government had yet to establish the tight integration required for the effective implementation of the test, trace and treat strategy. It had not undertaken any national campaign to distribute at its expense protective masks and face shields to the public. But it had reiterated the order for the police to arrest those who stepped out without masks or wore them improperly.

Despite assurances at IATF meetings of available funds to cover government vaccine purchases, the roll-out has been slowest in the region, with delays attributed to officials "dropping the ball."

Early consensus on the need for public–private collaboration in vaccine procurement has not helped speed up the process to enable private sector companies to purchase vaccines for their own people. At the IATF meeting on March 22, Duterte questioned the tripartite framework for vaccine procurement, long established and accepted by

* Catalina Ricci S. Madarang. "Philippines makes it to int'l headlines with anniversary of 'one of world's longest lockdowns'". *Interaksyon*. March 16, 2021. Accessed on March 24, 2021. https://interaksyon.philstar.com/trends-spotlights/2021/03/16/187709/philippines-makes-it-to-intl-headlines-with-anniversary-of-one-of-worlds-longest-lockdowns/.

† Katrina Hallare. "OCTA Research Warns of 11,000 Daily COVID-19 Cases by End-March". *Inquirer*. March 16, 2021. Accessed on March 24, 2021. https://newsinfo.inquirer.net/1407523/octa-research-warns-of-11000-daily-covid-19-cases-by-end-march.

private companies and local government units, vaccine producers and the national government as represented by IATF Chair Galvez to whom he had delegated authority. He also objected to the idea of a government fund to indemnify those possibly harmed by the use of the purchased vaccines. But he had previously approved the provision, which was already part of a law Congress had enacted.[*]

By March, medical frontliners were again protesting government management of the pandemic response, as they had done in August 2020, when the daily cases had not yet reached 5,000.[†] Again, the government had to decree stricter quarantine of more areas.[‡] On March 24, a group called AGHAM (Advocates of Science and Technology for the People) called for the replacement of the IATF with "competent people with medical and scientific backgrounds."[§]

In terms of its scope, intensity, duration, complexity and consequences, the pandemic caused the gravest crisis for the Duterte government. It was not an optional issue that could be set aside and ignored. Drastic, emergency measures, such as lockdown, inflicted immediate pain. Temporizing threatened the faster spread of the disease, higher casualty rates, and long-term costs to the public health system and the economy. It was also a problem closely monitored by the public, and successes and failures could not be concealed.

---

[*] Pia Ranada. "Confused Duterte Rejects Indemnity for Vaccine Makers after Signing it into Law". *Rappler*. March 22, 2021. Accessed on March 24, 2021. https://www.rappler.com/nation/confused-duterte-rejects-indemnity-vaccine-makers-after-signinglaw.

[†] Katrina Hallare. "Medical frontliners to gov't: 'Time-out,' revert Mega Manila back to ECQ". *Inquirer*. August 1, 2020. Accessed on March 24, 2021. https://newsinfo.inquirer.net/1315204/medical-frontliners-to-govt-time-out-revert-metro-manila-backto-ecq.

[‡] Bonnie Au. "Targeted Lockdowns in the Philippines". Video. *South China Morning Post*. March 17, 2021. Accessed on March 24, 2021. https://www.scmp.com/video/coronavirus/3125773/philippines-fights-new-wave-coronavirus-infections-lockdownsand-curfew.

[§] Davinci Maru. "Overhaul pandemic task force with 'competent' leaders, scientists, urges group". *ABS–CBN News*. March 24, 2021. Accessed on May 3, 2021. https://news.abs-cbn.com/news/03/24/21/overhaul-pandemic-task-force-with-competent-leaders-scientists-urges-group?fbclid=IwAR3EH5fTCh9HOKVIcq_PGUHrl9QxIfeJGSSA5VUQA9mk7OAv0yMPfE3tjy4.

COVID-19 will determine Duterte's legacy. Given the formidable political and management challenges of moving throughout the archipelago, the vaccine that has still to arrive in bulk, the betting is that Duterte will leave the Palace in May 2022, before the virus leaves the Philippines. His term will end with the consequences of a lingering COVID-19 crisis, which he did not cause, but could have managed better, and the damage inflicted by the inclination to resolve problems, including the pandemic, mainly through shock-and-awe strategies.

Afterword: Moving Forward

Voters will cast their votes for the 2022 elections on May 9. The campaign for national elective posts, according to the COMELEC rules, begins on February 8, and for sub-national posts on March 25, both ending on May 7. Regardless of rules that COMELEC has historically faced problems in enforcing, aspiring politicians had begun promotional campaigns in aid of elections in 2021. Mainline media generously publish their press releases. Netizens speculate about the chances of their own preferred candidates in social media. Opinion polls report results on the head-to-head ranking of likely contenders.

A single, six-year presidential term, established in 1987, spares the political opposition from the challenge of overcoming an entrenched re-electionist candidate; although, under the earlier system that allowed two, four-year terms, unseating the incumbent had not presented an insurmountable obstacle. Only Ferdinand Marcos managed in 1969 to win a second term.

Duterte will thus have to leave the presidential residence at the end of one term, which Donald Trump in the US also had to do because he lost his re-election bid. It would be a mistake, however, to assume that Duterte will be content to ride off into the sunset, without trying to influence the outcome of the elections and to retain political influence in the next administration.

Parallels drawn between the rise of the populist regime of Donald Trump and Rodrigo Duterte and their common one-term presidency suggest other similarities and differences. A short detour into the 2020 US elections might help cast a helpful light on the current Philippine political terrain, as long as we keep in mind our different environment and different problems.

The long, winding, torturous road to the 2020 elections in the US exposed an electorate sharply polarized between the two political parties. The ruling Republican Party had no problem choosing its 2020 presidential candidate, because the incumbent was eligible for a second term. The Democrats had to undergo a divisive, potentially damaging contest to select their candidate. The clash between the two parties remained intense.

Political polarization has assumed a different character in the Philippines. Under a multi-party system, more political parties have emerged, but these rarely represent contending political ideologies or policies; they are vehicles for rival politicians and their personal and family interests.

Duterte's 2016 election triumph on the back of PDP-Laban (Partido Demokratiko Pilipino–Lakas ng Bayan), the smallest political party, prompted the wholesale migration of the political butterflies to his camp. The price for membership in the supermajority was unquestioning fidelity to the president's agenda. The old, two-party system had allowed ample space for the party out of power to play a countervailing role to hold the ruling party accountable. Turncoat-ism has marginalized opposition forces, while submerging the rivalries within a ruling coalition dominated by the president. From one perspective, politics has become less polarized.

Nor does the Philippine electorate appear polarized, going by the high SWS "Satisfaction" or the Pulse Asia "Performance and Trust" ratings that Duterte has sustained through his term. Admittedly, at the margins where the zealots of the DDS (Diehard Duterte Supporters) joust with the few Aquino *Dilawans* in the digital space, the polarization sharpened in the 2016 elections has continued, sometimes with greater viciousness. But this enmity might be contrived; the fiercest digital warriors may be mercenaries playing assigned roles, receiving compensation for churning out views they don't necessarily believe.*

Polarized views have manifested themselves, however, on specific issues, including: the justification of the shoot-to-kill approach against

* Jonathan Ong, Jason Cabanes. "Architects of Networked Disinformation: Behind the Scenes of Troll Accounts and Fake News Production in the Philippines". *D&S Media Manipulation: Dispatches from the Field.* Accessed on March 23,2021.

suspected drug criminals, insurgents, and even aggressive lockdown violators; the veracity of EJK reports; the defense of Philippine rights in the SCS and the good intentions of the PRC. The president has taken one view, which the general public has opposed. This dissonance between the president's general high satisfaction and performance/trust ratings and the high rejection of his specific policies has perplexed diligent followers of SWS and Pulse Asia surveys.

It has revived fundamental questions about public opinion: how do people form their opinions? Where and how do respondents get their information? What and who influence their views? Can respondents be manipulated or shepherded towards pre-ordained results? In the July 2020 SWS survey, 51 percent of the respondents concurred with the statement that "it is dangerous to print or broadcast anything critical of the administration." The number appreciating the danger of expressing critical feedback rose in the November 2020 survey to 65 percent. Might this perspective influence respondent when they reply to strangers asking them questions on their trust in the president and satisfaction with his performance?

These questions are not new. But the environment in which we must now try to answer them has radically changed. In an age of Facebook and social media, big data algorithms, troll armies and disinformation campaigns, it has become acceptable to offer not just alternative views but alternative facts. Old questions have thus acquired greater salience. Should not polling agencies pause to review how they structure and develop their survey instruments?

In the context of the doubts on polling result, SWS has taken the bold and painful decision to omit the "satisfaction" questions in their 2020 surveys. The omission is a striking deviation from the standard SWS template familiar to its faithful followers. The silence on the issue of trust and approval is particularly eloquent at this time, when the country is gearing up for elections. In one of his *Inquirer* columns last December, SWS Chair Mahar Mangahas declared the ability to predict election results as "the litmus test of the quality of opinion polling." The public satisfaction scores on political leaders, often the SWS item drawing the most interest, establish the basis for this litmus test.

If SWS followers have become skeptical of satisfaction scores, Mangahas might find some comfort in the thought that Duterte himself takes a more honest view of his performance and disagrees with the rating. Else, he would not be publicly confessing the failure of his wars on corruption and drugs. In this respect, Duterte differed from Trump, who never owned up to a failure or a mistake.

Duterte will never experience the pain of losing a presidential election. But while Trump lost the election, eviction from the White House did not extinguish Trumpism. A significant segment of the American population remained loyal to Trump because of legitimate grievances that it blamed on his rivals and the policies they pursued on abortion, globalization, immigration. Supporters expected him to keep fighting to reverse those policies to which they attributed the widening income inequality and deterioration in their economic situation, the depreciation of their cultural values, and the loss of standing and recognition in their community. Even in defeat, Trump stood for values his base cherished and would fight for.

The problem Duterte and his followers face is the difficulty of locating a comparable bedrock of common values. What were the policies, original with Duterte and successfully promoted by him, which voters can claim as critical to their welfare and interests? Expulsion of foreign missionaries working with poor and marginalized communities? The closure of ABS-CBN, depriving many communities of their major source of information in a time of pandemic? The conduct of the drug war? Better human rights protection? Restrictions on access to SALN data? A stronger justice system? A more trusted police and military force? A more robust economy? More secure Philippine rights in the SCS? Counter-insurgency campaigns and anti-terrorism measures? Pivot from democratic allies to China and Russia? Management of the pandemic?

Absent this bond of shared commitment to policies with which people have identified and in which they have invested, the president's power and influence must depend mainly on command over state resources: the budget, the bureaucracy, and, most critically, the security forces. An ex-president does not retain the power that comes from access to state resources; that passes over to the next president.

With no re-electionist incumbent in play, the ruling coalition will have difficulty uniting behind one presidential candidate. A squabble has already broken out in the president's own party. PDP-Laban president Manny Paquiao, whose success in the boxing ring propelled his election to the Senate, rebuked some party members for politicking in the time of pandemic. Without his blessing or knowledge, they had signed in early March 2020, a resolution urging the party chairman, Rodrigo Duterte to run in 2022 for vice president, with Sen. Bong Go as the presidential candidate. This ploy would give the party a candidate with the advantages of an incumbent president. But it was no secret that Paquiao had been planning to run for the presidency himself and Sen. Lacson confirmed hearing this directly from him.*

Whether Duterte, protected from losing a presidential race, would risk losing as a vice-presidential candidate is uncertain. But the problem of the ruling party remains: what successes can it demonstrate to justify continuing in power? While Duterte can be blamed for the ruins he is leaving behind, he did not accomplish the damage himself. He was enabled by the people he recruited and retained in his government. What platform can they campaign on, when they have so closely identified with the Duterte policies?

The opposition also faces a difficult problem. Any opposition party must worry, not just about the relative appeal of campaign platforms, but also command of material assets, and, hence, about the capacity of the ruling government to tip the election scales in favor of a candidate. Consider the seven-hour blackout in the 2019 elections never satisfactorily explained beyond a "computer glitch." Who is going to ensure that no similar glitches happen in 2022? Duterte has expressed the intent to replace Smartmatic as the technology provider for the elections. Is there time to negotiate a new contract before the election ban? With no clear exit from the pandemic, manual voting can hardly be an option. Three commissioners, including the Chair, will be retiring in February 2022. Who will ensure that their replacements will protect the integrity of the elections?

Beyond these non-trivial, operational details, the opposition must also address its own weakness. On March 18, 2021, a new political group launched the 1Sambayan (One Country) initiative to take the first step to

---

* Camille Elemia. "Duterte for VP? Pacquiao warns PDP-Laban members over 'unauthorized'reso". *Rappler*. March 12, 2021. Accessed on March 24, 2021. https://www.rappler.com/nation/pacquiao-warns-pdp-laban-members-unauthorized-resolution-duterte-vp.

build an opposition party. The DDS will try hard to paint the 1Sambayan Convenors as discredited yellow losers. Br. Armin Luistro, OSB and Albert del Rosario, both served in the Noynoy Aquino Cabinet. Conchita Carpio Morales received her appointment as Ombudsman from Aquino as well, though her appointment to the Supreme Court came through Macapagal-Arroyo. But Antonio Carpio, perhaps primus inter pares in the 1Sambayan, cannot be reasonably depicted as yellow; it was Aquino who denied him the appointment as Supreme Court chief justice.

1Sambayan announced as its aim the formation of a common and comprehensive slate of 2022 candidates, from president to local government officials, to compete against whomever Duterte will "anoint" as his electoral preferences. The premise is reasonable. More people voted in 2016 against Duterte than for him. But the 60 percent of the electorate who did not vote for Duterte, split their votes among four different candidates and Duterte prevailed. As in 1985, the primary convenor mission was to persuade all pro-democracy forces to yield to one contender they would all support.

The first and fundamental convenor problem, then, is to find candidates to convene. This would not normally be an issue for an opposition party, especially in a multi-party system. But in 2019, the opposition party could not field a full senatorial slate of twelve candidates. The opposition party did not win a single Senate seat, something that has never happened in the independent Philippine republic.

Elected senators are prime, presidentiable candidates, because they compete in national elections. Blanked out in 2019, the opposition does not have available a natural pool of recently-tested election winners. Nor would it be easy to recruit candidates from the supermajority; precisely because most of them already bear on their brows the Duterte brand. The 1Sambayan Convenors may need to review and calibrate how deeply the brand has been etched and the threshold criteria that their prospective candidates will have to hurdle.

The 1Sambayan Convenors have a longer runway to the 2022 elections than that given to their 1985 counterpart to prepare for the snap elections. Their task is clear but not easy. It recalls the testy exchange between Presidential Legal Advisor Panelo and Sen. Ping Lacson on the government's management of the pandemic response. Bristling at the criticism of government mismanagement coming from all quarters, Panelo challenged Lacson: "What are those drastic and innovative solutions? Present them. If you're really that good . . ." Unruffled, Lacson shot back: "How about getting more competent people?"

Certainly, the convenors will need to find more competent candidates to present before the voters. Competence will be necessary, but not sufficient. Their candidates will also need commitment to the task. And courage to take up the burden.

1Sambayan must also reach out to the voters. Survey respondents show that they know and speak their mind in their replies to questions on specific policy issues. The electorate deserves the chance to choose among the candidates, the leaders more sensitive and better attuned to the challenges posed by this environment and more respectful and supportive of their aspirations for a life liberated from desperate want and endless "wars," a life of freedom, dignity and peace.

The voters, like the 1Sambayan candidates, also need help to muster the commitment and the courage necessary to exercise their right to make their decisions.

Abbreviations

AGHAM	Advocates of Science and Technology for the People
AI	Amnesty International
AO	Administrative Order
ARMM	Autonomous Region of Muslim Mindanao
ASEAN	Association of Southeast Asian Nations
AK	Authoritarian Kleptocracy
AWAT	Anti-War, Anti-Terror
BAC	Bids and Awards Committee
BAR	Bangsamoro Autonomous Region
BARMM	Bangsamoro Autonomous Region of Muslim Mindanao
BBL	Bangsamoro Basic Law
BJMP	Bureau of Jail Management and Penology
BIFF	Bangsamoro Islamic Freedom Fighters
BOL	Bangsamoro Organic Law
BTA	Bangsamoro Transitional Authority
C	Centralization
CAB	Civil Aeronautics Board
CBCP	Catholic Bishops' Conference of the Philippines
CEEC	China Energy Engineering Co. Ltd.
CHED	Commission on Higher Education
CHR	Commission on Human Rights
COA	Commission on Audit
COCOPEA	Coordinating Council of Private Educational Associations
COMELC	Commission on Elections

Con-ass	Constituent Assembly
Con-com	Consultative Committee
Con-con	Constitutional Convention
CPP	Communist Party of the Philippines
CSCEC	China State Construction Engineering Corp, Ltd.
D	Decentralization
DAP	Disbursement Acceleration Program
DDB	Dangerous Drugs Board
DENR	Department of Environment and Natural Resources
DepEd	Department of Education
DFA	Department of Foreign Affairs
DILG	Department of Interior and Local Government
DND	Department of National Defense
DOH	Department of Health
DOJ	Department of Justice
DSWD	Department of Social Welfare and Development
DEG	Drug Enforcement Group
ECQ	Enhanced Community Quarantine
EEZ	Exclusive Economic Zone
EJK	Extrajudicial Killing
EO	Executive Order
EUA	Emergency Use Authorization
FDA	Food and Drug Administration
GDP	Gross Domestic Product
GII	Global Impunity Index
GPH-MILF	Government of the Philippines-Moro Islamic Liberation Front
HCM	Hermitage Capital Management
HIV-AIDS	Human Immunodeficiency Virus-Acquired Immunodeficiency Syndrome
H1N1	A variant of Asian and Swine Flu
IA	International Alert
IATF	Inter-agency Task Force for the Management of Emerging Infectious Diseases
ICAD	Inter-agency Committee on Anti-Illegal Drugs
ICC	International Criminal Court

IDP	Indigenous Displaced Persons
IFEX	International Freedom of Expression Exchange
JLN Corp.	Janet Lim Napoles Corporation
LGC	Local Government Code
LGU	Local Government Unit
LMS	Learning Management Systems
MCHBII	Makati City Hall Building II
MERS	Middle East Respiratory Syndrome
MILF	Moro Islamic Liberation Front
MNLF	Moro National Liberation Front
MELC	Most Essential Learning Competencies
MWSS	Metropolitan Waterworks and Sewerage System
NCR	National Capital Region
NDF	National Democratic Front
NEJM	New England Journal of Medicine
NPA	New People's Army
OFW	Overseas Filipino Worker
OGCC	Office of the Government Corporate Counsel
PACU	Philippine Association of Colleges and Universities
PAO	Public Attorney's Office
PCOO	Presidential Communications Operations Office
PDEA	Philippine Drug Enforcement Agency
PDI	Philippine Daily Inquirer
PDP-Laban	Partido Demokratiko Pilipino–Lakas ng Bayan
PNP	Philippine National Police
PPE	Personal Protective Equipment
PRC	People's Republic of China
PRRD	President Rodrigo Roa Duterte
PSG	Presidential Security Group
RAM	Reform the Armed Forces Movement
RT-PCR Test	Reverse Transcription Polymerase Chain Reaction Test
SAF	Special Action Force
SALN	Statement of Assets, Liabilities and Net Worth
SAP	Social Amelioration Program
SARS	Severe Acute Respiratory Syndrome
SCS	South China Sea

SHS	Senior High School
SRP	Self-Rated Poverty
SUCs	State Universities and Colleges
SWS	Social Weather Stations
TFBM	Task Force Bangon Marawi
ULAP	Union of Local Authorities of the Philippines
UNA	United Nationalist Alliance
UNCLOS	United Nations Convention for the Law of the Sea
UNODC	United Nations Office on Drugs and Crime
WHO	World Health Organization